AF413665

# Praise for *Trembling, Still*

'*Trembling, Still* is jazz-writing at its most turbulently brilliant; tuneful and mournful, poignant and funny, heart-rending and mind-grabbing, skillfully improvisational, eloquent and compelling. Thank you, Stephen Jenkinson: only you could have written this, and I offer you my gratitude, paltry recompense for such a masterful gift to us all.'

— **GABOR MATÉ**, MD, coauthor of
*The Myth of Normal: Trauma, Illness and Healing in a Toxic Culture*

'Maybe Stephen's greatest. His writing is infused with strange staccato jumps then river-strong flow, with hawkeyed storytelling leading us on. There's dread judgement but also religious wonder, and never, once, does the book lose its mesmeric hold.

'This is not a domestic document. If you seek the unexpected, seek this.'

— **MARTIN SHAW**, author of *Liturgies of the Wild*

'A rare, real-time chronicle of receiving and reckoning with a neurodegenerative diagnosis, *Trembling, Still* is a study in how to remain awake, accountable and alive while the ground shifts. This book steadies us in this life, reminding us to tend without turning away.'

— **ELENA BROWER**, best-selling author of *Hold Nothing* and *Practice You*

'Even in its printed form, *Trembling, Still* bears the trace of an unsteady hand — raw, intimate, and unprotected. It invites the reader into the friction of receiving devastating news in the middle of an ordinary day, where life continues even as everything has changed, and charges even the simplest tasks with a great longing. It is a sober reminder that the ride does not go on forever — and a rare, unsentimental guide to what might matter while it still does. What emerges for me is a hard but generous question: how are we using the days when we still can?'

— **MATTIAS OLSSON**, founder and filmmaker, Campfire Stories

'Stephen has always been a bird with more than two wings, a rare creature. Given the pressing circumstances, he has recently learned to breathe underwater. He uses his pen like a straw that connects him to the surface. He's always eschewed superficial assurance. Now again. He keeps the transfusion running – his fancy stylograph is also a needle, and the ink is his soul's blood.'

— ÀLEX GÓMEZ-MARÍN, PhD, neuroscientist; head,
Behavior of Organisms Laboratory, Instituto de Neurociencias de Alicante

'In *Trembling, Still*, Stephen Jenkinson writes from the raw edge of a diagnosis with honesty and vulnerability. The book is a meditation on grief, dignity, and the fragile brilliance of being alive. For those willing to sit with uncertainty, sorrow, and the strange clarity that arises when the ground shifts beneath us, *Trembling, Still* serves as a profound companion through bewildering terrain. What emerges is not despair, but a fierce reckoning with what it means to live fully, even in the face of uncertainty.'

— ADITI SETHI, MD, founder and executive director,
Emberlight: Center for Conscious Living & Dying in Asheville, NC

'What an antidote to the prescription pill – a script, a plea. More than anything, this book is faithful. In Stephen's loving hands and radical generosity, Parkinson's disease becomes lucid, transparent, touchable. As we are let in on his human act of befriending the beast, we befriend the befriending. Reading *Trembling, Still* will not give us more years, but it does have the power to root us deeper in this world as Stephen's words turn flat Earth into round. This book is better than good; it is whole.'

— RONY ROF, MD, Sabar Health Hospital at Home, Israel

'There is extraordinary courage in this book, and extraordinary honesty. But what moves me most is its refusal of consolation. Jenkinson does not arrive at peace. He arrives at something harder and more trustworthy – a kind of sorrowing clarity that, as he writes, can fit you out for joy. In a culture of bypass, this is a direct, head-on wrestling with reality, and it is a pleasure to see how someone who has created some of the best maps actually traverses the territory.

'For anyone who works with the dying, loves someone who is ill, or simply has not yet figured out how to think about their own mortality – which is to say, most of us – *Trembling, Still* is essential reading.'

— MANISH AGRAWAL, MD, MA, cofounder and CEO, Sunstone Therapies

'Those familiar with Jenkinson's opus – listeners, readers, the counselled and consoled – may be unsettled by the profound unsettling Stephen recounts. Vulnerability is all too often dissonant in a culture obsessed with competence, perhaps all the more so when the one sharing their fears is assumed or expected to be unfailingly competent in the face of disassembly. Genuine devastation, as Stephen attests, brings with it a deep draught of frailty, it invites hard questions about consistency, it insists on a reckoning with the limitations of living, and it forces a fumbling acceptance of the inadequacy of much of our bodily being, and not least of button flies.

'*Trembling, Still* is, however, more than a wordsmith's journal penned while he steers headlong into the storm of self-loss. It is an honouring of the beauty and brittleness of pottery, the resistance of beans, the affordances of having a hand in the provisioning of our daily bread, and it is an invitation and invocation to cultivate joy and gratitude in the midst of troubling times.'

— DR. JONATHAN CODE, writer, teacher, kindler and craftsman

'Stephen Jenkinson is a man of both words and phenomena; I savoured every expression of experience from the depths of sadness to the peaks of triumphs, from exquisite reflections on body and mind to relationships close and casual. Gifted with letters, this man's words are authentic, masterful, painterly and poetic. Demanding life from his ailing body and confronting the terror of a failing mind, he wows.'

— DIANE DE CAMPS MESCHINO, MD,
psychiatrist and artist; associate professor, University of Toronto

'As a practicing end-of-life counselor, I have found no text more insightful, more trustworthy, more honest, than *Trembling, Still* for its humble look into the abyss of neurodegeneration and lament. There are so few who have sat on both sides of the hospital consultation room's desk that separates patient and practitioner and given us their account of the hurt of it all. Being of age and broken body to be obligated to inhabit both as well, I can confidently say that *Trembling, Still* is the truest account of the words the Rough Gods have spoken to anyone listening on either side of that desk.'

— JONATHAN HELLER, MS, CT, founder and director, Casa Ahava,
the first hospice and palliative care home in Mozambique

**Also by Stephen Jenkinson**

*Money and the Soul's Desires: A Meditation* (2002)

*Angel and Executioner: Grief and the Love of Life* (2009)

*How It All Could Be: A Workbook for Dying People
and Those Who Love Them* (2012)

*Homecoming: The Haiku Sessions* (2013)

*Die Wise: A Manifesto for Sanity and Soul* (2015)

*Nights of Grief and Mystery* (CD, with Gregory Hoskins) (2017)

*Come of Age: The Case for Elderhood in a Time of Trouble* (2018)

*Rough Gods* (CD, with Gregory Hoskins) (2020)

*Dark Roads* (CD, with Gregory Hoskins) (2020)

*A Generation's Worth: Spirit Work While the Crisis Reigns* (2021)

*Reckoning* (with Kimberly Johnson) (2022)

*Matrimony: Ritual, Culture and the Heart's Work* (2025)

*Caldera* (LP/CD, with Gregory Hoskins) (2026)

# Trembling, Still

## The Awful Clarity
## of a Mind in Eclipse

**Stephen Jenkinson**

Chelsea Green Publishing
White River Junction, Vermont
London, UK

First published in 2026 by Chelsea Green Publishing | PO Box 4529 |
White River Junction, VT 05001 | West Wing, Somerset House, Strand |
London, WC2R 1LA, UK | www.chelseagreen.com
A Division of Rizzoli International Publications, Inc. | 49 West 27th Street |
New York, NY 10001 | www.rizzoliusa.com



Publisher: Charles Miers
Deputy Publisher: Matthew Derr
Project Manager: Natalie Wallace
Copy Editor: Sara Bader
Proofreader: Nancy A. Crompton
Designer: Jenna Richardson

ISBN 978-1-64502-453-8 (hardcover) | ISBN 978-1-64502-454-5 (ebook) |
ISBN 978-1-64502-455-2 (audiobook)
Library of Congress Control Number: 2026008169 (print)

**Our Commitment to Green Publishing**
Chelsea Green sees publishing as a tool for cultural change and ecological stewardship. We strive to
align our book manufacturing practices with our editorial mission and to reduce the impact of our
business enterprise in the environment. We print our books using vegetable-based inks whenever
possible. This book may cost slightly more because it was printed on paper that contains recycled
fiber, and we hope you'll agree that it's worth it. *Trembling, Still* was printed on paper supplied by
Marquis that is made of recycled materials and other controlled sources.

Authorized EU representative for product safety and compliance
Mondadori Libri S.p.A. | www.mondadori.it
via Gian Battista Vico 42 | Milan, Italy 20123

Printed in Canada.
10 9 8 7 6 5 4 3 2 1     26 27 28 29 30

*For those summoned to the mind's wilderness;*
*For those staggered by it, stilled by it;*
*For those who stay close.*

# Contents

# Prologue

I may have, in a heated moment of indiscretion or inflation, told the Gods of my plans. Hindsight, and some disorder in the mechanics of my life, tell me so. I don't know about outright laughter, but there's evidence that my schemes for myself made mirth for the divinities with whom I share this place.

The drastic genius of that couplet – 'Tell them your plans if you want them to laugh' – is the notion that the Holy has a sense of humour. And just as drastic: it's likely a kind of humour that has no need of irony. Unless you are a Homeric Greek, it is more than possible that you've never said those words aloud, nor thought the thought that there's mirth in the sanctum sanctorum. If you are a secular humanist, it's less likely still.

That the makers of the whole carnage-strewn funhouse of life as we know it can be made to laugh: it's a perfect storm of wit and least likelihoods, an open invitation to the cynic and the siren and the saint.

But if it's true, I'll wager they don't laugh through their teeth. I don't think they sneer. In this world and in the other, a genuine laugh, a holy one, is a full throttle amen, a high-octane hallelujah of confoundment and affirmation. Laughter, joy of that kind: it's likely their invention. It's us, not them, mistaking a scythe for a walking cane and wondering and chagrined after those nicks in the shins, with no sense of humour.

The Gods are laughing most of the time. Maybe that's what life is: them laughing, and us invited and incited to take the hint, to get it straight.

None of us deserve the cruelty or the grace. That was Leonard Cohen's take on the ledger of healing. A lot of suffering rises from our investment in merit, in being one of the good guys. It's good to be good, sure, but it isn't a prescription for a good outcome. There's some other calculus that finds us, without finding us deserving. There are things in life that we don't deserve, things that we do. And the difference between them might be negligible, and hardly helps.

The work of being human in a crisis is a crisis. We are blessed, often, but not particularly favoured. Crises are crossed swords, crosshairs, crossroads, where several things are possible, and most of them are unlikely. Hope gets a workout, prayer gets an airing, and then things happen anyway. And then comes making meaning of those things, which is a hard and drastic business of dissonance and rupture and flailing for firm ground. Unknowing is the least of it.

If you have any moral compass, any sense that there is a moral order you can resort to, then you know how inscrutable, how anarchic are those times that are more conjectural than meaningful, times when the harrowing and the hurt, the cause, the course, the curse and the cure of them are untraceable.

I wrote what follows in the teeth of a storm. It shows. There are moments of opacity, self-absorption, perdition. I was prompted by receiving a diagnosis of neurodegenerative disease. It wasn't a book I went after, but a long shudder that I didn't proofread. In fact, I never read it during the course of the year that produced it. I couldn't have borne it. I couldn't have lived through many of these realizations twice. I had no audience in mind, or purpose.

So afterwards, when the hard weather had for a time played itself out, I embedded some scaffolding into the fray, after the fact, to hold up the edifice, to help the book make a little sense, to make the hardship of the storm sentient and sad. Those are the moments where I came down from the roof, to get a little ground beneath me and think about what'd come to get me. Much of the rest of it was a kind of seizure.

There are half sentences here, lots of them. There are sentences that are dense in the manner of dark stars, or black holes. There are drastic sentences and desperate sentences and dour ones. The difference between them is the difference between roulette wheels and steering wheels and prayer wheels. At the time, I couldn't live, couldn't see, couldn't write. So I wrote that way.

In my corner of the world, Anglo North America, the mind comes a distant second to the heart. There are 'matters of the heart', where the cursor and calculator uneasily wander, easily distracted, distressed, underserved by their intelligence. Yet for all that we favour the heart even still, favour its native land, its feeling tones. When there's discord in the house of love, the mind and its habits are often blamed. When disorder comes to the bone house, the body, then the mind, the wounded seat of thought – the 'psycho' in psychosomatic – is suspect. Emotional intelligence, or just intelligence? When the crisis is on, it's an easy call. We may not think about it much, but we don't doubt that the heart knows its way in the dark, that it's the real homing device. Nobody says, 'To thine own brain be true.' Or mind. They're too easily lost.

From the beginnings – and I can't find any sign of those first days, so subtle they were – my mind has been nominated by experts and by friends as more culprit than casualty of this calamity, this neurodegeneration that's come on. I overdid it. I asked too much of the lobes, burned too hot for too long, courted too much of a taxing kind of knowing. Not enough joy. When the news came, those convictions danced at the edge of 'why?' and 'how?'– leaving 'now what?' to care for itself, to fend for itself.

You have in your hands a rosary of shards, switchblades drilled through and beaded on a string. Yes, it is a chronicle, a this-worldly sequence. The news I received about the desertification of my brain – and it was terrible, utter news – caused *Trembling, Still*. It isn't a book about Parkinson's disease, or neurodegeneration. It's a book caused by neurodegeneration. It is an instant of detonation, and three hundred and sixty-four days and nights of wrestling angels, and unravelling and deformity. It is a scanning after the work of sanity, too. It is a wondering after redemption. It is wilderness, and a hurt primeval, and an assaying of the heart. It is a civilian's bedding down with rough Gods. It is a thinking man's meeting with a mind in eclipse. It is a drastic, awful, clarifying hymn, with the music mostly gone from it.

# Scaffolding 1

Days before Christmas, my family doctor says, 'Well, it could be stress. It could be a postural tremour.' 'Ok', I think, 'That sounds doable.' She pauses. Then: 'It could be Parkinson's.'

The room contracts, dilates. 'I'll refer you to a neurologist. Getting an appointment will take a while. A year, maybe.'

I call in a few favours, bypass the lineup, and see a neurologist on 2 January. We're two minutes into the meeting. He's been testing my reflexes. 'Oh yeah', he says, like he's commenting on the weather. 'Parkinson's.'

At first: what? Shambles?
No. That wasn't it.
A weeping, rearing, leaking, ruptured mind?
No. That came later.

A punishment? The cylinders on the cage door clicking shut?
No. I was thinking by the time I saw it that way.
*Before.* Before the figuring, the stance taking, the old recourse to fixes: what was I?
Before anything meant anything: what was I?

I was a single feather blown off a wing by the January wind,
pretending I was still a bird. Ever was a bird.

I was a small, illustrated book, every third page gone,
every third instant missing,
the intermediate pages of stepping, reaching, soothing
broken and torn out.

Yes. That was there, then.
But mostly I was cold and
without reasons. I heard the diagnosis. I didn't know what it meant.
Or who it meant. Those were the first few moments of a branded,
blistered life.

How is it my brain is crumbling, melting like
a sand mandala in the rain?
How could I know that,
and it be true,
at the same time?

Bits of my family standing in the parking lot after the appointment,
bits of me trying to decide what comes next.
Walk? Tea? Drugstore prescription? Asylum?
Staring down the street. There's the winter wind. There's the edict. That's it.
Is this me we're talking about?

Describing 'devastation' is trolling through a field of debris. The
impact's already happened, already so, already a cooling, impersonal
fact. The cartwheeling of personal effects has already happened,
the scree of corruptible days now a strewn, blurred smear across the
ground of an otherwise ordinary day. Unrelenting time has swallowed
the moment of impact, the ploughing up of ground. There's no fixing
to be done, no deal to be struck. No remedy. It's all already happened.
Ordinary morning street sounds bury the burial of 'ordinary.' This
isn't summons. It's news. Already I'm not a witness. I'm a subject.

Something's so utterly over.
And I didn't notice.
And I still don't know.

I was in for a hammering. That
was to come.
But just then, at first, on the second day of the year, out on the boulevard
in front of the clinic,
I was hunted, and seized, and brought to ground
in something's jaws.
And still I didn't know.

On New Year's Day I was fine. The next day, diagnosed. The next, on a
plane to California. No reason to go. Less reason to stay.
   In that state, I started writing things down.

# 3 January 2024
### *Plane, layover in Calgary, en route to Palm Springs*

To whomever this comes to rest upon:

Before we go any further, an apology for the penmanship. I'm told it's a sign. The longer this thing goes on, the deeper the perplexity in the dexterity, the smaller and more irrevocable the writing becomes. I found this out yesterday, although I've noticed a certain bewilderment in the fine-motor world for some time.

'Wear and tear' is what I figured at the time. Not being in my fifties any longer, those full-throttle days. But no: yesterday's news was that the writing gets smaller as things go on. The record will show that I've always favoured a small script. Starting out as a writing type, I held a high regard for paper and ink, and small script was my translation of that regard. The scrawl will signal diminishment from here on, even though regard is still there.

This time yesterday, my life was perforated, punctuated, punctured by a piece of information. I was told that all the signs were saying I had – have (a shift that needs practice) – Parkinson's disease. My wife and son were with me, my daughter on speaker phone. I relied upon them (more practice) to track the steady stream of information stemming from what seemed a cursory, overly brief survey of the highlights of this affliction. I squeezed fingers. I pointed to my nose. I touched certain coordinates. I counted backwards by increments of seven.

That last one was a strange encounter. I sensed that my competence was, for the first time that I know of, under scrutiny – in doubt, even. I found myself trying to memorize instead of calculating the rolling, reversing sequence. I found myself hoping I got the answer right, and then noticing that I was hoping instead of knowing. Then I was asked to walk down a hallway and walk back. 'Not bad', the neurologist said. I was grasping for affirmation by this time, even though 'not bad' isn't what you want a neurologist to say about something you've been doing since age two.

All the while, I was noticing myself engaging the sequences, watching my usually unstill hand, remarking on how I was focused on stillness in order to pass a test I thought would be rendered by a CT scan, or the like. But the survey of my affliction was simplicity itself: tracking a finger with an eye, rolling my fingers across imaginary piano keys while staring ahead.

It was strange . . . No, it made me a stranger to myself, trying to perform well while a neurologist sized me up. It made me wish I'd practiced more, paid attention to the gestures I thought were inalienable, inevitable, irreducible – barring an accident-borne puncture of the mind or spine.

Of course, the conceit is a kind of subterfuge: if I do well on this testing, then I'll walk out of here in better shape than I walked in. But, of course, I'm in the office, and *I'm already afflicted*, minus the information. What I'm hoping I might prevail over is already so. Has already happened. That's the oddness of this thing: *I'm already not the man I hope I still am.* All the new undoings are intact, none of them undone, undoable.

And that's what I found the hardest thought to think in the first few hours, post-diagnosis: *this is me he's talking about.* I've not much say in the thing. It's me there, in the crosshairs of his dismal expertise. It's me he is writing an anticonfusion prescription for. It's me he's advising to take my time and think over whether to take pills that will do precisely nothing to restore any lost dexterity or smooth running, or even challenge the oncomingness of what's already here. Already me.

We are, many of us, famous for our ability to get used to reversals of fortune so severe. That is the usual story, the suspect reassurance. I now think it more likely that we can get used to the reversal of fortune of others. It isn't indelicacy at work or play. It's just the brief, short distance between our tiny fickle well-being and the demonstrable fate of that person known to us but a step or two away.

Exhibit A: While I was writing the above paragraph, the flight attendant announced a 'medical situation' occurring in the rear of the plane, and inquired whether there was a doctor or a nurse on board. I instantly vacated the centre seat in the day-old degradation of my likelihoods, and something of me thanked the middle-aged woman who rose to the occasion with her studies and time in the halls of human suffering. I vacated the seat with no effort, no labour, no onset of comparison. Just this: for a few minutes beyond my noticing of it, *it wasn't me*. That's all. I don't know if that is misery finding its company, or a contorted suffering forgetting itself for a while, or me gladly taking the opportunity to set the last twenty-four hours of dissociation aside unawares, until this moment. Then this one. *Gladly*. And gladly I wish the medical situation and its actors well. But, finally, for a moment, it's not me at the centre of affliction.

The cross knot of despair that wrung every particle of wonder out of every moment of the last twenty-five hours is untied somehow. I am a casual voyageur in the sky, as so often I have been. I have to remind myself who I am now, looking out the window on the scheme of roads and buildings and lives down below. I am a Parkinson's man. Or I was. Or I'll be again. I'll have to decide whether I'm avoiding things, or whether I've come to my senses, or whether my as-yet-uneclipsed abilities in the human striving for life have come around again. I'll have to make up my shaky mind. When everything – OK, not everything, not yet – connected to your mind, when everything that convenes in your mind seems to be shaking, the mind, bless its soul, seems to go along for the bumpy ride. 'Turbulence' is what they call this condition in the sky, and turbulence is a close enough descriptor: some unseen force from without sees to it that all within heaves and churns and shuffles. There goes the kilter.

Yesterday – diagnosis day – time broke. Time passing turned into rough acreage. I hauled myself over it, through it. The night before, when everything was still pending, my daughter and her ex-spouse equivalent, his five-year-old by another woman he is no longer with, my son, my wife, a guest from Ireland, my partner in a music project and his spouse equivalent, and I ended up at my ex-wife's place, the same place she bought after leaving me, the place that was now a staging area for arranging the recon mission into the neurological unknown that was to follow.

Several times one of us said aloud, 'Well, this is weird.' Everyone except my ex-wife – something I've never called her – who said she didn't think it was weird at all. Bless her. At one point, as I sat in her living room, it seemed to be a kind of pre-op theatre, and I was wondering what my life might already have become, without me really noticing. It could have been weird, and no one might have noticed.

If this is a tragedy, then we could say that tragedy might make useful, purposeful even, what the statutory found weird and discredited, even forbade. A room full of people that tragedy brings together might as readily be a village as an oddity. The misfortune of one in their midst might be the occasion for communion. Afterwards, attendees might bring shards of integrity back to the corners of their worlds. They've been to prayers, to the opening of the holy books. Tragedies are holy books: hints, inscrutables, skewed instructions, the index finger of a startled mind running down the chapters, the verses, the fissures.

I'm glad it was weird. I'm glad my kids in their mid-adulthood could see their parents and their parents once-removed in the weirdness, see them fallen down, though not all at once. *Weird* needs the contrast of 'ordinarily OK' close by, the way light needs something to illumine. Like light, *weird* is gone soon after it appears, so it needs its amanuensis to take a little fugitive dictation. (The writing is deteriorating just now. I'm right about that, though perhaps not about why: there's turbulence in the air above Nevada, or wherever we are, and it affects my spelling, too.)

## 4 January 2024
### *Desert, Joshua Tree*

One thing I very much want to do: call out, 'You don't understand.' Or, 'I don't understand.' I don't know who I'd call that out to. 'This is all badly misunderstood, and that's underneath it all.' I couldn't tag the understanding. But I know that I want to have been wrong, fundamentally wrong, somewhere along the way. Wrong in the examination room, say, when I misheard the doctor's directions and hesitated, revealing a neurodegenerative symptom. I review my performance on writing out a sentence he asked me to reproduce, something about 'a dreary morning was upon us.' It was a poor sentence. Poorly imagined, poorly spoken. I couldn't get behind it at all. My heart wasn't in it, and it showed. And *that's* why I'm here, I want to say, shaken, in the California desert, adrift in my unsettledness, a day into the disease, having last night paid through the nose for an oversize rental car at an airport in a foreign country, unable in the dark to solve the locked gate's combination to the house kindly loaned us, everything gone awry, every ordinary obstacle now utter defeat.

Some part of my mind would almost decide on such an account. I can feel the willingness of that part of the brain – if that's where these things happen – to bring all of this down to a breakdown in nuance. Some part of me seeks salvation just now, and a missed flight might just be the way out. The three airports yesterday, the lost baggage, being upsold at Thrifty, the rules, the cards in my wallet bearing my ID that are more vital to the fact and the process of being modern than I am: the strangeness of the twenty-first century washed over me all day, razed my ability to belong to it. This is not a good time to sprout infirmity. It's not a time that is kind to not knowing your way around the place. The intelligence necessary to navigate this international travel fracas is already artificial. Scarier still: the word 'artificial' in this world isn't scary at all. It's another kind of 'real', the newest real there is.

Not quite, though. My discomfort on the matter is newer than the artificial intelligence is, and just as real.

I remember tonight a woman, maybe in her fifties, at a presentation I gave a few years ago. I'll leave her whatever privacy is left, and say only that she appeared hollow and hard-driven by whatever carried her to me. The question period came. This is when people ignore what's just been said and restore their reasons for coming in its stead. She was the first questioner. She began with a common enough litany. She'd been diagnosed recently. She'd been unnerved and riven by the news – and it had been news. She'd had no expectation beyond something being off, something that was usually kind to the long-term allegations of life. This part of the story she knew well, well enough to be singular of purpose in the delivery. But, as is common, I could hear the uncertain end of her tale looming. In another moment, it appeared she had lurched to a halt. Galled at the suddenness of the thing, she reached for something that would continue her question, her life. In the name of all of that, she said, 'I'm afraid it's too late to do a lot of things.'

'It is', I said, 'it's too late for a lot of things.'

This cauldron of calamity – these very days – are what I meant.

I've already decided – this may change – that I'm not going to become a Parkinson's do-it-yourself expert. I don't have any sense that peace of mind, or stillness of mind, awaits those of us afflicted as we calve off hours, then days at a stretch in search of expertise in what we can do about what we can do nothing about. So, I'll remain uninformed about what the internet would bid me do.

Before that decision took effect, though, I engaged my dread, my word voodoo, and looked up a couple of things. I avoided the word 'Parkinson's' entirely and went for the less damning 'tremours'. And it was in that brief review of contending likelihoods that I came across the word 'dopamine'. I've heard it before, as have you. It is the physiological seat of contentment, or joy, or bliss or well-being. The neurologist I met the other day slandered that idea. The 'happy gland', he called it, and then promptly discredited the possibility.

Still, in what I read, there seemed to be a link between Parkinson's and some kind of dopamine disturbance. In my case, there's probably something to all that. It's fair to say that I haven't made joy or happiness a core goal of contemplation. It doesn't figure largely in the work I've done in the last twenty years. As best as I could understand it, happiness was a consequence, not a cause.

But this isn't happiness thinking about happiness. Could I have been wrong about happiness? Are there different kinds? Does it ask as well as give?

Already in the wake of the appointment with the neurologist, I have completely forgotten that I am charged with a diagnosis. Twice, that I remember. Each time I realized that I was going about things – reading an idle magazine for no reason, thinking about very little – as if my life is exactly what it was a week or so ago. Some game show trapdoor snapped shut just then, and I yanked myself back into the present, the foreclosed-upon-present, the harshly lit, intolerant, blasted, Godly present.

It shocks me, twice. Once when I realize I've forgotten to be diagnosed, and once when I feel the moral obligation to be utterly changed seize upon my fidelities. How will I manage with this oversight? How will I gather up the current crumble of my Parkinsonian thoughts if I forget I am afflicted? Is this forgetting *grace*? Is it the disease?

When the neurological appointment slumped to a halt the other day, I could scarcely stand. Once up, I could scarcely walk. I couldn't find a reason to. I wrestled with my coat. I shuffled into the waiting room. There I locked eyes with a late-middle-aged man who was perched at the edge of his chair, awaiting his turn, his worn wife beside him. His affliction rode him so mercilessly, the misery so palpable, so postural, so infernal, the suffering so final in him. He was stooped, looking up at me from a hell of drastic clarity. His eyes were pools of misfortune. We nodded, one to the other, as prisoners do shuffling to and from their lostness. In that moment I thought: Ah. Here's what's coming.

## 5 January 2024

The name of the afflicted part of my brain and the name of the drug of choice for contending with the affliction both have the word 'dope' in them. 'Cope/Hope/Dope', I used to say in the days I worked in palliative care, the death trade – 'the holy trinity of death care in a death-phobic culture.' Now here comes the dope. I imagine the other two will not be far behind. 'Dope' is slang now. It describes a mind-buggering substance, and it describes the devotee of said buggering. Hope struck me for a long time as slouching on the future's doorstep, refusing to go inside. To go inside, you see, would have to make it the present. That takes a lot of nerve. 'Hopeless' has as much slouching involved, plus enough nihilism to warrant the posture.

I wonder if coming apart from the cognitive insides will change any of this, whether it will give the changes and the reluctance to change their due. They've impulses, they've reflexes, each of which initiates and imitates necessity very well, each of which, when tangled with, take a lot out of you.

Can you take things seriously happily? Is sobriety tolerant that way? Is discipline funny? Is funny happy? Is devotion happy? I am nursing those and a host of other crises.

This being diseased is me standing on a pier, the boat of everything before now casting off, all ashore who's staying ashore. Or, it's me soloing in a stripped-down outrigger, watching the pier of old understanding recede, taken in by the mirage of the earth's bend manifest on the horizon.

Of course, nowhere is it written by the Ancients of Days or their heirs that mirth banishes discipline – that would be neither joyful nor disciplined. And we've heard of those Zen masters whose meditation discipline is taken up in chortling. They may have the usual incidence per capita of this affliction of mine, chuckling or not, but their particular grace under pressure might enable them to laugh their way through that, too.

Sobriety and solemnity are Anglo–North American twins. I'm not the first to forge them, even confuse them. With very little time in with the ecclesia, still I was heir to their resemblance. So, is it too late for me to have lived as if this was a choice and not a given? Is it too late for me to have undertaken the work I did with the happy gland turned on?

Yes, in every way 'too late' can be meant, it is too late for me to have been that guy. Is it too late for me to be that guy? Close, yes, habits of the heart and eye and mind being what they are. We'll see if we take climatic measures that slow the recession of the glaciers. And we'll see if I choose latter-day recourse to joy.

One thing about dragging around a diagnosis that I have to remind myself I have: an agile, emotional part of me knows I'd better practice being grateful, at least for the big things.

The little things help with that. Your wife makes you tea – without asking. You're not thirsty, but your thirst is not the point. It's one way she puts her hand on you, while she still can. That's easy to forget.

If you wait until you feel grateful to say 'thank you' aloud, you would be waiting a good while. You receive things you didn't ask for, don't want, don't need. There's not a hint of the beneficiary's gratitude in you. That's magic hour. That's when you get all those things you don't feel – benefit, satisfaction, a need met – into your voice, and you shape them all into that empty place and give it the sounds of thanksgiving. I'd guess that's why it's called Thanksgiving: not because you got something, but because you have something – thanks – to give.

# 6 January 2024

Airport layovers are where you invent needs. They are culinary casinos: mealtime is all the time. The allegations of blood sugar are edicts. The decor is drywall deep. There are themed carbohydrates. The same half-dozen items are sauced, tossed, flash fried, fricasseed. Eighteen travel hours of unrelenting, self-abasing reward for denying yourself and eating well the rest of the time, when you're at home.

Mall half-light fools you into thinking you're eating because you're hungry. You're not hungry. You're dancing with the timing of your connecting flight and the sprint time to its gate. This is an ideal time for existential unmooredness.

We chose a Greek theme for the lunch-approximate, time-consuming layover scheme. No identifiable Greeks behind the counter. We focused on roughage plus unfarmed protein, a great challenge. It's mystery meat all round.

Flying the day after my diagnosis, I was in no shape for moral discernment and the rigours of a hundred-mile diet. I was in an airport on the Canadian prairies, halfway between the Ontario home I wouldn't see for months and the California high desert, and I didn't know who I was.

All those fugitive habits of personhood and adulthood were cracking and peeling off in handfuls, as if too long in the ultraviolet. I pretended I was hungry. I pretended to eat. I was scanning myself for signs of disassembly. This is how I'll identify now, choosing my brand of transience.

I notice now that I've begun to notice the autonomic capacity of everyone else around me. Of course, I don't really know how they're doing in the depths of their lives. I don't know if they know it, either. But they're unchallenged by the lost-gear shuffle of the airport gait, just as I once was, as recently as my last run of the *Nights of Grief & Mystery* tour in Australia, when that young man in the departure lounge sat across from me, so deep in his tremours and his misery, and I didn't know what I was looking at. I know now. But minus a diagnosis, my fellow travelers are mostly upright and moving along to the 'all together now' of sparsely examined competence, the same competence that bore me for work to the southern hemisphere and back, unaided, less than two months ago.

# 7 January 2024

I don't know if I was just keeping my stand-and-deliver ratcheted up tight. I don't know if the demands of the road and the shows were the binding agent. But the diagnostic gamut has unravelled a tremourous ensemble. It is as if the encounter with the neurologist five days ago was a starting gun, or an overture, or a countdown. The tight knot of imprecisions that were once at my periphery have displaced my official self and its smoothed repertoire. In a few short days, I'm moving like someone in one of those little children's books you flip through to induce movement – jittery, the intermediate moments melting away. One short week. The psyche is powerful business. Disempowerment is powerful business.

I was halfway through the Greek food in the airport. I wasn't sure if I was slower in the hand-to-mouth business than I'd been. I've been doing it for so long that it scarcely registers. But I think I've begun to track the subtlest of hesitations. I still have the motor confidence of the usually abled, but that might be a mastery habit enjoying its autopilot, blithe as to what is incoming. Compromises in self-mastery are the hellgate for Anglo-North Americans like me.

I noticed a few grains of rice on the table. There were another few in my lap. Before I brushed them off, I looked under the table. A few more. Not enough to resemble a spill. Enough to look like inattention. I was flustered. I was gyrating. I had an instinct to go the Greek counter and explain myself to the kid working there who'll have to sweep up after me once we shuffle to the departure gate. I won't really do it. It's a nightmare of etiquette breakdown: the jitters, the neurologist, a staggering affirmation that only happened yesterday. The bamboo fork is my prosthesis. He might be the first in an uncharming list of people who'll be cleaning up after my unravelling. My chemtrail.

In my mind, I hear the first-person account of my burdening years coming on. Unable to rearrange the cargo below decks, I'll be listing to port or to starboard. I'll have to oversteer and course correct as I sail off on the raft in my coming years, as strangers I meet in the shipping lanes of life give me wide berth, recognizing, as they eventually will, the tattered ensign of compromise whipped by the breeze.

I spared the Greek place guy. I spared myself. I nudged the rice into a little pile with my shoe. He'd probably think a kid did it. I wondered what of all this showed. My first thought: the whole business was an interior opera. We're maybe twenty yards down the concourse. I asked my wife whether she noticed. She nodded, yes, which was crushing. What it crushed, I don't know. The eggshell of my plans for myself, maybe, for my agedness, if there'll be any agedness. I am guessing the time will come when I'd want her to know what's going on in here without me telling her everything. But it's too soon for me to be able to be translucent like that, to want to be illuminated, backlit by time passing, and my evenness with it.

I've eyed the end. Not the ending. That's different. If we're talking about life here, then endings are graduated things. There are loads of them, but they're not all easy to recognize. You need a lot of oncoming, ongoing courage to eye those things rolling through, taking so few prisoners as they do. Endings are eleventh-hour stuff, and they can go on for years.

The end is easier to get in view, because it's ultimate. It's the Big Bang of your life, but you don't know that yet. For the longest time it's in the 'yet to be', an idea that you can practice on. It's an idea that will come true sometime. It's not a belief, really. It happens to your beliefs.

Along with its misgivings, misfirings, misanthropies, the end can have its mishearings. Some of them are tragic. At least as tragic as the hearings are. Some of them have no consequence that matters. Some of them can be hilarious.

A few hours ago, my wife watched me end a phone call, inefficiently. Eventually she'd seen enough. She started to dress herself for the cold wind coming in off the desert. Before going outside, she looked directly at me and said, 'I'm going outside. I don't want to be a raccoon on your neck.' I've spent ten minutes – ten minutes I'll never get back – wondering why she'd ever be a racoon, and whether racoons get on your neck, and why, and how she knew all that. I like the idea so much I don't ask what she actually said, in case that wasn't it.

## 8 January 2024

I wasn't raised with tea. There was no tea, either hot or cold. There was coffee for the grownups. There was a bit of the paraphernalia for rousing coffee in the mornings – the grinding and the brewing, or whatever it was. There was never an invitation to join them in the ceremonial doings. Strictly adult business. Vague allusions to 'strong stuff' and 'octane' and the like had me understanding that coffee was lysergic in some way, that it was altering, conjuring stuff, barely containable, elevating and revelatory and narcotic. They'd drink it down cold and unadorned, just to have it inside themselves.

Plus, it was insolubly joined to cigarette smoking. It was a two-fisted devotion. Their smells were incantatory, phlegmatic. They were a cold mist in the air above their devotees – shamanesque. Any outlier winter's work was performed in the blue haze and the rolling billows of the strong, acrid stuff: as close as we got to sacred. Since I've been asthmatic from an early age, I've steered a wide berth around them both. Occasionally as I grew, I'd hear of someone my age being allowed a jolt of coffee by their parents, a reckless arrangement I didn't really envy.

Time went on. Coffee and café culture appeared out of nowhere. I remember peers hankering after these meetings, but I couldn't fathom sitting for hours in the same place, eating nothing and slouching over lukewarm brew. Still, I knew I was short a bit of sentimental sacramental education. There was no religion in my house, either, so I was dissolute in that way. As a nonaligned, back-sliding, nonpracticing and lapsed Protestant type, my beverage habits were iconoclastic and envious, if I'm honest.

There was no tea, not for the longest time. It was to me the weak sister to the coffee, unable to pull its own ceremonial weight, no match for the java. And it came in bags, which turned the leafy stuff and made it granny-grade, elderly business, no match for those café denizens brooding over their grains. The swill that came from tea and milk, or cream, the overwrought preciousness of the cup with its curlicue of a handle. Tea service gear: all housebroken, ecumenical, feral, faint.

And so it remained, until I found myself in Japan in my mid-thirties. Japanese tea culture wasn't a revelation – it was the discovery of a new continent. The elaborations in the tea shop beggared me. The tea ceremony, even in its abbreviated-for-Westerners form, even in its vagaries and boredom and very slowness, broke my heart. I had, it was now clear, missed so very much. My education and my soul were incomplete. Seeing this upswell of tea savvy in me, my Japanese host took me to a pottery shop, and there I discovered the raku teacup, where the makings of a cultured way of life were to be found. No porcelain for my late-to-the-scene soul. No slip. No glaze. The elaborations of clay made elemental and holy by fire in hillside kilns, all the devices of finger, palm and thumb vitrified and made over in the image of the Great Conjuring of the world. Or so it was for me. Febrile, caldera in your hand. Holy ground in the round.

At once, tea opened to me, and I to tea. Returning to the West I had to make a study of this revelation, surrounded as I was by the disposabilities of a 'to-go' world. Years of solo tea education followed, visiting the shops, drinking two handed, looking for the one true cup that could contain this for me. She appeared then. The cup was the work of a Canadian from the prairies, and it was the sum of all that I'd lived without. Time went by. I married, I sired, I fathered, I moved homes more often than called for. The beautiful things were put up high, out of reach of infants, those human wrecking balls, and then put away altogether, wrapped in newsprint, mute, safe.

Children grown and gone off, houses built and lost, matrimony in ruins, a public life rising from ash, notoriety coming round, age gathering round. Deep into the second act of my three-act play, twenty and more years ago, strangers asked after my take on the troubles of the times. Interviews, more interviews as the Death Guy. One day someone asked me about beauty, a rare inquiry. 'What is the most beautiful thing you own?' he asked. Though I hadn't seen her in years – the cost of preservation – I knew the answer at once. Interview done, I rooted through the boxes until I found one labelled 'Good Stuff'. The date of the newsprint told me it'd been a decade since she saw light, tasted tea. On a shelf by herself now, I vowed to make a ritual of tea part of my life, the part that remains. Slow going, inefficient, tea making.

Later that day, I took the cup down, passed it from one hand to the other thinking of something else. The cup slipped from my grasp, fell on the counter on its edge. It made a bad sound, the sound of a dent, a concussion, a fissure. I was thinking of nothing else, maybe not thinking at all. I made myself look. There was a y-shaped crack running from the lip to the cradling bend in the bowl. Waves of recrimination, acres of remorse, the whole thing gone, the original intention gone, flawlessness flawed, all the closeting care undone. Set beauty apart from the world, and it's beauty that suffers, and maybe the world doesn't know. A thousand blandishments, things never really working out, every tired recrimination and one-size-fits-all indelicacy levied for the sake of the delicate: I piled that upon myself. Preservation: a tax on beauty.

In his book titled *Platero and I*, Juan Ramón Jiménez tells
the story of riding the intuitively gifted mule Platero up
a mountain pass late at night until reaching a derelict
customs house. A menacing civil servant emerges,
demanding to know what taxable goods they carry.
The rider holds open the saddle bags, and says, 'See for
yourself. White butterflies.' The customs man doesn't look.
He dismisses them in disgust.

# 9 January 2024

The first responder in me wants to rid myself of the brokenness, the intact reminder of brokenness. A creep of unworthiness comes to claim me, other things. The less beautiful things gather round. I remember the interview, 'the most beautiful thing' question, how frail things become when they carry that designation, what becomes of all those other things set aside. Is there a 'most beautiful word'? 'Most beautiful thought', or 'moment', or 'look in your eyes', or 'possibility'?

Intact, it was, yes. But watch this: 'intact' doesn't really mean 'all together', or 'whole', or 'sound' or 'fit.' Its root means 'not touched'. The word whispers something truer than you wish it were: the way we go about our material life, the 'wholeness' of a thing doesn't include our employment of it. There's an essentialism in our language and in our psychic style: a thing, a thought, a moment, a child, maybe, is only whole starting out, undiminished and pure potential, the bloodless blessing of what could be, before the fall. With appreciation commences depreciation – deprecation, too.

Now there may be beauty in the untried. No, there is, sure. And beauty in the single, staggering moment before the sun breaks the horizon and day comes on, sure, or before you say 'I love you' for the first time, or before the first child comes in the house, before the first word is written for the new book. Before you know how lucky you are, how anointed you are with ordinary life. Before all that begins to end, or ends outright. Before it starts shedding all its could-bes.

But there's another kind. The song's taken up, the aria joined, the polyphony counts itself in. Already bound for silence, beauty's there in the one less measure, the strophe playing itself out. The song's beauty is there, in the certainty that soon it won't be there. The stillness has been touched by sound, its silence by the strophe and the stanza.

'What you have to do now' changes with age.

The a priori defeat of 'always' by 'now,' by 'this': that's beauty born and bathed and blessed and bound for goneness.

A cup taken up into the rafters of storage and safety is beautiful the way an idea is beautiful. Rescued from the fray beforehand, before anything has a chance to happen, it is a gesture's beauty. But it's not a thing's beauty. A thing is beautiful according to its appearance among us, as it takes up its place, as the rest of the world takes it up in its hands and chants. Or drinks.

So down it came, into this world. Its perfection cracked. It's 'most beautiful thing' cracked. It's 'best above all'. Like a divining rod, the raku cup went earthwards. Like that rod, it was ambivalent, tending two ways, not choosing from among them, divining, beautiful in its austerity, beautiful in its . . .

And unable to hold water anymore. Don't leave that out. Didn't hold its tea when it could, can't hold its tea now.

The time without tea came on, the time without tea went by. Somewhere inside I wore widower's black, abstained. Somewhere along the way I must have told the story, perhaps at the Orphan Wisdom School. Someone in the school, perhaps an angel down from the shelf, offered to get fixed what for me was unfixable. Unfixable in the way that I am.

## 11 January 2024

She spirited the cup away. Occasionally there'd be an obscure reminder: she's working on it. She knows somebody who knows somebody. She's moved to the West Coast. I all but gave the cup away by this time and made a vow not to elevate one shard of beauty over the others, at least not verbally, when I got the chance. Beauty, I seem to have decided, is a savaging of the heart. It belongs to the world, but it's a tough go for everything involved. The presence of beauty is radioactive and radiant, as deforming as it is affirming. It says of itself, 'If I live in this thing, at this moment – and I do – then everything else might bear some beauty, too.' But it's not clear that it does.

I want to contemplate and approach the silence of God while I can still hear. I hate to say it, but I don't trust peace of mind. It's not vigilant enough.

Just as I wrote that last sentence, a lash of wind tore down from the mountain behind the stone house I'm in, tore around the building until it found me wrapped against the desert cold on the veranda, writing about tea and beauty, and all but lifted the table I'm writing at out from underneath me. I had just enough time, maybe a second and a half, to decide what I was going to pluck from the tempest. I chose the raku cup I'd been writing about. I chose it over the writing book. That was just as I pondered beauty's power to demand communion with its setting. I held the teacup in my hand, mindful that it could fall again, and watched the plants, chairs, the garden stones with their heads in the wind, anything above ground riled up by the tempest and ready to pull up stakes and sail.

Ten seconds later and it's all but still now. Still in a way I'm unlikely to be again, nothing to show for the moment but a shakenness about and the undoing power of beauty leaving a shimmer in the leaves. As if it was a thought, and so had never been. I've left the cup on the floor of the veranda in case I have the whole thing wrong. In case the whole thing was a wild, mindless coincidence, or in case the wind picks up again.

What a grievous thing beauty is in this life. A wanton and grievous and dexterous thing it is, grating, fierce and open in its face. 'What shall we do', it says, 'now that I'm possible? Where do I end? Where do you?'

## 12 January 2024

Years later, I was in Switzerland to preside over the first-year anniversary of matrimonial doings undertaken at my farm in Ontario. The gravitas of matrimony in an era of vibrant and seamless celebrations of love was unnerving. In this part of rural Switzerland there was an echo of old ways, of village-minded ways, and they helped the beauty of matrimony come round.

The teacup woman attended the ceremony. 'I have something for you', she said. I knew what it was. You know what it was. I looked at the bumpy bubble-wrapped package in her hands. Frankly, I didn't want to open it. I knew that she'd gone to great lengths to make repairs, years of effort, crazy effort there, so there'd be loads of expectation heaped on my reaction. But how can you unbreak something? Are you going to anoint a teacup that can't hold tea as a differently abled thing? Staples? Sutures? Crazy glue? Another casualty up on the shelf for the sake of decor, decorum, gratitude?

I asked her to do the unwrapping. I could tell she was pleased. The last layer shed, the raku teacup was there, after all this time. No effort made to hide the crack. No smoke, no mirrors, no looking the other way. Instead, the breakage was enunciated and honoured by a ribbon of gold, forked lightning all down the cup's depth. Jewelled frailty. Jeweller's stuff poured down the brokenness, the crack in everything adorned, given its due, throne for enduring disassembly. 'The Japanese', she said. Ah, of course. The Japanese. Those who gave us raku gave us raku's *ma*, its unadorned, conscious emptiness. Not nothingness. An earthen caldera, gathered around the soon-to-be goneness of tea. The dust-to-dust of clay, the only-for-now of tea, the sharp mercy of the broken cup, its mind, the gold seal upon understanding. The here for now and all but goneness you can hold in your hand, you can drink and be warmed by. You can be stilled by.

awaken: 'a', an Anglo-Saxon adjective/preposition meaning something like 'of', or 'from'; and 'wake', the 'web and ebb of consequence that fans out from each intended and unintended thing'. To be awake: 'to draw nigh to the doing and undoing of being here, responsible and claimed by the sentient world.'

The endless, enduring Alps were framed by the window. The few of us there gathered around the steaming kettle. I poured the water into the broken cup. Only water. Tea now would be too sudden. Two wonders came to pass: the brokenness held, and all the water's surface held a cloud of gold dust, as the horizon all around holds the night sky. The genius of whoever repaired the brokenness fully at hand. The cup wasn't washed. The repair wasn't tested. It was done, and then it was let go of. And then it was in my hand.

We passed the broken cup, and we drank down the emptying magic of it then. And for a little while, there was gold inside and out, and we were awake.

I don't know if this Parkinson's affects the hearing. The affliction seems to have its way with most of the body's business, so I would not be surprised if hearing isn't spared. Everyone's hearing, maybe, whoever's attending to the symptom list.

I know life affects the hearing, although I don't know in which directions. Maybe a half dozen years ago, I found that ambient sound was tending to elude me. I was no longer able to discern with certainty which direction some sounds might be coming from. I used to carve marble with pneumatic chisels and hammers. I wore masks and earphones, but you never know what's getting through to you. The ear doctor asked if I'd done a lot of ocean swimming. Never, or near never. This is the kind of hearing loss that's triggered by cold-water excess. That phrase – hearing loss – was stilling at the time, like a signpost on the road heading out of the town called Intact.

So, is the hearing 'the mind'? Is it the most direct route to the mind's routines, no delays, nothing underdone, no soft balls? Or is hearing the will's fetcher and fixer, where preference and habit have their day? Is the mind a clearing house of wild and uncalled-for translations of what the audio nerves dredge from the sonic depths?

A half hour ago I was doing some yoga on the floor. That's a laughable declaration, given what a latecomer I am to the exertion. For the moment, I imitate the postures and the way of getting to them. Many decades of habit are in the way. But my wife is persuaded that I have a moral obligation to whatever's left of my dexterity to get some yoga into me, even at this, dexterity's eleventh hour. For the sake of whatever she's going to have to do for me later, yoga – proximal it is.

I was at the tail end of the bowing and the scraping, unravelling now to assume what I think is called the corpse pose, the least emphatic and maybe the most demanding of the morning's postures. For all its elementality, laying prone and prostrate, as if you are truly done with life and life with you, is not so easy. The torque of life is hard to renounce, as the desert saints have attested, and in crunch time, life, even its misfortunes and demands, will do. More than do.

Down into corpse pose I descend. Halfway there my palm is pierced by a micro-agony that makes me wince and gasp. It takes me a second or two to realize it's what's called a 'goat's head', a burr of exceeding precision in its extremities, both sharp and barbed. A standard desert design it is, fending off the wild's opportunists by clinging most persuasively to them to get the seed strewn, punishing the point of contact with infernal persistence, the way a memory of imagined pleasure gained and lost the hard way persists.

My wife, on the alert for infirmity of all stripes, asks what's what. 'Burr', I say, still trying to assume the corpse pose. 'It'll pass', she says. 'Focus'. Jesus, I think, this isn't going to pass, focus or not. It's stigma. I'm trying to get corpse-like, which is counterintuitive for a living person in most any condition, but any touch of clothing or carpet drives the nail, so I'm trying to avoid the warming blanket my wife is draping around me to keep me from chattering.

'It's in my palm,' I say. She says, 'OK', tucking me in like a malingering patient. She says, 'Show me.' I say, 'You won't see it without your glasses.' She's on the verge of losing patience, since I'm messing with the yoga gold that's supposed to be in the corpse pose. She pokes at what she can't see in my palm. The goat's head goes in a little deeper. 'Can you take it out?' I ask. 'What?' she says.

It's then that I realize that she thinks I said 'burn', as in 'rug burn'. Or 'brrr', as in 'chilled'. A short moment goes by, and then I think to

'Yep. This is what the future includes: clusters of near-symptoms, near-misses, mishearings – each of us poking at the tea leaves, reluctantly trying to get the lowdown in the latest round of diminishment that may have come on in the night.'

## 13 January 2024

Time was that I could get up in the early morning, get dressed with care as if going to work, leave the house undisturbed, make tea as if making communion, retire to a writing room set aside for the purpose, and write. I did this in Tepoztlán, in San Cristobal, in Ikaria, in Badajoz, in Guadalupe, in Tramore, in Istanbul, in other places. I sat for hours, wrote by hand. I welcomed the room, and the room seemed to welcome me. No technology to fail. A decent pen, decent paper, a sense of well-being. Later, when the eyes dimmed, glasses were called for. Being easy to lose, I had to craft some devotion to keep them close. The windows opened, one to the slate grey Mediterranean, one to the bronze Bosporus, one to a sun-bleached courtyard, one to a monkey jungle, one to the River of Abundance and Time. One to silence, one to the wind in from Africa, one to Ulysses's way, one to the whale road. Another to the silence of the boreal winter, another to the Plaza Matamoros.

I would sit, open the book, date the entry, begin. Begin as if I'd done my part, done my stations, ablutions and absolutions. Much more often than not, the beginning was routine enough as to pass without notice. It came to my coming to it. The devotions murmured round the room. I knew I was fortune's son. I knew I was lucky. Even with the advent of fine motor fuckery, in the form of scrawl, I was a lucky writing person. I could read everything. When the time came to transpose to the computer, I knew what I'd written. I was doing something of what I was born to do. I had the grease. I had the bones. By the time I learned to love writing things down, I was being loved by wherever good stuff comes from. That's how it seemed. Necessity has always seemed kind to me. I was glad of the discipline, glad of the mandate.

# 14 January 2024

When a fitting subject came around – money and soul, death, elderhood, pandemic – it clarified itself according to my discipline. I put on my best things, out of respect for the concern at hand, out of respect for the grace accorded me by fortune, the allowance granted me by whatever skills had settled in my joints. I was discharging the burden. I wrote. I loved it.

When properly adorned in the threads of office, when the shoes were shined and the graces met, I drew down the rough attentions of the Rafter Dwellers, the resident deities of place. I wrote because I was obliged to write. There was no arguing the matter, no argument at all. It came to me that we humans can argue beyond what we can know or remember. In fact, when we are caught up in argument like a fly in amber, memory is the first and enduring casualty. With hammer and tongs we go at it, and a day or so later have a frayed and unreliable memory of what the fracas was about. We remember mostly who won, and that we fought and contended, inventing or seizing upon new reasons to do so as tinder for the witless ordeal. But the life blood of the argument? It hadn't any, beyond the storm and fears and devilry we take up as we go.

I reckon that is sign enough of our design and purpose: what we've been granted by way of nature and proclivity and indwelling purpose isn't wrought round argument. God knows we can mobilize around any curse, and gather the slights into something like reason enough, and crusade our way. But the fact is that the memory doesn't do strife's biddings, that the reasons for a slagging match are lost in the slaggings, enriching the barristers and solicitors. After a while, we're railing to retain the point of the thing with surrogate reasons and principles, with replacement values to fuel the contention. It all persuades me that the mind we're granted simply has other business.

That business: you heard a story you found compelling and important, but due to a lack of training and other things, you can't remember how the story went, which is galling. So, in some kind of faith, good or good enough, you sort of half tell the part that you do recall. Just there, in the act of recollection, a bit more of the story uncoils, and in some mycelial fashion your story – the one you cannot recall despite mightily wanting to – begins haltingly to tell itself, using the design of your mind to do so. A story comes on. Not quite the one you heard, more likely the version of that story more needed now than when it happened.

Your mind is not an arguing thing. It is a storying thing. That is its maker's mark. That is its sixth sense, the soul's pattern and mould.

My discipline was recollection, mostly. I washed and dressed for the telling, not so much the tirade. And when I began to travel to older parts of the world, that difference and that discipline seemed to be recognized. Laid claim to, even. In places where conversation is still an art form, where inflection was a blessing to hear, I had a hearing.

I sit down this morning, and things are different. I am still dressing for the occasion, but I may look more like a veteran dressed for a Veteran's Day parade.

# 15 January 2024

The mechanics of scrawl, for one, are a clutch of details, which like those of breath, say, pass with no notice when all is in order. But the mechanics of scrawl are an altar, too. They are a place where all the fumbling after gratitude can be waged. They are a place where the profanity of grace can be assayed. It's holy ground there.

> profane: 'that stretch of ground before the altar place', 'before'
> in space and in time, in a place where holiness goes in revelry to
> renew its vows. Profanity is a vestige of that time when the Holy
> held the world sacred, high priest of the ordinary. High
> priest, hierophant of the profane.

With the oncomingness of disease is coming a survey of degradation, slippings away without notice. Unsteadiness is not a different ability. It is becoming – quickly, too – the back forty of ability. I watch my writing hand contract around the pen as an unsteady swimmer contracts around a buoy. Contraction increases the erratic motions of the nib, magnifies them into a seismic sensitivity, registering every tectonic weave or wobble in me.

I'm right-handed – or I was. I am, at this point, residually right-handed – right-handed by default. My left, the more palsied hand today, wavers and signs according to the writing exertions of my right. It's an odd, unfruitful sympathy. It is a land of puppetry, a broken echo of an old, unvaunted skill. The right hand guides the pen, the left exaggerates the gesture until it's semaphore more than it is writing.

It seems that my writing may be a precedent for my general dexterity and gait. It is a detonation of a stagger of regret, a flash flood of bitter sorrow boiling up around the slow extinction of unvalued creative skills. The antics of my left hand might be a signal flare of distress, punctuating the midnight sky of my agile days.

I have said and written many times that having been born into a time of trouble and a pantomime of grace and culture will, according to the decision you don't know you've made, be either an affliction or an assignment. I will say now that I am entering into the weather system of wishing I'd been born into a time that cultivated a scheme of gratitude in me, gratitude for what rises and sets upon me, what waxed and waned in me to conjure the ordinary days and the redeeming nights of my little allotment. I do wish there'd been more inheritance, less drastic miming and invention. I don't say this to save these days from regret. I say it to give shape or scale to the enormity of . . .

Of what? Of culture, I think. Culture is what gives us catalytics to render down limit and frailty and goneness until they belong in the little lives of its citizens. This time of dischoreography, discord in me, this arrhythmia in the poetics of my mind: it's no good for crafting a diction for sorrow.

What you want is this: to be marveled into existence by the ordinariness that won't ever end. You want to be ready for the ordinariness that is even now ending. Maybe that's how readiness comes to be so: knowing there's a time of never ending that happens before the endings start. It's not insurance. It's assurance.

They say – and it persuades me – that there are domains of sensoria that, in addition to prevailing when the ordinariness is upon you, also compensate for those times when the code of ordinariness is broken, like heightened hearing does when there's no vision, or heightened heartbreak does when there is no village.

Maybe these senses have their equivalent in worker bees or drones who walk the perimeter of what works, who, when misfortune or a fraying of the frontier happens, are reemployed on behalf of a neighbour state, maybe a feeling state, or a fine motor state. Mercenary maybe, or maybe angel.

My heart's dominant hand was versed in tragedy but nursed in terror. Its right hand could do terror's work, patrolling the perimeter of well-being in the dark hours, card-carrying citizen of the state of siege. Oiled with adrenaline was I, nerve sheaths in panic and necessity, burdened by the obligations of governance, the first born in a fatherless house, but ill-suited for it. Adolescence was entered into that way. Adulthood was bent to it. There was mayhem enough to vouchsafe it. I was terror's legionnaire.

My heart's left hand was full of compromise, as it now is again – compromise and tribulation. When the Chinese medicine lady tapped my sternum and said, 'Much sadness here', it was my heart's left hand she was tapping. Sadness has been its trade, its workshop and its work. Grief monger in my later years, I made my living as grief's amanuensis.

So now the spheres of influence are blurring. Dominance is coming undone. There's new work at hand, and the undoing of habitual work. The terror of my unravelling needs unravelling now. The broken heart's brokenness is my right hand's work now, please God. My left hand, involuntary tally maker of dopamine's decline, is fitfully fingering the invisible rosary beads of the ordinary of this little life's going out. I'm fumbling for the door. I never said I knew how to do this. No words to eat there. But the sadness of this moment takes my breath.

The word 'fix' is a floppy one. Whoever wants to learn English shouldn't start with 'fix' or 'fixed'. They're asking for it. People learning languages, most of them, want rules to go along with this work of poetry and the seeking of direction. There's nothing fixed about 'fixed', as you'll see.

There's being 'in a fix,' which is a grandmotherly way of saying 'in the weeds' or 'in trouble'. If there's an arch quality to the delivery, dripping irony, it probably means 'in the shit', which is worse for the person in question and funnier for those looking on.

There's the verb 'to fix', which can also mean 'repair'. It can also mean 'locate', or 'identify', or 'establish', or 'pin down'. It doesn't really mean 'reassemble', though, because it's possible to fix something without restoring it to its original condition, according to the blueprint. In fact, it's possible to fix something that's not broken. You don't need something to be wrong to fix it. You just need something. And that kind of mind.

Even that kind of mind, mind you, can't work in a line of constancy between being in a fix and fixing. That kind of mind can't fix fixing.

There's the past tense, the passive voice: to 'get fixed'. This usually means interfering with reproduction on the farm. Somebody doesn't want a lot of extra mouths to feed, so they fix the rutting instinct, or what it could lead to. It's doubtful the mammal in question feels fixed, as in 'repaired'. It's questionable whether there was anything broken, or wrong, or not working, outside of the questionable assumption that one life form owns the reproductive future of another. But that's a longer question. It's a problem that's fixed (stationary) in us, thanks to our inheritance and legal precepts, and so unlikely to be fixed (repaired) in us.

There's 'getting a fix', a narcotic solution for certain troubles, and there's 'needing a fix', which is one of those troubles.

There's a 'fixed point in a turning world', say. Nothing's wrong there, nothing that needs repair, except possibly the hankering after fixity in a life in flux. A fixed point opts out of the whirl. That could use a fix, or some tampering with. It's a make-believe place, like Disneyland, so it's nothing to worry about. In a world like this, a fixed point doesn't happen by accident, if it happens at all. It's a conceit, or it's a bone of contention or a bone in the throat, or an inattention to detail, all of which can be fixed.

Finally, for now, there's 'fixed', as in 'stable', 'immovable', 'reliable', 'trustworthy', 'of sound mind or character'. There's a lot of hope riding on this kind of 'fixed'.

I mention all of this for two reasons. One: there's not much to me that's fixed in the last sense of the word, or will be. Tremours run up my left-hand side and down again. Left hand for now. I'm told I'm neither fixed nor fixable. There's a drug I've been offered to push back and palliate the shudders and staggers and jags. Not there yet. It won't fix anything anyway, in any sense of the word.

The other reason: I needed the exercise. I wanted to see if I could still think of things I hadn't thought of before, parse them, write them down.

The semantic wildness of this isn't that there's no reasonable resemblance up and down the barber's pole of this word, but that there is.

## 16 January 2024

'Everybody knows they're going to die': that's the allegation that is used to thwart the efforts I've made to democratize any death wisdom that's not yet in general atrophy and prolapse. It relies on the demonstrable, oncoming fact of death to lazily make the case that the crude fact of it readily and insurmountably translates to awareness, consciousness, awakenedness. The case can't be made, though. Facts don't inevitably translate into anything, least of all to life wisdom. Work is in order for that to happen, and work is where we can find our least inclinations, if we're inclined to seek them out.

No, we trade in this lesser fact: 'everybody knows that everybody else is going to die.' The deaths of all those that occur before our own only go so far as to teach us that lesson. The lesser fact is that we're around for all those other deaths. We *see* them, after a fashion, the unadorned fact of them. The lesser fact on the other side of everyone else's death is that after those deaths, *we're still here*. That's the abiding lesson: death is usually a third person event, sometimes a second person event.

It takes something like reckless courage to nudge the stone of someone else's death up the intolerant hill of your own persistent perusal of life. There is, on the face of it, no good reason to trouble the waters.

Human life – the postmodern, secular, humanist kind – is a weft of decorative assurances draped across a warp of habits of the mind. And most of those habits work, in the way all addictions work. One of the more persistent and persuasive of our habits is immortality, particularly the immortality of our intent. When it comes to our intent to be here, we prevail.

The blunt force education which is the death and disappearance of another person from the fray is lost on most of us most of the time. We go with the lesser education of our infirmities, of prevailing over our infirmities, instead. So far, we've made it through. The strange math goes like this: if I've made it through so far, there's no reason I won't make it through again.

Well, there *is* a reason you won't make it through again. It is the same reason, forced through the cool entrails of an actuarial: each time you make it through, you've one less possibility – at least one – of making it through again. The actuary's evidence is not gathered around what kind of good person you are, nor of how your merits warrant an extension of the number of times you'll make it through into a perpetual grace period. Having made it through until now is by most standards your grace period in action.

But the actuarial wisdom and calculus is merciless: the odds are you draw closer to the time of not making it through with each time you make it through. The actuarial of your life does the same existential math that you do, and comes up with a different sum. There's an unknown number of narrow escapes or feats of persistence you are born to, and you work your way towards the completion and exhaustion of that number with each success, each persistence, each feat of survival.

You can see now, can you not, the courage that it takes to draw down this life lesson from the evidence at hand? Everyone's removal before your own: that's where the tale of the tally is told. That's where you get to learn it. Your own success at persisting throws you off the scent of limit, frailty, finality. You just go the other way. So, *the presence of the absence of others*: that's the gold. The willingness of others to encounter the limits of their days in the presence of everyone not doing so now, or yet: that's the village-minded gold of this little life of ours. Hide it away, privatize your losses, your sorrows and frailties, and you're stealing that gold from others. Not hoarding it, stealing it. When you hoard it, it isn't gold anymore. It's alchemy, then. It's bitterness. It's dross. It's scree across the landscape of our mutual life.

So, the one habit: I'll persist. Very likely.

The other habit: I'll likely do so for a while.

The small 'b' Buddhist take on this: the problem is that we think there's enough time.

# 17 January 2024

There's time. Or time enough – almost the same thing.

Even the fringe players, the desert dwellers out here where I am, seem persuaded in their feeling habit and buying habits that there is time.

All except the middle-aged woman trolling, lurching down the sidewalk of the main drag of a twenty-first century desert town called Joshua Tree with a small shopping cart and a small dog and a megaphone, blasting away at the twenty-first century and its persuasions. 'Wake up, goddammit' was high on her list of citizen obligations. 'They're killing you with the water supply.' 'Get out of your cars' – not popular in the US from what I can see. And 'the matrix is coming undone', of which her despair and recourse may have been a sign. Her broken faith, her reneging on the deal she likely struck in childhood with what 'good enough' was like, was itself a raw, unfiltered business. She, clearly, was brain-boiled.

I was waiting for my wife outside the health food store. I slipped the car keys into my pocket so as not to be tagged as someone unwilling to leave his car by the roadside and walk with her into the sunset or the desert or the Old Testament. I hoped that would get me a pass from the worst of her jeremiad. She was bearing down on me. She was awash in the drivenness of betrayal, as a widow must be with her man gone to the war and lost in it for no reason that stood the test. The drivers passing by who weren't taking her advice and resorting to the merits of the pedestrian honked and high-fived her, probably unaware of the sobriety and persecutory lash of her message. They were high-fiving her despair, her unhinging, as any coliseum crowd might, windows up. Some who'd tuned her in while idling at the red light flipped her the emphatic bird, which she took as affirmation – and how could she not.

The dust of a glaring desert afternoon was kicking up. Weed knots were boiling down the sidewalk. There was grit in the prophet's voice. She was taking no prisoners. She was spoiling for a good old-fashioned Pentateuchal throwdown. She knew her apocalyptic stuff. Her nerves were at an impasse. Mine, too. I was in a borrowed hoody. She was in a long green velveteen oracle's great coat done up to her chin. And there was precious little time.

The clarity of the thing brought her no comfort at all. That could have gone the other way. Ambivalence usually brings torment, and torment can ludicrously clarify, and clarity of that kind can crystalize into singularity of purpose. In matters of biblically scaled certainty, the desert doesn't warm the heart. It broils the mind. Clarity of that order is carnage. Clarity, and other people. That great compromise of the infinite which is other people.

She rolled on by as if I wasn't there. I was spared.

## 18 January 2024

A sane culture, as I used to say, is not a culture with no crazy people. It is a culture where most of the people at any given time aren't crazy. Sanity comes from an understanding of 'crazy', not from its absence. You realize you are faring pretty well once you encounter brokenness in a human form, and that realization isn't put to rest by relief. A deep realization of this kind doesn't provide relief. It produces gratitude, and it produces an acute awareness that your current excellence is very unlikely, and as temporary as the excellence of the other guy who's currently raving. And however much your excellence brims with merit, it's balanced on the fulcrum of timing. The preponderance of the fact that enough people in one place burdens the circuitry and the edges, frays the fine print, wobbles the gyre, means that your good fortune bears with it the rest of your fortune.

Foreknowledge of that fortune might be the key to sanity in modern times, just as it may have been God in the God house of former times.

This affliction that has come to me in the last while is not a silver-lined, secret-sauced blessing whose message is just waiting for me to locate the bright side. It's early days, and it's neither wise nor fitting for me to cobble some wounded certainty from it all. But from here it looks like I lived long enough that heredity, frailty and some habits of the heart have coalesced. My mother's line tended to die early, and the men, in particular, who I resemble from the neck down, were prone to cerebral haemorrhage. None of them got out of their seventies. My father's line tended to have a long go of it. When it comes to genetic preferences, it's not easy to know what to want. For every favourable dimension, there are two whose alchemy is beyond easy reckoning. Living long sounds good when the weather is fair, but living long brings on obsolescence, brings on a certain failure of the instruments. The general war on frailties and limits and endings of all kinds has done us few favours. It's a regime of gross intolerance. The infirmity of any and all around you becomes one long haunted cautionary tale, a manual of disorder and defeat.

We tend not to be buoyed by the three dimensions of other people, but warned by them. The three dimensions of their lot, including the hard business – especially the hard business – should deepen our tuition, should radicalize the education of our sentiments. We should be tempered and tested and trued by our neighbour's strange days, not warned off them.

I realize – or think I realize – that it's often hard to tell in these strangest of days if I'm realizing something, or contending with it, or fighting it off, or prematurely knuckling under or overly cooperating with the proceedings, a strange enthusiasm. I realize that what I'm doing here is grappling with the immovable, trying to make a dance out of a stumble, wrangling a murmur of a conversation from the silence of God. I suspect that's what's happening. These are soundings, little bits of sonar, stones down a dark well, shouts down the mouth of a played-out mine, maybe. They are not the makings of a new competence or a kind of para-competence. They are the best of what's come out – ragged, unexpectedly frail.

## 19 January 2024

I am amazed – and not in the best way possible – at my scrambling after the fugitive roaming down the street called my dexterity, or strength, or capacity. The day clatters towards the evening, and I'm all set to carry on as if I'm still on tour. And there's a chronometer somewhere that registers the ticking away of hours, and then of days, from the bag of days and hours I've secreted under the writing desk, knotted and pulled tight around the emptiness there.

## 20 January 2024
### *San Diego suburb*

This won't go well, this fierce, fearsome tallying of the days, the rendering down of them into good days and bad, or rough, or broken, or lost. After all, every day since the 1950s has been a last day, each one that I've been granted, all the sunny ones and the ones spent in torment or torpor, each and every one I didn't see go by – and those are plentiful – are lost. There's no saving them, nor sorting nor stacking them up. Take your vitamins, or no, count your blessings or your shekels, or no, race through the mansion of your days or take your time . . . where? Where'll you take it? Into the present, that vault of certainties? No, you will not. The tariff of joining up with the present is to have the past there, row upon row of lost days given over to the ferryman.

Just as I wrote 'ferryman', I hear from as far away as I can hear the torqued whine of a motorcycle set loose, full-throttled and screaming down the coastal highway. By the end of the next sentence, the sound and the hurtling machine are gone. Early on a Saturday morning on the unrelenting shore of the great, great Pacific there's someone leaving this place behind at a speed that would scatter him like a field of debris if anything went badly – maybe has already done, out beyond my hearing. And here I am, dressed in mourners' white, sitting almost stock-still in a stranger's house, managing the point of a pen's nib, writing things down. And we each, in our fashion, are in the first hours of a day we're losing, the latest last day. And what might separate us is the way by which we are losing it, or how we remember that, or how we forget it.

It is bracing to see how faithfully coincidental is this habit of 'What is life for now?' with 'How many days are left?'

No, they are not gone, these days that are passed – but yes, you lose them.

## 21 January 2024

The poor cousin of the raku teacup is the bamboo whisk. I've had this one for years now. It brings the matcha tea powder to a foam. Foam is not your first thought when you think 'tea', at least not when I do. But, like the idea of cold noodles, the idea of frothy tea came to me as part of my *gaijinness*, my foreignness, when I was in Japan a few decades ago. I was let in on what was probably an abbreviated form of the tea ceremony. It was boring, as you might imagine, and moving, once I caught up a bit with the respect of the made world that was manifest there. The simplicity of the thing devastated my attention span. Of course it did. That's what 'boring' is most of the time. It's a generous simplicity brought to bear upon the consumptive force of habit and addiction to novelty, plus time enough for the frustration of habit to register upon the lion's share of one's convictions.

I've come to admire the ways of the masters of ordinary necessity. Their calculations are the stuff of redemption. They train their discipline upon the unavoidable, monochromatic necessities of life, the sustaining ones like breathing, or bending over to pick up something they dropped, or walking down the street. They raise the stakes by raising the alertness to mechanics and details until everything matters, again. I've tried to do that with speaking.

The tea people do that with hydrating. Somewhere someone with nimble hands makes their way down the bush rows picking the leaves that will one day be read, pinching the clusters. Someone takes the leaves, bruises them to release the tea spirit. Someone else sees to the fermenting and drying, to the storing and packing, the shipping. Others see to the lore and its transmission, its practice and preservation.

## 23 January 2024

Ceramicists, kiln makers, mineral gatherers and haulers are at work, sellers and buyers, afficionados, high priests and low, the aspiring among us and the spent, the cracked and the sound and the lost and the found and the sick at heart and the blown apart and those quietly come to table and those scarcely able, all alone and altogether: all of us gathered round for the communion of tea.

Over the years, I have sat down to tea, the elixir of all their labours. I don't have stacks of paraphernalia for sitting down to tea. I do avoid the plastics and the tinware, which are as affordable as they are regrettable. My son recommends a very advanced kettle that comes of its own accord to 209°F/98.3°C – pearls on the ocean floor, as the practitioners prescribe, so as not to burn the water. But the precision dissuades me. I don't know enough to be a purist. I have my preferences, most of which are the sediment of experience coalesced into easy opinion. And I have my cup, the gold-healed raku cup, when I travel. I have a carrying case for it so it can travel felt-lined and silver-clasped and leather-thonged, and be fine. I have the bamboo water ladle which honestly never comes out to ladle water. I have the curl of bamboo they use to teaspoon out the tea, but I couldn't put my hand on it right now if I wanted to. And then I have the whisk.

The whisk is a marvelous and meticulous thing. Fashioned from a six-inch flute of bamboo cane, having the girth of your big toe, its topmost four inches are split lengthwise maybe eighty times to make a sprocket of prongs – a nest of needle-girth filaments that curl inwards at the ends. Not a wire whisk, not a fork, not anything you'd otherwise employ can stir the matcha in its innermost depths, nor call it to come rise this way in breathy suds. With the whisk, it is as if the tea has been petitioned by God to rise. It is as if the moment's very breath is conjured from the tea.

## 24 January 2024

The whisk is a tea whisperer. With a whisk in hand, and the steady lineage of all those tea workers by your cup, you are – in each of the important ways – a wealthy one.

And yet, an aged whisk is a paltry thing. Stained for good by the work, the old whisk is missing prongs and filaments, the way an old lion misses tufts from his mane, or an old human misses teeth from their gums. It has stiffened now, and the handle is cracked and irreparable. And none of this really showed, at least not to me, until I bought a new one a few days ago. The new one is boisterous and garish, perfect and primed for work in unappealing ways. It is uniform and standard and unable to speak, an artificially intelligent thing, shining and unbecoming, waiting to be plugged in.

The old whisk has the tang of the tea it has called into life. It won't be cleaned. It has no other work to do, no second life. It is what it has done, and now will do no longer. It ages the tea it wicks up, all tannic and briny and old.

I am far from home today, far from my things. Still, I will make a place for the old whisk, maybe alongside the raku cup. They've both done their work, and it shows. Because of that, they look more like each other than they do clay or bamboo. I'm in the shade of their working lives, here in the shade of my own.

Insects outnumber us many times over, for now. There was a time, must have been a time, when we took comfort in outnumbering what was around us – as it is in the cool comfort of cities. In misanthropic times, we're probably comforted by being outnumbered. Soon though, no comfort to speak of.

Three weeks into the pronouncement of my plight, into the regime of affliction, and it's begun to happen, as I might have known it would. The prayer wheel has been spun, and it turns and turns. It draws to itself dust of the ages, all the prayers and all that has become of them.

I have begun to grow accustomed to the dread. I've begun to look past it. To plan even, in a fitful way. The fallings away have begun to slow, even to reverse. The forgetting that comes with custom is at hand. And now something in the clicking by of days and the tremours is wondering whether that first visitation of terror-tinged clarity, that crisis, that catastrophe, that dread-born simplicity, isn't called for. I am, I think, calling for it, that it comes down from the rafters or up the cellar stairs and walks with me awhile, since I can still walk.

'What's with all the blessings and the vows, the prostrations and the stations of the evening, all the toiling and the tolling of the bells?' That's what I ask of the monastic life in a piece of the *Nights of Grief & Mystery* show we toured with, called 'Still'.

And I answer: 'That's what you have when you put away things of this world. Without them, nobody'd survive the stillness.'

Those things are the jostled memory of a feverish seeking after a spirit's sanity in a time loomed over by a colossus, I see now.

## 25 January 2024

There's the unlofty business of getting used to the Beast. I might've known this was coming, a vampire at the throat of my sorrow, taking the life blood of its urgency away.

There's mood and there's mind. There are feelings and there are afflictions, and there's fight-and-flight and despair and the relentlessly honest assessment of the prospects. And there's precious little difference between them, hour upon hour, come daylight, come twilight. And they are remorseless. Of course they are, playing back and forth there across the back forty of my awareness – colossal, unremarkable, senseless.

It is the mauling surf of a midnight king tide come to claw away at the shoreline sediment of agility while I sleep, the wave of unsettlement come, and the next and then the next.

My understanding has the shakes, you might say. I can add, still, but I don't do well with the exponentials. I'm calling out to my understanding now, so that it might bear down upon the moment and not be drifting, so that it might take up the hard business of making room at the communion table for disassembly.

I am in a basement room, outfitted with air-con neutrality, surrounded by beige things easily replaced, the quintessence of Airbnb. I am close to the ocean, but I can neither see nor hear the water from here. It is neither winter nor summer as I know them. The sun is at an oblique enough angle, or my room is so subterranean, that the sunlight can't find a direct way in, and so insinuates itself into the place instead.

I am on a regime of herbals whose bitterness I need to wash down with unusual amounts of water, and so the self-care available to me includes frequent trips to the porcelain portal. I'm walking because I've been told to walk. I've been told that somebody walked his way out of Parkinson's. I don't believe it, but I walk anyway. The mandatory walks through the leafy neighbourhood I undertake with urination in mind, scoping from alley shadow to closeting bush for several miles at a go so as not to be taken by urological surprise.

Now the toilet in this place is a hit or miss thing, in its mechanics. It looks expensive, but each depression of the handle seizes up the gears inside the tank, so each depression is a raising of the tank lid, flailing about for the seized plastic in it, nudging it accidentally, releasing the pent-up water into the tank, ready for the next time, replacing the porcelain lid, ready for the next time. It's a drain pretending to be a toilet. It's cold in the sunless bathroom, the toilet cold to the touch.

That toilet situation is what happens to my focus when I train it upon a shaky limb or appendage. The shaking stops when I do. I seem to have dominion. But each time I have to start again, as if it never happened. There's no retaining the quiet or the calm. I'm still for a second, perhaps, or two, and then we are back to the beginning, as if the victory had never happened.

And then I realize, 'Well, there's no victory now, is there? No more than there's victory over the king tide at midnight with you a mile or more inland and asleep. No more than there's victory over having to pee. There's no victory at all there. There's getting up to pee when you have to. There's fumbling with the buttons until you realize that button flies might now be a thing of the past for you. Not enough dexterity to fix them.'

And I can't tell any more if that realization makes it a good day or a rough day. The purpose of the day isn't clear anymore. It isn't to prevail. It isn't to be all right. There's not much that's alright, not really. A good day is as bewildering as a bad one is disconsoling. Setting and resetting of the compass of reasons: that's the workday now. Agree that there are reasons still, and go out, and walk among them as you're able. Foggy days and feeble ones, the sun and sky as before.

I mean to pursue simplicity as I imagine the monks and the desert saints have done. Certain of them were let out into the world, I suppose, and sealed back in at dusk. Certain of them worked the clay or the fleece, and others the earth and the seed, as their vows of stillness permitted. And certain of them we know were allowed the labour of the pen, with which they flayed their solitude and afflictions of their spirit until they were praying with it.

I am flaying too, flailing as I do.

## 26 January 2024

Nathalie is obliged to return to the farm. I am now, for the first time, alone with this. Even with my benefactrix one floor above me, I am alone with this.

Living in the world with other people and slipping the reins of honest distraction: can it be done? Is there time enough?

## 27 January 2024

It is as if a beaker made of fine glass has tipped over in my mind, and some vital violet liquid is leaking out of its watercourse and trickling out to sea.

It is as if the movement of the air itself is wicking away the lubricating mental gel, and the moving parts are heaving down on each other with no membrane between the vertebrae or the plates to cushion them. Now there's no glide to them, nothing there to ease the mind's bones into service.

It is as if in the night, the quiet full-moon tide mounts the shore and takes all the sand away, so that morning light finds beached cobbles and sheets of sediment blasted free of the sandy subtleties that let me walk there just the day before.

It is as if I am losing some war I'm fighting in the night, so that all the headway I've made in this amoral storm during the daytime is gone by first light, and I begin the day in defect and disorder.

It is as if a stiffening spell is already cast, cast over me with the same words I myself spoke, and with the same signs I myself made, the same opposable movements of articulation of tongue and hand, the same utterances and benedictions.

It is as if the old accord has run out, expired, and I am now governed by a rogue state, a faithless theocracy, an entropic machine, and my citizenship in the land of the mindful has lapsed, and old revelations have gone opaque.

It is as if all day long I spend myself pushing this weighted halting pen across acres of empty page, as if pushing a blunt stick through wet clay to write messages of plea and warnings of eclipses and landslides, and the wash of my own attention has scoured them away.

It is as if I am alone on the only mountaintop in sight. No, the cactus desert. I am alone in the desert with God, only God doesn't think I am in the desert, nor agrees that I am alone.

It is as if every subtle, supple thing entrusted to me has forsaken ambivalence and gone all in on rigid orthodoxy and singularity of purpose – stiff with clarity, important, ruinous.

It is as if my old life has pinwheeled midair until it lost all integration, then has strewn itself across the terrain of my plans for myself, a debris field of reasonable expectations.

No announcement. No apology.

## 28 January 2024

The shaking is like semaphore. It's worse than metaphor. It's like waving at somebody no one else can see, in a language that's never been spoken yet, or signed, with no real hope of translation.

(Note: After several weeks in stagger and recoil, it seemed considerate to invite alumni of my Orphan Wisdom School to a call, in which I would try to find the words. I didn't really know why. I felt some obligation to them, given all we'd been through together. And I suppose I wanted to hear what I would say, if I could say anything beyond 'Goodbye', and 'Sorry'.)

# The Reveal Call

I want to thank everybody for rerouting your day or evening or middle of the night in some cases, or your life and plans, to make the time to get in on this, as I have done. And I'm sorry for the impersonality of the machinery, although we're all used to it. But we've all met in person, I believe, and so maybe that compensates to some degree.

What am I doing? What is this?

Well, I don't think I've ever done it before. There hasn't been call enough to do it before. Although you could say that the madness of the pandemic was right up there with reasons why. And I guess we did find our way towards each other in this format in those days. But these are different days, and I have a different purpose this morning, as you're about to hear.

And so we're going to play something for you now that comes from the *Nights of Grief & Mystery* tour that Gregory Hoskins and I made much of the latter half of last year, 2023. We were in Penzance, in the U.K., a real place, and we had the great joy of playing in kind of a punk palace that was staffed by guys who were extras from . . . What's that wacky rock-and-roll film, what's it called? *Rocky Horror Picture Show*? No, oh not *Rocky Horror*. The touring band, and they're buffoons basically. *Spinal Tap*. That's it. These guys were *Spinal Tap* extras, and very kind to us. The piece is called 'Still', and it found its way into the set list fairly early, and it kind of bossed its way into the proceedings and elbowed its way in. We were glad of it, and we were glad to have played it every night. It became a kind of set piece for us, a fulcrum for the evening.

It went something like this:

It happens from time to time in your life that the phone rings, and against all good advice and prior experience, you pick it up and you say, 'Hello'. The voice on the other end asks for you, and you acknowledge that you are you, in fact. The voice says, 'This is your life speaking'. And you're brought to a kind of standstill involuntarily when moments like this happen, because you're not sure suddenly. For the first time, you're not sure who you've been or what you've been doing all of this time. If this is your life on the phone calling you, whose life, after all, have you been living up until the time when your life called? Well, you don't know, but you acknowledge that you're you. And then your life asks you if you're busy. If you have any good sense at all, you say, 'No', and you put all your busyness down.

Your life announces to you that the times are tough. In fact, the rough Gods are on Main Street, and things are not as recognizable as they might've been even a generation ago. The likes of you have been called upon to see if you can answer the bell and fill a certain gap that's emerged in the proceedings, which has the approximate shape and size and even disposition of you. It asks you if you're available for steady, acute employment. The first thought that comes to you is the first thing that comes out of your mouth, something on the order of, 'I'm probably not worthy, I'm not ready, I'm not capable, I'm not that guy.' *Your own life has made a mistake in calling you*: that's what you come back with. And then your life sits in the silence for a minute, and then says, 'If you've been called, it's the only sign you'll ever really get that your worthiness has already been established. All you have to do is see that. Whether you feel it or not is beside the point.' Finally, you knuckle under to your life calling and so you say, 'Alright, I'm in. To the extent that I know how to be in, I am.' You say to your life, 'Is there anything I can do to prepare for the upcoming?' And your life says, 'Be still.'

This is called 'Still'.

**I.**

Now, if you ever had a mother, well she probably made you lunch.

Yeah, she probably made you sit down and eat that lunch. Because mothers can be Zennish, too. You know it. Isn't it true? She was messing with your momentum, the way all the good teachers do. She was arresting you. Because she knew that momentum just makes a slurry of your moments, that you can't tell the difference between them when you're all metronomic and, baby, you're on the move.

Don't they call religious politics 'movements', and isn't that for good reason? But you know, the spirit mechanics amongst us, those of them left, they're forever working on the brakes.

Stillness and quiet, they are the black of the inner life, or the white. They are all of its repertoire, all of its colours, all at once. Or they are all of its colours gone. That's what happens when life relents and grants reprieve, undesired, with you undesiring. Or you relent, or you repent. Or both.

So there's a monk and there's a nun and there's a mendicant. And they've got a good chance at stillness. For they have left this world behind. Still, I wonder, what's with all the rules and the vows, and the prostrations and the stations of the evening, and the orders and all that toiling and all the tolling of the bells?

They replace what you lose when you lose this world. Without them, nobody would survive that stillness.

So you retreat to your undivided room, sure. You'll have your divisions, friends, even so. And you complete your undivided self. And sure, you'll have your incisions, even so.

**II**.

Now if you go for stillness in this life, you take your chances. Without this world to blame, you take the suicide's risk: that it's no better – that it's no different – there on the other side of all this.

And so you pray for clarity, that's all. And you get it. And oh, it's too much, O God.

And so you pray for mercy instead. That's all. And yeah, you get it. And it's not enough, O God.

And so you pray for clarity instead and you get it. Too much. Mercy instead. You get it. Not enough.

You pray.

**III**.

Now when you're dying – I've seen this – something takes over, and it's so much bigger than you. It won't let go, and it's terrifying.

That is momentum. It brings you to the cliff edge of this life. It brings you over it too, just barely. Then it will be done.

And that's the purgatory. For the dying is dead now, and the death, it's dead, too. And everything's gone ordinary and still, and all of your wanting is gone. You are a contemplative's dream.

But the habit of your wanting is still there. And you'll want that gone, too.

So why is the body 'remains'? Why is everything else 'effects'? Why do they call it 'a wake' when it's all finally done?

Well, it's a still point in a turning world.

Or it's a chill point in this burning world.

Or it's a nil point in a learning world

or it's a kill point in a churning, churning world.

It's a will point in a yearning world

or it's a thrill point in this spurning world.

Maybe that's what it is.

**IV**.

So, does peace finally happen when all the troubles cease? When you're finally out of range, and you're finally out of reach? When at last you're out of sight, and you are finally out of mind? When you're falling out of love with this beautiful, bright blue spinning world? Is that it? When your homeless intelligence is mapping the nap of this world instead on that broken little screen? When you are caught up now in career, and you're camouflaged and baby, you are desperate in your digital nomad neoprene?

It's pitiful, Lord knows. It's cityful, all of this conquering of the hill.

Do you still want to be still?

Then be stilled.

Wow, that was a treat for me. I was there. I was really there. I was there again, too, just now.

So, I want to tell you a little story now. It was nine years ago almost exactly that I was in a medical specialist's office, and I was far from home, in another city, with breathing troubles, my life's constant companion. And he had me do what they call a pulmonary function test, which has you blowing through something that looks an awful lot like a spent toilet paper tube.

But it's high tech, I suppose. I came out the other end of all that blowing to be told that I had about 30 per cent normal lung capacity, which was a little worse than I thought it was. As things can be sometimes: a little worse than you think they are. And I said, 'What does that mean?' He said, 'Well, I understand you've got a plan to fly out of town tomorrow. Is that true?' I said, 'Yeah'. He said, 'I strongly advise against it.' He said, 'Your lungs can't take any shenanigans with air pressure and cabin pressure and all that sort of thing, and it'd be a one-way ticket for you, man.'

I thought to myself, 'Well this is January, this is eastern Canada, and I have a one-way ticket to Mexico. It doesn't sound awful.' And so I thanked him for his advice and for his strong plea on behalf of remaining stationary. And Nathalie and I, the next morning, bright and early, got on the plane and flew down to Mexico.

The first morning I was there, I sat on a flat roof of the building we were staying in, and I watched and I listened to the sounds of that little village coming to life as it's done obviously for centuries, the clip-clop of the donkeys coming down the cobble stones, and the cooking fires and so on. Very cool in many ways.

Somehow, I made the trip, but obviously I was on some kind of timeline. Things weren't good. I wondered to myself as the sun came up, 'What do you do in a time like this', considering the fact that really there's no such thing as 'a time like this'. There's just 'this time'. You suddenly are fully the only occupant of this time that you're in. And I thought to myself, 'So what does a man do and what does a father do, and a husband?' And I was all those things at the same time.

This is going to sound a little vainglorious maybe, but I imagined that when word got out that I had expired in Mexico, there was likely to be a brief but maybe somewhat intense flood of emails of some description, compassionate and commiserating ones, certainly, but somewhere in there there'd probably be a fair share of requests for more. In other words, had I left anything behind? And, of course, you always leave things behind. But I just thought that of all the sort of hard-to-bear things at a time like that, being asked for more from the person who's no longer among you wouldn't be the most favourable. 'And so could I do something about it?', I wondered. I had a pen. I had a book with me. I just began to write all the stories I could remember of my time in the death trade.

An amazing thing began to happen. I mean, I wrote these stories down basically because I had nothing else I could figure out how to do, and I was sort of up against it, you see, and not able to breathe very well at all. But it was a kind of sedentary enterprise, and so easy to undertake. I began to write all the stories I could remember. Not the finger-wagging cautionary tale kind of stories, just the stories . . . Just the human debris field of people trying to make it through, stories that I was very privileged to be in on in those days. After about three days of doing that, six or seven hours at a sit, something began to happen between the stories. While I was sleeping and during the nighttime, they began to grow some kind of mycelial rumour or web, one towards the other.

You couldn't call it 'meaning', exactly, and you couldn't call it 'purpose', but you could call it a kind of radicalized kind of coincidence that these things were emerging at the same time that I was telling these stories, in a kind of random serial fashion, really for the first time. As some of you, most of you probably know, I'm telling you the story of how *Die Wise* came into the world. That's literally how it happened. A roof top in Mexico, on the lam. No plan. A little bit of desperateness from someone who was far from home, trying to figure out what his job was when virtually all the jobs normally available to him were suddenly in the past.

Twenty-five days ago, I was in a medical specialist's office far from home, again against my own inclinations. I sat there, making a cursory investigation of certain abilities that I had or thought I had, 'touch this', 'bring your fingers here', 'write a sentence on a piece of paper', 'do it five times', a few other things like that. Not very high-end medical technology stuff, but at the end of it I got a diagnosis of a similar kind of arrest. I was told then, and I'm telling you now, that I apparently have Parkinson's disease.

That's when I found out for keeps: twenty-five days ago. It was early in the morning, on the 2nd of January, and I staggered out into the light from the office and I couldn't think, I couldn't see really. I couldn't see myself. I couldn't find my life. I was treading water. And I was certain on some level where certainty doesn't serve you that they were talking about somebody else. I couldn't simply locate my life in that little piece of information. In fact, in the days to come, I couldn't remember the name of the affliction either, which is a sign of how remarkably agile your mind can be at defending itself. I couldn't actually remember the name of the thing until it occurred to me, 'My God, it's almost your surname: Parkinson/Jenkinson.' It became easier to remember when I could say it like a rhyme.

So, the next morning, bright and early, Nathalie and I were on a plane that brought me down to Palm Springs, a place I never thought I'd go, and subsequently to a place called Joshua Tree, to enjoy and deeply appreciate the avails of a friend who extended the use of a stone cottage in the desert. And for two weeks in the Joshua Tree desert, I tried to find out what I'm here for, or what's left, or something. And I have to tell you, I was not able to locate much of a reason, much of a purpose. Certainly no plan. Nathalie witnessed the rather drastic disassembling of my capacity to put one foot in front of the other, really. But because her license had expired, I was obliged to drive the rental car through the desert at night in the rain, in that condition.

So it was kind of funny and tragic and ludicrous in a Samuel Beckett sort of way: driving through the desert, not capable of doing so, but no plan B. And so what have I done since then? Well, I sat on a porch with the sun coming up in the morning. I sat on a porch far from home at someone else's house again, yet again in another country, and asked myself again, 'What does a husband and a father and a man do in a time that is clearly like no other?' – the difference between that time and this time being, it seems, that there's a little more foreclosure that's in the wings now that may not have been there eight or nine years ago.

So, I wrote. I don't recommend this to anybody. I didn't write to stave off what was happening, and I didn't write really about what was happening. I don't think I began to write because it was happening, or because certain things that had been happening for a long time were beginning to not happen in the way that they'd done before. I did everything I could to control the fine point on this pen, and discovered that in this kind of condition it's no longer a fine point, no matter how fine it was when I bought it. It feels like a stick that I'm dragging through the mud when my fine motor control is beginning to head out of town. But anyway, I did everything I could. And I'm fifty-something pages into some kind of new book. I don't know what it's going to be, and I doubt that anybody would want to touch it, publishing-wise. But if there's a last thing that's undertaken in the presence of all of this that I'm telling you about, well I suppose this will be it. If Nathalie wants to make it available to people when I'm no longer in the position to make those kinds of decisions, at least there'll be this. So, I want to read you a couple of little things from it.

By the way, I've got a lump in my throat, and I'm very sad about all this. And I want you to know that.

I don't know why I want you to know, but we've been a few places together over the years . . . or maybe not quite together, but together enough. And who else would I tell? And a lot of the old gospel songs say, 'Got to tell somebody.'

So, here's the first piece. This was written on the 4th of January.

[*reads entry*] 'I remember tonight a woman, maybe in her fifties, at a presentation I gave a few years ago. The question period came. This is when people ignore what's just been said and restore their reasons for coming in its stead. . . . "I'm afraid it's too late to do a lot of things."'

That was her question. Everybody in the room looked at me. I know what the expectations were, what needed to be said in a time of generic, standard, government-issue compassion. But some of you on this call at least have a sense that I probably didn't obey that instinct. I just left it for other people to do. Clearly, they'd already done it. This is what I said to her instead of all that. I said, 'It is. It's too late for a lot of things'.

And this is what I'm saying to you: these very days turn out to be what I meant. It's a hard business on a Sunday morning, on any morning. Before

I go on, it's good to remember that. Life continues on the back end of all of this. But until it ends, I'm going to do this for a few minutes more.

This is the second bit of writing. This is from yesterday. Yesterday morning, around this time, I woke up as I oftentimes do, with a kind of claim that's already been made upon me, in the form of a phrase usually. The claim simply says, 'Get your ass up and write this down.' And then I negotiate with it: 'Can it wait?' 'Will it still be there in fifteen minutes?' No. And there's no snooze button. Wherever or whoever these things come from doesn't take no for an answer. So up I got up, and I wrote the first one down, and it turned into seven or eight more.

Here they are. This is me trying to understand what's happening to me. Because it is *happening*. It's not in the future, and I'm not even sure I wish it were. But it isn't. And so, this is my attempt to try to give somebody who's not quite here, Nathalie included, a kind of feel for the grainy daily or sometimes moment-by-moment realities of this thing that's come to call.

[*reads 27 January 2024 entry*]

Wow, 'pinwheels, a debris field of reasonable expectations, and there's no announcement and there's no apology'. The likelihood of anybody wanting to publish stuff like that: probably not so great. But that's the first time I've heard myself read them out loud. And if I may say, that's not too bad. I'm rather pleased that those things happened yesterday morning, and I was there to catch them.

I am coming to the end of the things I want to say to you. There's a kind of p.s., and then I'll try to give you a glimpse of the near future, which I promise you now, if I didn't promise you before, is the only kind there is. And this occurred to me way in the beginning of this, three weeks ago, and it's a kind of plea, it's a kind of prayer.

You remember, some of you, how fond I am of that Provencal prayer: *God help me, for my boat is so small, and your sea so immense.*

I used to say that with great verve, basically unafflicted. Now that I am afflicted, I say it with a kind of a solemnity that wasn't really available to me before. So, in the spirit of that brevity and that clarity of purpose and voice, I dare say I have my equivalent, and this is what it is. I haven't memorized it, so I have to read it from the page. It says:

*I want to contemplate and then to approach the awful silence of God while I can still hear.*

If you're like me, some of you may be scrambling now to send me all kinds of alternative medical information designed to deliver me from the oncomingness of all of these symptoms, and perhaps even the fore-closing reality of the diagnosis at all. I appreciate the thought and the gesture, if that's in your mind. I can tell you this: I've been very derelict of duty, I think that's what it is. I haven't gone on the internet one fuck-ing time on this matter. It's nothing to be proud of, because I know that people around me are doing so partly because I haven't, so I can't defend that. But I knew in the early going that the last thing I wanted to do was disappear down the do-it-yourself rabbit hole of self-administered alternative realities.

When it comes to Parkinson's: I've come to hate the word, I should say. I don't hate Parkinson himself, if it was a him, but man, I don't like the word. I don't like the surname. I don't like the resemblance to my own. But there it is. So, if you send your plans for me for salvation or deliverance, I really appreciate it and I am sure you'll understand that I probably won't be able to get to respond to them in the manner that acknowledges the care and concern that you invested in sending them to me. I'm not sure I can really look at them all. I'm not sure if I can enter-tain eighteen, twenty, or thirty alternatives to the low-grade misery that I have been living since I heard.

'Misery' is probably not the right word. I'm just sad all the time.

I'm sad because I pictured for myself a kind of agedness that looked a little bit like this: I'm sitting in a corner, preferably outside, but you never know. And I have a walking stick that I don't really need, but the style of it is undeniable and I need the style for sure, And it's a kind of a worn thing, but it may not have been worn by me. I don't know. I'm not wearing rehab clothes and I'm not wearing easy-to-fit exercise wear and Lycra and all of that. I'm wearing linen and it's just a little bit worn, but it looks pretty good – and maybe some leather here and there. I'm sitting there, and I've got a hat and I've got choices where it comes to hats already, so I'm not petitioning for more, but it's a wonderful thing to have. The hat's tilted down to keep the sun out of my eyes. Most of the time nobody's talking to me. Most of the time I don't mind, because after all I've done my fair share of talking by then. You could easily make the case that it's enough already. 'Move aside, let somebody in their forties take up a little room.' Well, they don't need me to step aside to take up a little room, because by that time I've already stepped aside. But occasionally somebody backs into me by accident and we stumble upon the beginnings of some kind of conversation that turns mighty with nobody noticing.

Really. That's what I pictured for myself. If I were allowed to picture anything. Now some of that might still be available, the trappings, the decoration of the picture, but I'm not sure that the availability that the picture implies is going to be there for me. I'm going to leave you with a consideration of sorts, which is going to sound maybe like life advice . . . But come on, we know each other by now. I don't have any. Or if I did, look where it's got me. Whatever you do, don't listen to me when it comes to life advice. But I'd like to imagine out loud with you a kind of story that might serve you well in time to come.

You do get a chance. You're shocked by the reversal of fortune, which becomes your life, but you do get a chance to know that in principle it is coming. One of the great aching difficulties of being a human being in real time is how to change your mind so that you're not any longer anticipating this thing, but you're accommodating yourself to it instead. Because it's already true, and you don't get a choice about whether it's true or not. That's the place I find myself, and I don't know how to inhabit it. The irony is not lost on me. How long I spent with how many people who turned the corner magically, alchemically and sometimes tragically from 'going to die someday' to 'dying, of course'. It's probable that that moment with those people is what drew me to your attention, when and if that time ever happened.

Here's what I think I'm going to try to do now. I talk a good line right now because it's not a bad morning as these things go. The extremities are a bit shaky, as they are most times, most days. The mind seems obedient for the moment. So I'll just, I'll tease it a little more and dream out loud with you about what I think I'm going to try to do with this time that's allotted to me.

I don't pretend to know what the arc of the career of a Parkinson's patient is. I honestly don't know. I don't think of myself as a Parkinson's patient, actually. I'm taking a handful of Chinese herbal medications that I found down here in California because Mr. Allopath at home hadn't much for me. So I'm trying something. But this is what I wanted to say, so as to not let my mind drift too much out loud. I'm trying to figure out whether 'business as usual' in the face of this particular storm is bravery, or sanity, or cowardice, or no big deal.

It's occurred to me that trying to continue as I once did might be the least responsible thing available to me – the most appealing in some ways, but not the kindest to myself, nor to anybody around me. I think what I'm going to try to do is live in the teaching house on the farm for a while when I get back, maybe in April or something, I don't know. I think I'm going to take up something of the life of one of those desert dweller types that we've all imagined ourselves to be at one time or another. I'm not going to imagine it – I'm going to see if I can do it. I've got so little of that kind of discipline available to me that I'm going to be wrestling the adversary most of the time, and I don't really want anybody else in on that gnarly opera.

I don't know if anything writing-wise will come out of it. I came down here with a plan to finish a sequence of five small books. I can lean in with great candour and say to you, that's not going to happen. I can see now I'm going to try to do something – a series of things – with my ally down here, Kimberly Johnson, but I don't know if I'm physically capable of doing it or keeping up my end frankly, when it comes to thinking on my feet, which has been kind of my stock and trade. I can feel it compromised already. I'm terrified at the prospect of it, to be honest.

So I'm not trying to fight it off. I'm trying to engage what's left for me with what's left of me. I don't know how it includes any of you. I don't know if it does at all. I don't know if we get a chance to do anything together as we once did. I can't begin to tell you how mournful a proposition that is to say out loud. We all know in principle that that day was coming. The hellish thing is when principles turn into days, and you're obliged to acknowledge something that everything inside you screams, 'Anything but that'. We may be able to do something if I'm still in fairly good condition in the summertime, towards the late end of the summer, maybe in August sometime. We'll see if we can do something that is multi-day, which is a very daring thought for me to think now, but I am thinking it. Maybe it's the school that never was that we'll do. Maybe it's a school that will never be. Maybe it's some attempt on my part not to summarize a life, but an attempt to live one instead. I'm not sure. And maybe some of you would be interested in getting in on that. And so we'll let you know in plenty of time if it's floating, if it has air, and if I can manage it. I don't want you to come all the way there and just watch disassembly in action.

I kind of seized upon this moment not knowing what to say to you. I don't know if you can tell. I didn't know what to say, but I know that I didn't. And with the help of the other people on the screen now, I got a chance to kind of carve out a moment before things turn so remarkably ordinary that I grow accustomed even to this, too, which I pray doesn't take place. But man, let's not kid ourselves, right? Our ability and our desire to get used to things is as strong as any desire we have.

So maybe that's it.

*I want to contemplate and approach the awful silence of God while I can still hear.*

I just want you to know that I'm mindful of you. I'm mournful because of that, but I'm really glad about it, too, and I'm glad we got the chance to do this. I apologize that there's not back and forth for now. It's largely because I couldn't really manage the emotional fire hose, which would be you responding to what I've said, to me. I don't think it would be pretty. I'm finding that getting cold and getting emotional both drive my limbs to their own extremes now. So, we won't do that, except to take an opportunity in a few seconds just to say goodbye to each other for now. I'm not pretending this is it, but I don't know what 'from now on' includes. But somewhere in me it includes you, if you don't mind lending yourself to me that way.

Anyway, that's it. That's all I can say for now. Thank you for listening and tuning in.

## 29 January 2024
### *Aftermath of the Reveal*

These days there are surrogates galore – stand-ins and golems and virtualities like bobbing, blinking buoys in the ocean. We bet on the off chance that there's merit, that there's somebody there behind the anonymous content. You can get your messages out there before there's a message worth sending, before it's even occurred to you. It's like mouthing a thought . . . or humming one, before you know what it is – instead of knowing what it is. Nobody in twenty years will hold the AI surrogates at arm's length, in dismay and derision, as I do now and will continue to do. No, all of it will be required business, just as a phone per student has become pedagogical fair play in the classroom, along with missing stressful exams and AI-authored essays and mental health days. There's no truancy now.

Being there in person is not exotic yet. It's not vintage. It's just inefficient, clumsy, unsophisticated, you single-tasking when you could be doing other things.

When you've been told that your brain is no longer up to keeping you supple and subtle and fine-motored, I promise you that one place whatever's left of your mind goes is a flash card memory of being around shaky old people when you were young. No one explained it, and it didn't seem out of keeping. You had to make up your young mind about the shakes, and you did. It was some kind of brokenness come to call, untraceable to any particular terrible moment. Something just clicked by, and the old people pendulumed along, rattling off the walls of the invisible house they lived in. Is my house invisible now?

Me, I've a fifth finger now instead of a thumb. Things have begun to acquire a degree of difficulty they didn't used to have. When I was maybe ten or eleven years old, I remember finding out that advanced math had advanced beyond my mind's reach. I remember hearing the gears of my mind grinding, the math problems like pea gravel in the machinery. I just couldn't think that way, and I never did. These early days are like that. I can hear the mechanicals. It's like hearing a car's engine – a car you've relied on to get you to your life and back – and starting to have to think about what it's doing, having to decide on the merit of repairs. It's like having to *try*. There's always been work to do, but this isn't work as I once knew it. This is working on work.

At the farm we have a young boy who was born there, one of a dwindling number of people born to a genuinely working farm. I named the boy, a remarkable and weighty honour. For as long as it lasts, before the distractions and derisions and disenchantments of a public school education set in, before he wises up to the call of the great, wide, complicated urban screen culture, it's a wonderful and beautiful thing to see him tumble into the farm's ordinary wonders: the very excitable dogs knocking him over and him having no sense of frustration, no sense that a good day doesn't include being knocked over by a dog or two; the uneven snows' depths snaring him on the way down the hill, and him pitched over on his face waiting to be fetched up, doing what we call on the farm 'the dead cat'; him repeatedly getting knocked off-kilter by trying to carry around a four-foot spirit level – he is all of three foot tall – that he saw us using to build the new chicken coop, utterly unthrown at being skewed by his burden. We've never seen him just put the thing down in the name of getting on with his day.

If you slow yourself down, you can watch his mind grow. It doesn't seem to grow sequentially, but exponentially, mycelialy. It tumbles over itself. It doesn't grope along the thin line of safety like a cave walker with a torch. It veers. It careens and gambols sideways as often as not. It seems to me unconcerned either with success or advancement, or being thwarted. It lingers over a new impossibility, slides its mind-hand along the new thing, the impossible thing, as if it were the flanks of a never-before-seen animal in a field. It seems at once amazed and incited into mystic communion with the made world. It clambers up over the things of the world, and it is the clambering. Into the soft storm of the made world his mind goes, not seeming to want another, even for a moment.

And I wonder: is he in the shallow end of his life, his work prototypical, a practice run for the main event, barely real? Is almost everything yet to come, with him and his shadows dancing in the off-stage of his awareness? Is he *coming to be*?

Or is he in the deep end of everything, the water of life up to his eyes and ears, the great din of life murmuring to him, promising him, vowing him into the mind of mystery itself? Is he among his makers still, lent to us for a time that we might yet remember the strange days of our own making?

As we come to our days, are we rising to them? Is ascent our momentum, then? Are we emergent, improving, and provident and headed for home? Or are we, one thought at a time, tottering away from them, the near past making its claim on the simple sight we're granted at first?

I wonder: what is happening to me? Am I circling the ancient tower now, the eternal return, a passenger in the pushcart of my plans? Is this the broken ground beneath me? Holy ground? Am I meeting the farm's young lad on a path I can't see, me taking him by the hand, or him me? Are we the beginning and the end of something endlessly beginning through us and then going on without us? Am I lapping him, or him me? Are my soul's staggers and confusions on these matters coming from the forgetting of all this, or from the sudden recall of it all?

nostalgia: from 'nostos', Greek, 'reborn', or 'restoration', or 'recall'; and 'algia', Greek, 'pain'. So there is a pain upon returning, and there is the return of pain.

# 1 February 2024

I'm leery of the silver-lining sonatas that the well-intentioned hum into your ear in a tough time. Bless them, though, of course. The heart is there. But silver linings seem to shine too hard. You can't see very well when the silver linings beam out from a dark place.

A good fire is a welcome thing at night, in the cool of the evening. I welcome it. You can see the people gathered for a warming, the old conviviality on their faces. But their faces are all you can see, and most of them are in profile. There's something about the eye that seems to squint for want of the roundness, the soft distribution of the firelight. Try to look beyond it: the dark is like a monolith with a cancelling power, an occluding power of its own. With firelight and with silver linings, its often either there or not there, no nuance, either black or white. 'Thank God it's not that simple', Leonard Cohen reminded us on his way out the door.

Habit: where all my best disapprovals come from.

I suppose I am like my eye in that way. I seem to lose track of the subtle presence, the ambivalences of the other world when it carves or quiets its way into this one. If I was a blind man, maybe it'd be a different story. Maybe there'd be revelation at hand, and any light, even a silver lining, would be every prayer answered.

Maybe I *am* a blind man, and that's why I see things this way. But they say that there are suddenly-seeing people who, with the cataracts gone, recoil from the light, can't understand its severity or its syntax, go mad from the oracular, ocular moment. I'd as likely be one of those, raving then as I might be raving now.

I've a fondness for the half-thereness of shadowy things, an alertness to them, even: eclipses celestial and existential, the ebb of the dying, the shafted light in the hay maw towards day's end, the unopened book of poems, the old of almost anything I can think of now, the dilapidation of a building, all the voices there.

I don't know if that means that neurodegeneration suits me. I certainly don't feel as though I'm in the grasp of something I've known before, or am akin to. It is, so far, a dark place, full of details I don't want to learn. It is, for all that, a darkness I don't want to lose track of. It has the darkness of a cloister, of a ruin.

The Beast has sometimes taken the form of a cascade of worsts. Today was a worst day. It began well enough: my writing hand seemed to work independently of my left, more altered hand; my posture was mostly vertical and upright. It was a rainy day – what the Californians call bad weather, with nobody out who doesn't have business out – and I rewarded myself for some scattered but sustained writing work with a rainy-day excursion to an art museum. It started off well enough, but about an hour into that shuffly stagger of attention from one display to the next, the bottom floor of the bone house that I am gave way. It was all I could do to stand still. I would have looked like a drunken man, or somebody in insulin shock, or in the electrical storm of psychosis, I imagine, seized up in the confines of a public place. Where did most of me go? I wondered.

The subtleties of brain chemistry, histology: laymen like me are tempted to see the works as hydraulic business, gaskets that either hold or blow, fine tubing snaking down into the cortical basement, pulsing lobes fitted for the cranial canal of blood flow, like that glycol that keeps your in-floor heating system from seizing up in the cold up north.

By my guess, that's not true at all. There's blood pressure in the vascular work, yes, but the whole thing must be prodded and prompted, governed and ground to a halt by humours and alchemy, by deities that ride the brain, remember its memories, harry its imaginings, raise and lower its extremities.

Until they don't. When the mechanics fail, I'm persuaded to believe that the reasons aren't mechanical. They're natural, which is to say that they're deities as the Greeks imagined them: fond of tumult and quick to riot or to calm, prone to exaggeration and . . .

## 3 February 2024

Am I to grow accustomed to the leaping in my limbs? Is this the prize? Is that where I've landed, if I'm wise, St. Vitus dance in the extremities and me doing well by keeping time? It is as though I've a small salmon in my hand and I am trying to pass him through a hoop that's just out of reach. I don't know much about dancing this way, and so I don't know if there's skill or wisdom in cooperating with the intemperate conductor at the console.

## 5 February 2024

It is as if one extremity or another has been nailed to water and an irregular tide is coursing through, rising, falling away.

## 6 February 2024

Woke up, rolled over, got dressed, took the measure of myself, walked out into the place, washed my face. Hearing my footsteps, thought about the bitter handful of Chinese herbs waiting for me, made tea instead, turned on the computer to work on the matrimony book, took the measure of myself again, seemed a bit vague but fit enough for sitting, did a few dishes, peeled back the blinds to allow the grim daylight in, thanked God, I hope, but not too convincingly I fear, tuned up the bathroom since it's been a while. I took receipt of a plate of breakfast that the bodhisattva upstairs brought to me, knuckled under and sat down finally to do the editing thing I'd committed months before to do.

Ten minutes in, I began swimming against the current. Not just the tremours, but the recounts too. Same paragraph six or seven times, same line even, and nothing happening, no sign I'd done so or that I cared or knew how to care, or knew how to think, or whether that would ever return.

It erased the mind like it was an Etch A Sketch screen. I started again. I could watch myself thumbing the file cards of things I used to do. Nothing. And I knew there was nothing going on except for me knowing what was happening, and the exceeding sadness of knowing that and little else that worked. I could still envision, and envision I did.

I pictured myself in a facility, in a corner for safekeeping, moving food around on a tray without purpose, stained in front, just recurring, shuffling, autonomic in the mind, persuaded by special fears and forces, people tiring of it. I was sorrowing in a pixilated way, in slow motion.

I thought about a walk outside in the drizzle. Never really a walker, I couldn't warm to it. Somewhere in the executive suite my still conscience, or something else, advised it again, required it, removed any other possibility but walking in the drizzle. Stiffly dressed, I put everything on for fear of a chill, so I looked upmarket homeless. I jittered out the back door, disputed with the key, gave up, left the door unlocked, walked.

I didn't feel any better outside, any more than I did inside. I was self-conscious, like a person disfigured in a crash in a way that is just starting to show. Kept walking nowhere. Imagined getting lost, remembered I put my wallet in my pocket in case of an emergency different than this one, imagined what I'd say by way of being lost to someone who's trying to decide if I'm confused or if I'm a criminal casing the street, creating intricate strategies for roadside mayhem, considering how addled I thought I was.

It was an amazing, conjuring combination: the drizzle and the wind and the not wanting to walk and the turgid fears and the not knowing where to go, and the walking. I'd like to say I was in the desert with the desert saints, but I wasn't. I was in an inglorious 'this foot, then that foot' stance about the whole thing. I wasn't glad. I was grim, for sure. But I was walking as I grimly walked, and little else. Some thinking, maybe, most of it ghosted and shuffling and anti-walking. Still, walking. Yet walking. And walking. But walking down the surburban street on the southern edge of a foreign country and sure of mishap, and walking. Without a witness or a plan, ludicrously self-conscious, early-stage something, and walking.

They say that there are ways of meditating that seek some kind of distance from the monkey mind, all that chatter. And there's that impossible stillness on a cushion, or not on it, where all the distractions melt into pain and give you a decent focus. Some Zen monks chuckle to themselves in meditation. Some, they say, walk. Maybe that's what I was doing. Minus the discipline, the self-awareness, the meditation. Empty walking, with anxiety earbuds in. No peace of mind, no well-being, no escape into health. Just everything as it was, and walking.

It was something I could do. I did it. That's all. Goes alongside the things that are slipping my grasp. Don't know how long I walked, how far. Eventually, I turned back, went indoors, sighed as I took off the shoes, the damp jacket. Assumed the position that an hour before was futile. After a while, something lifted, or softened its lameness or its grip.

So far as I know, I could walk from now until I couldn't, and that would never happen again. I'm not sure even now that anything happened. I am the same hesitating man who walked. And the desert rose up to meet me. And saints were there.

## 7 February 2024

I wake up mostly as the person I was. Each morning of the last forty or so, I rise, swing legs over to the side, find the floor, heave up as I have done on the farm, on tour, hotel or home. There are a man's memories waiting for me like a suit draped over a chair. Same sort of memories as when I left them the night before. Then there's a kind of waking dream sequence. I try the pants, but a pocket is in backwards, or a pant leg goes inside the pants. The jacket fits only one side, buttons are behind the lapels. I don't know what happened. And it's only then, a few seconds after rising to the occasion of the day, that I remind myself that I am misshapen, unaligned, cracked and leaking a vital fluid. I am not as I was. I am not coming back. I have a neurodegenerative disease. I'm leaking a vital fluid. I'm balanced enough, but I'm not squared away any longer, or trued or framed up well. The head is cracked, a vial broken. I won't be fixed. I am as good now as I will ever be. This is me, in this spirit in this basement room in this bed in this country.

The walk of the other day tuned me for despair. I did dramatically imagine myself as lost on a street I didn't know, approached by a stranger, being asked who he should call. I told Kimberly about it, chuckling a bit. Today she left for a few days to work out of town. She didn't want to leave me here. I told her it was fine. I was fine. Then from her purse she produced a folded piece of paper. On the outside, painted flowers. On the inside, my local address, contact names and numbers. I looked up at her: 'An "if lost please return to . . . card?"' 'Yes', she said. Which was hard to take for a minute, and otherwise funny.

## 8 February 2024

I am sad for my body.

I haven't said much about all this to anyone beyond Kimberly here and my wife at home. It's a hard thing and unkind, too, to lever this down upon them and then retire to fatigue or silence for a while and leave them trying to sort out the etiquette of responding. There's so much to say and so little of it is called for. So we all flail at the thing.

There've been a handsome amount of fifth column reveries and testimonials come in, many of which I can't bear to read. The psychedelics advocates are well represented. I'm not keen. Transplants and implants at great expense, crowd funding recommended. I couldn't ask people to send me money with a straight face.

But here's something I've noticed: it has to do with movement. It began maybe three weeks ago. My wife and I were in the stone house in Joshua Tree, and it was dusk, and the moon was coming up. We'd figured out the speaker's mechanical mystery – I didn't, she did – and we were playing a Doors record called *L.A. Woman* at my request. We'd each had a glass or two of mezcal and the monumental sadness was off in the corner just then. My wife stood up, extended her hand. She wanted to dance. I'm a lousy dancer. But I knew this wasn't a time to be typically awkward. 'It's just us', she said. So I took her hand, rose to the occasion, listened to the groove.

Nothing happened. My right leg more or less obeyed, but the left was parody dancing, like it had no serviceable tendons. It'd go forward, it'd go back, but it couldn't syncopate at all. I couldn't tell at first. But after a few tries, it was like calling a number that just kept ringing. My wife was still dancing, still looking at me, her eyes saying, 'C'mon. I want to dance with you.' And I realized then that I couldn't. Not 'I can't dance a samba or a waltz.' It's 'No, I can't dance. Can't move that way.' I made myself say it. We were both suddenly embarrassed, or something close. 'It's OK', she said, and stepped back to let me sit down. I didn't want to sit down. I was in shock, or something close. I couldn't move my leg. When did this happen? It wasn't weak, it was unresponsive. Barely there.

Ever since then, any move I make to do some yoga or tai chi, or anything similar, I get weepy almost at once for all the things that this body will probably never do again. It's not defiance or resistance. It's grief, in waves. I'm so mournful over it, this body.

## 9 February 2024

We begin in light, we end in wisdom, if the Gods prevail.
We begin in water, and we end in dust, they say.
And life is us drying out, mostly.

## 12 February 2024

In the earliest days of this, when the allopath passed his judgment, satisfied, I just recoiled. Couldn't find myself in it, or I refused to. There was no path, no way, no reason to anything. Just the severity and moral quiet of weather. I was in the prevailing wind, that was all, and it was in from the northwest, just as the strong weather so often comes.

It was in that first week that my handwriting went. Not utterly, but surely. It was in that first week that my leg forgot how to syncopate and shuffle or dance in any way. Little weaknesses on the left side had me listing and refusing inside to walk. I went walking outwardly, but everything else refused the incessant labour of it, the exercise. It was in the next week that I found the silent shudder, as if the earth of me, the ashes and dust of me, was sliding into the sea, and with it my home. I would hang on to my wife as if I just met her and suddenly the boat on which we sailed across the channel was sinking for no reason, as if something vast below deck had given way.

The great dread I have now, besides imbecility, is forgetting, or being set upon by this but not dying, seeing the dying only. At four, I forgot the surfacing after the meningitis and the spinal tap, the plate glass in the door and the being looked at as though I'd never be seen again. There are only so many seizings and summonses per lifetime. Few get to recognize or learn the hieroglyphs.

I've taken the discipline of bedtime to appeal to my left hand to stay in the race by this ruse: I will brush my teeth as usual with the right hand for the sake of the teeth, but at the same time I will screw the toothpaste lid back on the tube with the left. It's a Rubik's Cube of a job.

## 17 February 2024

This is my best guess at translating all of this into a life that isn't over: something of the fundament of the life I've meant until now must change. It's hard to say why. It's not a war. It's not disqualification. More so, it seems to me today unbecoming to live a life where the powers of the mind will last as long as the powers of the metabolism or the heart live, or longer.

Life, under the gun: it isn't repentance. It's closer to reckoning. I ought to give up what is mine to give away. Be deliberate with what I say and to whom.

I credit the people painting Lascaux with forethought, and with the intellectual power and discernment to engage nonviolent demise with genuine pause, as though it asked something that the tiger at the cave mouth didn't ask: a willingness to occupy another time in life that didn't resemble anything coming before.

## 18 February 2024

Another day's end. I could catalogue the things I've done. I could count those remaining as short one or down one. But a few minutes of recounting the goneness of another day? What would the next one be for? This is neither discipline nor brinkmanship nor candour. It is pulling the wings from a bird to see how it flies.

You've seen mites of dust airborne? So slight they obey almost nothing. The subtlest of air, maybe. They are rotating and spinning, and barely land if they land at all. And each of them is an ability spirited from me without real purpose. The ability had purpose. Its goneness, not so much. I am dust, with nice clothes.

## 21 February 2024

I've thought of the term 'getting old' lately. Like most people I knew it was out there, but I tended to avoid using it. Never liked the fore-closure the term dragged around with it. There was a feeling of collapse about it. We might better say 'gain' than 'get'. You gain age, acquire it.

We say that so-and-so or such-and-such catches up to you, as if you slow down or come to a rolling stop and the aforementioned latches on to your stiff leg. Are we sure, though, who's doing the moving and who the standing still? It takes humans a powerfully long time to slow down. The sheer entropy of our style takes the likeliness out of dreams for con-tentment or contemplation. We are a'movin, we are, and it's more likely that we catch up to those lingering truths. If we're wise, or if we're on the receiving end of some reversal of fortune, we might see a bit of life there in the near distance. If we're wise, we slow down to let it pass, and we get a good look, and finally we get to really decide on a few things.

Have to slow down. An irony for a mind in eclipse.

## 23 February 2024

I'm no longer in the desert, now by the ocean. That's a lot of mythic ground covered. You don't go down to the shore to breathe in the thin air of the saints. Too many people here, far too many solutions. Too much health. Here, best to keep your afflictions to yourself.

One such affliction is the trmarkling of a marked life, the way of healthy people and people not seriously tested in the way of the calendar and the clock. How many more years or days are left to me? One less, at least, since the last time I asked. And so goes the slow march of devaluation, the days taken up in subtraction. The quality-centred people – quality, not quantity is their logo – are want to wring the neck of each day for a bit more of the vital fluid of life, the waning elixir. In this regime, any day that doesn't give up its storeroom of vitality is a squandered day, a crime committed against those you leave behind, against potential.

I had spinal meningitis at a very young age, three and a half. My keeper teeth were still in my gums. I remember nothing of the onset, but something of the care and feeding allotted to one so young and uncertainly here. There were the two hands of the nurses, where hospital meets patient. They made a claim upon me to keep me among the living. There was the relenting of that claim when my death became likely. There was the sitting on the stool and the being bent over, the nurse laying atop me for the spinal tap, the overriding terror and insanity of the thing. There was the end of visiting hours, and my mother looking through the glass at me as if she'd never see me again. There was the long convalescence indoors in the summer.

It is that last one that sits most heavily upon me. My association with convalescence is so fraught that I'm weighed down by it, lumbar puncture–prone. I can't pass a day indoors but that I feel somehow an invalid removed from life. It made studying for exams very hard. It makes resting very hard, and taking it easy, and picking up a book, and idleness, and contemplation for its own sake hard.

But this problem with being idle is just the measure left to me by which I might know that I am devoutly alive. It isn't a skill with octane. It's a bad octane habit, maybe. It isn't my alacrity or dexterity. For which I thanked God, until recently.

## 24 February 2024

It is a stunner of a thing: you can think a thought down to its finest details and still not have the thing have its way with you in the full three dimensions of life. You can have taught the thing, or from it, or because of it, and still know nothing of it in your bones. I've told the bulk of my childhood near-death fracas, and the grief therein, recorded it even, made something of a living from it, too, and know so very little of where it lives in my bones and my sinew, and what shuttles me around the place.

I held the notion of counselling, of paying for the privilege of telling someone my life's staggers and jags, at arm's length if not in contempt, for a very long time. I couldn't find the merit in it. I provided counsel for some years, repented thereafter, and left the enterprise to its devices. Something has happened, though.

It started with being unable to muster more than a front and back shuffle when Nathalie asked me to dance. At first, I was knocked over with dismay of the most acute kind. It took telling it several different ways for the familiarity of the thing to stay put for me to see it anew again. I saw it through an old lens, and thought I recognized the awkwardness, the maladroitness of the moment. But, historically at least, it wasn't a physical disability I had. I felt awkward, unaligned, incapable in the way of dancing. So I disowned the desire to be able to dance, for example, the way I disowned the desire for a father when there wasn't one: all but utterly.

That disowning went deep into the bone house, into the tendons and sinews, staunch declaration, a stance of a kind, a posture of stiffness. I was an involuntary Tin Man, clanking and banging dry joints. A posture that is so much like the posture I would now curl into within days, it seems, if I wasn't walking five miles a day, writing a book, learning the rudiments of chi gong, and getting counselling from an old woman all but deaf in one ear, costing scads of dollars for an hour, and each session going over time.

I am so arrested by the unexpected flood of sorrow and compassionate regard I have for my body as I begin recalling these stories that I know so well to this stranger.

## 28 February 2024

I've agreed to devote five online teaching sessions, two hours each, to the standard *monies* – patrimony, matrimony, ceremony – that have claimed me in my adult incarnation. I didn't want to do it. It's amazing how the inclination to agree can entirely bypass willingness or preference. I was afraid I could not answer the bell any longer, and I wanted to see if that was so.

I survived it. I'm not sure my particular notoriety survived it, but I did. I felt a kind of survivor's victoriousness at the end, and the afterglow of survival lasted several hours, included joking with the strangers who lingered a while afterwards – something I never valued in my former life.

A few days later someone who'd once claimed me as a certain influence wrote in to demand a hundred-dollar refund. One item he cited in support of that claim of injury: that I'd got up halfway through the online proceedings to go to the bathroom. Which was true. A $100 self-care episode.

There are lots of things to make peace with as this goes on.

## 29 February 2024

It's hard to tell. Everything has the look of a symptom now. Is there any movement I don't choose which isn't the Beast? The acupuncturist says everything that's got me is in the lungs. Nothing shocking there, nothing unforeseen. I'm not good at lungs. I'm good at lung infections, at the upheaval in the inarticulate parts that, traditional Chinese medicine-wise, are a dead giveaway for trouble behind and trouble ahead. I've rarely been thirsty in my life, for example, and I have to remember to eat, signals which have been lost in translation.

I do my best now to elaborate and articulate the length and breadth of the Beast. It's what I can do, instead of sitting still. No more sitting still for me. No more calm demeanour. Given the leaping of my left hand, I am wearing my heart on my sleeve, in every way one can. Minus any voluntary aspect that might accompany that candour.

I have been saying for years: 'If you can't say it, you can't see it.' These days, I cherish the elaborations and precisions of the tongue and of the mind that are still available to me. It's better than playing Scrabble, better than ball-squeezing rehab. I find it literally sharpens my 'mind sight', the part that sees the thinking, that speaks its way into things.

I've begun fingering rosaries. I don't have the beads yet, but I am cultivating a couple of habits. One is tracking my usual 'no' response to anything I formerly found uncomfortable or uncool or unstylish, and mobilizing an autonomic 'yes' in its place. I'm not persuaded that all of these yesses are good for me, which would be neither true nor wise. The fact is that I've no idea if any of the supplements I'm taking are good for me, or whether they are working. I have no standard for any of them, and I'm desperate sometimes to find my feet and mobilize on behalf of a better day.

Another is keeping a promise I made to my daughter to not be so cheap in deciding which redemptive measures to take. I'm spending 'fix money'. In days past, I'd be more than reluctant, but it's time for a wide net – and for keeping promises made to loved ones. Whatever it is that you want to remember, you have to be doing now. If there is a future, this is where it is made. Right now.

Another is admiring admirable things aloud. Even marginally admirable things get the treatment, in case I'm wrong in my assessment. Doing it aloud, lending your tongue to the words, is where the alchemy lives. Say it, and the heart gives the benefit of the doubt to most candidates in line for the treatment. Basic behaviour modification. Very useful in a crisis. The standard bearer of the mind is careful with the treatment. He's had his day, frankly. This is not the time for parsimony of the heart. It is time to lower the standards, until most ordinary things weep beauty. Say it aloud, and the anaesthesia wears thin, the cool remoteness loses its grip.

I remember Robert Bly telling of a conversation he had with the poet William Stafford about writing and discipline and morning light. Stafford told him of a practice he'd come to: write a poem every day, then get out of bed – in that order, with that unwavering fidelity. Bly asked him what he did about the unvanquished, unimprovable limits of the aging human bladder. What about standards? What about bad poems? 'Ah', said Stafford, 'not all the poems are good. Not even most of them. When that happens, I lower my standards, and then go to the bathroom.'

I still love the cagey, agile disciple's devotion of that story, especially now. It's so sane now.

## 4 March 2024

Reach.

At one time, my reach was exclusively something I did. If something was beyond reach, I moved until it wasn't. It was just a question of closing the distance.

Now all those things in my reach are heading towards the undoable. All the biomechanics of reaching are giving way. The fluid gesture is broken into grainy, flashcard bits that tumble eccentrically over each other. As I move my hand through ordinary space they pile up, as if something impedes them, then gives way, impedes them again, microdoses of stillness that won't prevail. The arc the hand makes through the unclaimed ground between it and where I'd have it go describes broken promises, broken openings.

## 6 March 2024

I suppose I am moving closer to a kind of monkish life.
The old persuasions are barely hanging on.
The boots and guitar and jacket and hat that I
kept by the door are still there
but the door's hardly swinging now.
I'm here by the ocean that's taking its time in
taking my heartache from me.
It's at night when I'm most afraid that
I've left the unventured ransom of a king on the table,
an unconsidered, autonomic day.
Behind me is a sound that will be obeyed.
There's no time for sleight-of-hand deals.
I look for a sign that I've not overstayed
now that staying's not part of the deal.

## 14 March 2024

The Beast is curled around the brainstem. It's there in the filaments.
The Beast lingers over one element in the periodic table – the one beyond living and dying, the one linking vital to vitality – and leans.

The Beast ripples along one tendon, flares down another, particulates another, dervishes another. The Beast pronounces over the likelihoods from the wings, does all the unsuspected rewrites, insinuates itself into the drama, works the room from the rafters, wanders into the footlights from backstage.

Before me are five years of shudders, I've heard, by way of consolation. Then, a few more of the staggers and jags, if there's no intrusion of mortality.

These unravellings might include stutters, a bard's soul desolation.

After the desolation and the withering of words, I'll be haggard, the raiment in rags.

## 15 March 2024

Of course, the Beast is, more than I am, mindful of the windy caves, the bellows tree, the heart's ventral companions, the lungs.

In the early going, everything causes everything. Except reversal, or restoration: nothing causes that. There's no cure. Aside from that cindered heart's desire, it's a cascade of symptoms and signs and 'we can't say for sures' banging into each other in the prognostic dark. Efficacy all but untraceable, I imagine I'll probably go all in, palliatively. I have other reasons now. Soothing has merit of the kind I never credited before. It may all come down to the dermatologist's dictum: if it's dry, cream it. If it's damp, dry it. It's an MC job for your psyche, probably, but it is employment. It's a day's work, and a night's work for my moral and mortal extremities. It keeps them responsive so as not to be jumpy, which, given it all, is welcome.

But what employment is there for the lungs, beyond what exertion obliges me to? What are tremours to the lungs? Are they that other SOB: shortness of breath? Is it time for COPD? Am I to lean on a stick, gaunt and greyed in the cheeks, blowing for all I'm worth? Am I to be spent in shuffling?

Are my shoulders to be grafted to my ears, frozen in perpetual shrug, gawping at the air for air?

What are these glimpses of what's likely for? Are they different from those glimpses afforded me of the reasons for living when I was well, the odd hint as to how? If I don't like what is shown me, does it mean that I am threatened? Am I to begin crossing out words from the holy murmur now, when they've run out of assurance? Am I to purify my sorrow's tongue, now that I can't talk my way through this?

## 17 March 2024

Can you imagine dying? If you've not been close, if you've not been penetrated by the cold steel of the thing, you'll have a hard time doing it.

But that pales alongside imagining someone dying on you. Leaving is thing enough, but the storm of someone leaving you and you so solidly being left is fierce.

There is the business of wringing the neck of every day for its milk. It's something the ordinariness of days won't tolerate for long. The ordinary is not built for milking or for throttling. Spectacle takes too much preparation to be borne. Despair will take its portion. And time will.

I'm thinking of how monstrous the incremental life becomes when the slow leaving of it is at hand. You are leaving, say, and because you are and because it's not imminent, you ask those who'll be living on afterwards to mind the increments, mind the stuff that is already outlasting you. There are things the moths will eat. They and their unravelling take some minding, even if it is only for disposing. There is the fracture of planning. It galls you.

You ask the living to join you in the eternal now that you've only a passing acquaintance with and were never really good at. In your moments of despond, you're disappointed if they rest from you, now that you are burdensome, now that your daily life is freighted with infinity, now that it's under this kind of mortal scrutiny. That's where most of their lives get lived now, in the busyness, and it's a place you scarcely occupy. The brinksmanship that you practice is too severe a place for them. You'll have to practice forgiveness all day long, and at night you'll wonder after their easy way of taking their sleep, leaving you to the cool companionship of the shadows and the stars.

And all the while you'll be leaving mementos not seriously meant.

## 20 March 2024

The best part of the mind grows fond of defeat, just to get by.
The best part of the mind doesn't seem to favour habit, running down the routine life. It seems to favour losing most of the arm wrestling we do with what comes to call, the being defeated by greater things that Rilke recommended. It's like a limb hanging out over the edge of the bed. It wants something prevailing that it cannot be, can never be, what it isn't, to rest itself upon, to save it from flailing.

## 21 March 2024

The handwriting is all but defeated. A transcriber's unnerving. A point of pride in years' past was the near absence of scratching out, of reassessed lines describing a change of mind, a second guess, a migration of idea. Time was that things were written down just as they came, all but fully made and fit for the world. The music in them came with the moment, the cadence clear and clarifying all at once. I loved that music.

Now the hand's voice wavers as the finger pivot wanders, audible but missing nerve. The right hand's memory is good, and its will is there. The left hand is wild for this consolation, feral in its flailing. It covers four times the distance the right does, up and down like a bilge pump with the water gone and the gasket shredding. The right hand knows the tune, but the voice isn't what it was. And just as it goes once the recital is done and the hall empties and the cleaners move in and there's a lone chair left on the stage and all the house lights are up, so it is as I await the solitude and the waning of my writing hand's song.

I waited all of forty years to pay large money for a proper pen, a writing machine for the ages. I wrote all the time, but never felt the work warranted that kind of expense. I bought one in Australia, when my wife said, 'A man like you deserves a pen like that.' A wild compliment I didn't debate. And now, months later, I'm hesitating with it across the page, slower than ever in realizing a letter, backpedaling to trace over the indecipherable until with so much ink it becomes unrecognizable, and then making crude, uncalled-for flourishes, piling a third hump to my 'm', a second cup to my 'y', uncalled-for augments, liftoffs from the line.

I don't know if this fine pen amplifies my hand's mutterings until they're no longer words, the way a coffin chair does – those upholstered slouch chairs that come with retirement, amplifying the inability to rise up on command. I've never succumbed to ballpoint, never will now, so I'll never know if there'd be mercy in the sludge in that chamber, in that nail point nib that has the alacrity of a fingertip or the end of a burnt stick. For now, I suppose, I'll stick with this amplifier of my imprecision.

I am writing in hieroglyphs of heartache.

## 22 March 2024

I'm on a Zoom call early Friday, video on, with someone I haven't seen or spoken to in years. He's in a world of hurt, separations and undo-ings of all kinds. I can feel the gravitational sway of my old efficacy as I strive after it. He's looking at me for a long time, seeing if I'm still me, still here. I'm trying to see the same thing. Occasionally, I'm looking for a word. It was a rare occurrence in the old days. But it has me on something like AMBER alert now.

I am not quite hitting the mark. There are little delays, nothing socially awkward, but strange for me. The sound of that delay: wind through winter trees, the odd recalcitrant leaf shuddering.

## 24 March 2024

*Forgotten Pillars*, the five-part series I intemperately agreed to be a part of, has ended. I learned that for now I can think and speak aloud. I learned what a blessing it has been these many years to have that ability, and the opportunity to do it over and over. I learned again – what a notion that is – that there's been merit to what I've done. Testimony has come in that bears witness to it – premature eulogies. How a mature eulogy differs, I don't know. I learned that the strain of a live in-person audience is harder for me now, but a remote live audience is an anticipatory hell for which I'm ill-suited. I resorted to walking before the livestream, but it didn't help.

## 25 March 2024

The time for leaving here is coming on, is gathering in the wings. Winter is beginning to end, obliging me to be homeward bound. I've packed my bags a thousand times, it seems, until there are more gonenesses than bags in the hallway. This touring, travelling version of living I know well. This is the chi gong of departure, the fine gestures of gleaning, pulling up stakes, all those things upon which I grew to rely now left behind in their rental place. Trying to remember where everything was, counting on housekeeping to restore them.

Leaving, you could say, is practice. Everything is there: the wardrobe of departure, the place thick with memory, the linger of a day without all of this, and then another, and then all of them in the order of descent, working backwards from now.

And practice, you could say, is leaving. Don't walk through the days, I tell myself. Don't ghost them with rumours of what's yet to be, and what will never be again. Inhabit them four-square, I tell myself. Leave, emptied of 'shoulds', until sadness is only sadness, and losing's all that's lost.

## 26 March 2024

I watch the law unto itself that once was my foot. Happy enough to be part of the gang of extremities, now its bottomless agitation makes it a fringe dweller, much in the way any discontent that believes overly in itself refuses to dance. Refuses the hand-in-hand, the discipline, the sequence, goes off and sows doubt in the company. Maybe its agitation is a superior guile.

I watch the rearing tendon murmur down my arm, drum the fingers on a virtual table top, piston plunging and priming and emptying some cistern no one sees, no regulator, no governor. Its reasons it keeps to itself. Its methods are a mimic of generosity, a model of impatience, as is someone who waits so inelegantly that in his agitation he can't recall the messenger he is, or the message he brings, whether it's divination or damnation.

Such are the shakes so far. I've no notion at all of how close my old silky poses and artful gestures are to disassembly. The act of feeding myself can go to ruin through no fault of my appetite. I just lose the purpose of the thing, I elect to go out walking and bid the balance of my dexterity farewell. My head leans forward, and the rest of the machine follows suit on down the road.

Where has the timing gone so out of time? The tuning so out of tune? The matrix is a metronome whose weight has shifted, like the cargo below decks wrenched to port or starboard by a stiff and nasty set of waves. There's a maelstrom on my sinister side, and the chains are broken, and the satellite states of my once tithing and obedient hand and foot are rogue, and failing and feral. They conduct an orchestra I can neither see nor hear. They count in the absent players, bring on dysphony. A finger tapping anarchy.

## 27 March 2024

It turns out that leavings upend me. I've more experience with them than I need, although probably not more than the average person. And yet the practice doesn't help. My kids were here for a few days and have flown home this morning, and I'm unable to get through last night's dishes for the relentless sorrow of having them gone. About my own departure, there's contraction and the surreptitious anxiety. I'm close to ectopic, again. The diaphragm is knotted, the writing hand pivoting on an invisible dime.

Some old me wants my attention, the one who wailed at departures, the one who can scarcely bear waiting on a promissory visit or call. I storm out to nowhere, unable to sustain myself. I flee what I wish would come.

The oncoming of the mind's darkness requires so much work, friends, so much looking behind doors, so much opening doors, heading down into the whirl of the unwelcome. We gather symptoms around us like life buoys, like teleprompters that might bring us home. But home is the sea now, dissolving places, dissolving destinations and strategies for calm. The great undifferentiated is what begins to gather now.

I get up without knowing why or what for. On a whim I walk from the writing desk and into the kitchen. Nothing awaits me there. I'm the one doing all the waiting. I stand in the middle of the room, assume some kind of chi gong stance, decompress my diaphragm which has become the site of strange weather, no surprise.

In a clinic, maybe thirty years ago. Tap, tap on my sternum. The Chinese medicine lady, upon whom I have an irreversible crush, looks at me long, says, 'Too much sadness, here'. In a month or so, upon being told that I just can't swallow the twenty-six bitter herb pills, no matter how much tea I'm given, she'll say, 'Ah. You don't trust me.'

Your breath gives you every opportunity for panic that you'll ever need or seek, every detail to lose yourself in. Left to your own ministrations you wouldn't think of more than a handful of them. But breathing will announce them all. This looking down the road and waiting, it's a chance to get the exhale caught up to the inhale. But there's panting, too.

I was at the beach most of yesterday.
I read Eliot's *Four Quartets* for the first time in forty years.
It seemed time. 'In my end is my beginning', and so on.

The hand is unruly, the one I depend on to make this clear. Transcription will be punishing. It'll make mince of the pattern recognition protocols of my mind, just when that's all I might have going for me. I will deliver myself into the hands of others, for translation, for safekeeping. And I suppose, too, that I will be rendered, approximated, and I'll have become mostly brain-uncertain, and, 'what he'd have wanted' will be the currency.

'There's a rare state of mind that makes the Head obsolete.'
— John Moriarty

## 28 March 2024

I've not walked a step beyond the sill of this place yet today, and I am feeling the lack of it. I'm not sure what that lack feels like. There'd have been nothing to talk about there in times gone by. I'd have never 'gone for a walk', or next to never. If I had something to do on the farm, I'd walk to do it. So 'not walking' wouldn't have been noticed at all. It's something I would have done if there'd been nowhere to go. I'd have walked to get the work of walking done. It delivered me to a purpose. That was its only purpose. It was conveyance.

But walking now has been shorn of its easy utility. It is its own work now. I'll have to learn to peregrinate, to move as those pilgrims move whose end is there in their beginning, with them each step. I move and learn walking as I soon must learn thinking. Such stride or murmur I'll have to gather towards me.

There'll have to be whole steps, marvel at the ankle's work, wonder at the matrix of a knee without benefit of the astragalus bone. I'll need to walk as a man might do coming to after a terrible collision, as a man might do once he's suspected the loss of walking has begun, once he's figured on this intrusion upon infinity which is one step, and then the other.

The only time I've walked that way is in woundedness.

I am in woundedness now.

You'd think the coincidence would help.

Walking, I'm told, is the help.

Walk, I'm told.

Minus going somewhere.

*Minus why*.

## 29 March 2024

You move involuntarily.

Ordinarily, that might be called 'driven', as in 'driven into Babylon' or 'driven by drink or the devil to do it' or 'driven to drastic measures'.

Or it might be called 'possessed', as in 'what possessed him to do it?' Or 'a clear case of possession it was', or 'possession is nine-tenths of the law' (not much of a law, that one) or 'your possessions are your prison'– none of which binds us to clarity or conscience when it comes to worldly goods.

There's 'haunted', 'beset', 'overwhelmed': all reasons to move that aren't really yours.

It isn't quaint, all this movement to no end. It isn't cool. There's no firm ground or steady hand or – so far – inner stillness in place of the outer stillness. It's the jangled repertoire of a scatterling I have. It's a leaping frailty. There's no volition, no vote to be cast, no midnight reprieve.

The choices are few, but they're there. I can choose to fight the jags. I could, although the likely outcome is more jags for my troubles. Like fighting the flu, or the plague. Or the blues. Or the ocean.

You could think you're choosing to give in and get God, or get smart or get lost or the like. Choosing to give in sounds good. It sounds right. It sounds sound. It may be made of a thousand brief choices. Or there may be no real choice at all, just a sequence of shrugs, as you do when you can't find the door in the dark.

You could choose old prairie grass as your patron plant. Once rooted by feet upon feet of subterranean tangle, then torn up by the plough, now little tufts of temporary defiance, going about the magic of their appearance, going all in, rearing up towards their end, curled upon themselves, seed cast on promiseless ground, without conviction but with reason enough to start. And then to stop.

Well, now. We'll find out what kind of animist I am, soon enough we will. We'll see if I can take dictation from wild grass.

## 30 March 2024

When you've run afoul of the Beast, or when you've your suspicions, you'll see its mark everywhere. Clusters of sightings will trouble your mind and your sleep. There'll be a young man sitting across from you at the Adelaide airport, misery written across his face, his palsied left hand cocooned in his right. Your future wringing its extremities. There'll be an old Japanese woman serving your bento box lunch in a sidewalk restaurant, her whole ensemble atremble. There'll be a man walking the beach almost hypothetically, as if the ground is shifting beneath his feet, his footsteps washed away behind him, no evidence that he's here.

You'll want to say something, but you don't know what it is. You once looked at those so afflicted from miles away, from another country, vaguely sympathetic. You once looked upon them as if they were a murmur, a Cyrillic script, an uneasy illuminated gospel of human affliction, what the modern times still tolerate of the parade of deformity and devastation that would have been market day in a medieval town. They're closer now, though, less exceptional but still scant.

Because they are so few, you've the sense that it's you and maybe two dozen others scattered across the normal, able landscape, negotiating the vagaries, shuffling to Jerusalem, Byzantium, a tolerable but ignoble troop of involuntaries. Struck.

This divestiture will have you considering things unconscionable even a half year ago. Cureless remedies, say. You might not go all the way, but you'll probably get close. The straight and the crazed of everything will be offered up, and they'll sound different now, not as reckless as before, or as casual, or as groundless and desperate. Bits of bark and fungus, jungle juices, stuff that grows under the stairs out back, a wondrous working man's *Materia medica*. Bitter herbs and balms, heat pads and gem blankets appear.

Everyone knows someone who knows someone who beat your affliction. There's a hero story under every rock. Somebody just walked away from the disease. So you start walking five miles a day, maybe fourteen thousand steps at a go, hill and dale. Somebody loosened the grip of the Beast with nicotine patches. You start thinking about a pipe. You start second-guessing every position you've ever taken. There's merit aplenty in being unsure of yourself now. In frightful moments you'd rather be anyone but yourself.

You start reasoning with your brain and its habitual business. You've a notion now that there's something in the feelings and the affect and the hurt circuitry that's done a good job of initiating you, and its routine toxicity could be a culprit. Trauma's a raging business now. There are sympathetics and parasympathetics and the rudiments of the nervous system to make peace with. The poor old diaphragm could use a break. There are the disfigurements of mouth breathing you've read about in bestsellers. There are the habits of fret, and the time has seriously come for a mindful encounter with the orthodoxies.

This taxes the ordinary mind. It beggars, or seems to beggar, any mind with the Beast aboard. Ordinary anxiety becomes a tangle with absurdity. My anxiety – my anxiety about being anxious – replicates and recombines itself. I can feel it rappel the palisade of good judgement without a sound. There's nothing to notice beyond a certified vagueness, and an incoherent concern about it that won't clear off. It's so beyond sensical, cause-and-effectual, consensual, that it's a challenge for anyone caring for you to enter in the moment, to understand enough to look at you through the fog and see you for the internally writhing thing that you are. You'll be beyond reach to anyone who doesn't care for you.

This morning, I got an email from a stranger, short and to the point: 'You are intellectually interesting but emotionally unavailable', it said. The Beast bites down to the bone that way. I am discerning, but seem to be powerless. Maybe that's the Parkinson's Personality Profile: intellectually interesting, emotionally unavailable.

People you know and people you don't know promise to pray for you. How wise a course is that to go along with?

> Years ago, I was on the road, this time in Texas. Out of kindness, a local couple offered to put up a sweat lodge for a friend and me out on their ranch, to take the road weariness down a bit. 'How would it work?' I ask the friend. 'Oh, they'd preside over the whole thing', he said. I thought about it. 'Nothing personal', I said, 'nothing against them or their kindness, but I'm not having just anyone praying over me.' 'Hell no', my Texan friend said. 'I understand.'

But it's hard to understand. Does everybody know what prayer is? How did they learn it? When they bear down upon your plight in prayer, what happens next? Is it only prayer when it's good? Is prayer where safety and sanity go to hide, or prevail? Is there conscience employed in prayer, or does it get the day off for good intentions? What happens when they promise to pray for you and don't? If anything?

# Scaffolding 2

This was becoming a spectacle of failure.

Neurodegeneration can fool you.

I thought I was getting the hang of it, a few months in. Meaning: I thought I knew what I was looking at. I thought my despair was a working despair, lending itself to the strange inquiry. I saw a kind of neurosomatic counsellor for a while. I was still able to talk the talk, and I think she enjoyed the encounters. But I genuinely didn't know what I was doing. I was watching parts of me scale off, and then describing them, age regression and all. I was being lucid about fearing the losing of my mind, and I couldn't tell if that was called for.

I took to yoga, conceding that it was late in the day for such a thing, but probably called for. I walked for hours to the donut shop in the next beach town north, and back again, every other day. I was going to this Green Book, the one you're reading now, with crafty stuff, depositing it there for safe keeping, I thought.

You know how it is with impact: the kinetics drive the dust matter up for a moment, force's path of least resistance. The dust fancies itself on the rise. Then, something like a mushroom cloud. And then it begins to fall.

I was trying to register the devastation, I can see now. But it amounted to me setting up a seismometer where the tremours had already rolled underfoot.

I was in the desert, always a rankling, second-coming kind of place, and I was trying to be okay. I was on the Pacific coast, white wellness world headquarters, unable to figure out what 'well' meant anymore. Deserts, chimera, affliction: you need a biblical repertoire to make a go of anything, or you court a megaphone-toting, shopping cart-pushing madness.

I was trying to make it through — though 'through what' I couldn't have said. I was desperate to make sense, though I couldn't have told you why. Habit, probably. I was feeling culpable for my affliction, but I didn't know how. I was inundated with schemes for restoration, redemption, to the point where every day not taken up with a new lifestyle or pharmacopic repertoire was a day in perdition.

The sheer panic was useful. It was a kind of driver. But two months in, it was wearing off. That turned out to be the beginning of not knowing what to do.

# 1 April 2024

There are so many contenders for my self-interest, so many people who've heard of someone that heard of something that really worked this time. When the Beast comes to call, your standards for self-care swell to unrecognizability. Someone sends a kind of Santo card that advises me to 'wear your seatbelt, recycle, forgive some awful sinner'. Sound advice that I'll try to take. Someone sends mushrooms, which I might take once persuaded that they're not do-it-yourself mushrooms. Someone sends an email – scores of people do, so many that there aren't hours enough to respond – that holds bodywork up as the real deal. Suddenly, I can get behind bodywork in all its unregulated, florid, ready-to-wear diversity.

And that's how I became one of those guys lingering in the park. Not *those* guys. The chi gong ones moving in exasperating slow motion, swaying to an invisible, inaudible, metronome-like something that stalks the breeze, in their pyjamas, solemn as a spire. There aren't many things as alienating as watching yourself being watched doing something that foreign to you and that simple, in public. The movements are so see-through that they reveal every imprecision, uncertainty, hiccup and failing my untutored body is capable of – three-dimensionally, in slow motion.

On a gloomy overcast Saturday morning, in a city park, maybe twenty of us, sporting various degrees of dexterity compromise, various tones of athletic wear, each of them seeming to be deeper into this remedy to their compromise than I, fully engaged in the frame-by-frame metaphorical depiction of a heron, a crane, a tree, a wind, a sea – believing every moment of it. And I move in the back row, with a few other chi gong acolytes, way too acutely attuned to how all this looks to those people walking by, of whom I was one maybe a year ago.

# 2 April 2024

I left Toronto three months ago with a spell of facts and foreclosures clapped upon my mind. Shorn of my old understanding of myself, I was suddenly what I'd never be again.

Your soul wants a story at a time like that, not a Jesus-nullifying diagnosis, not a short-circuiting fingertips-on-desk drumroll for your old life marching out the door. Do I blame the neurologist for his bloodless practice of symptom box-checking, speaking about me to my family as if I wasn't there? Of course I do, yes. I was dog paddling towards a buoy heaved up and down by a riptide of fortune reversing, and if he saw the symptoms arrayed before him in the form of me with clarity, then he could have seen that in me as well.

For two or three weeks I was in a terror/misery tango that need not have been, I don't think. It would have had its own shambles. But three months ago, there began a regime of information and counter-information, and a torrent of schemes and counter-schemes which made no place for the Beast in their beastiaries. There's rough training in medicine – I know; I was one of the trainers for a while – and medical school is a survival of the fittest ordeal. But somewhere in the sordid sanctification of allopathy there should be a breviary, an invitation to ambivalence, so that the slighter souls among us might find rest and kinship as we tangle with the Beast of Mindlessness.

Many days I do wonder how it goes for those with little time for stillness, how it goes for those who have impatient companions, prosaic companions. The Beast frankly commands us to set down the sorcery of 'steady on'. I am on another shore. The last downturn in energy or understanding is sand in the circuitry. I am because of it a prone man, a citizen remote. The Beast is my country now. How do those upon whom it gnaws set themselves up for a day of tremouring and imprecision of the mind? Who is there to call them from the stupor, who will ask more of them than the Beast draws out? Who will remind them that this miser's contraction needs them to rise, however unsteady, and walk the fields? Who will bid them learn the Beast's *dance macabre*? Let there be a bead on the rosary string for them.

## 3 April 2024

As the subtle atrophies appear I get an uncommon chance to see the habit mechanics show themselves. It is wild to see how I settled for my mind/body predilections as if they were fiat from on high. I'd no appetite, for example, for years. I figured that was an aging person's adjustment to waning physical activity. Probably a good and fitting sign of me obeying my age, taking it to heart, I thought. I had no thirst, least of all for water, for years. 'Did you drink anything?' was a janitorial mantra around the house. I was, in the latter days, a touring musician who neither ate, nor drank, nor slept during the day. Gregory Hoskins, my faithful partner in the *Nights of Grief & Mystery* project, would boss me around: 'Stay at the hotel until 5', he'd order. But I didn't want to miss anything before the show. That's what I said to myself. I didn't want to shut it down and miss anything after the show. What was rest to others was deprivation to me. Shades of the meningitis days.

Without some other me to seriously contend with the habituation, there was only me and my habits. Without me noticing, by middle age they'd become the same thing. I defended them while I practiced them. They were the push/pull of life, the gravity circuitry, the necessity/adversity matrix of the daily thing.

I see now, or I am beginning to see, that the regent of all of these accommodations I made to flawed instinct was my breathing regime. I see it now because the Beast pulls at my diaphragm. It uses any breath to fret, to foresee mayhem, as a necromancer might use the entrails, the gizzard, to hazard guesses about what's oncoming. Its claim upon my breathing is so resolute that I cannot until now separate it from breathing. Breathing, it turns out, is how I've panicked, how I grieved, how I grew wary and readied myself for the carnage. It sidelined me in public school. It mainlined me at solemn times.

'I can't breathe', I've come to see, is a confession sometimes. There's plenty of air. Minus an obstruction, minus a persuasive compromise in the form of a tumour or a collapse, or when someone means you harm, their hands upon you, the truth is that 'I *can* breathe. I'm just not doing so. I have my reasons.' Every habitué does. Why anyone would cling to such a disabling scheme could bewilder – unless you credit the real possibility that the reasons for not breathing, the associations, are more persuasive than the asphyxias are.

Terror, for one, takes your breath away at least as efficiently as beauty does. You can negotiate beauty apnea as an amateur. You can get at-home technology for sleep apnea. But you need chops, time-in, razor courage to tangle with terror apnea. An engagement with terror starts with a fixed diaphragm, and digresses and distresses from there. Terror hunts you down in the woods, takes you in for questioning, waterboards your nerve. It fills your lungs with ethyl alcohol, dares you to take a breath.

Dread can go chronic. Terror is always acute. Once underway, terror means whatever you say. It doesn't need a voice, or words. It has yours.

The Beast very clearly has intelligence on these habits. It has spared me my dominant hand for now, but is making sport of my less elegant left hand. It found I was awkward at dancing, and so made a dance of the awkwardness. It learned that I treasured grace under pressure, and so has induced subcutaneous leaping that in my mind makes me a marionette whenever I am due to give forth in public, or to eat.

So God help us in our time of need, if there's anything to be done that isn't collapse, wither and contraction. It will find me on the terrible road. I am obliged now to contend in ways unknown to me. Whatever my abilities, they're being pressed into unnatural shape. I pant on the acupuncture table. I pant at the prospect of conflict, at the possibility of awkward social encounters. I pant and contract on the highway, whether I'm driving or not.

## 6 April 2024

I left the Pacific shore a few days ago. The umbilical tether that binds me to the places/people who've been kind has become so taut and intense that I'm bereft when I leave them, dissolving and disconsolate, like a child looking out the car's back window at a receding, waving friend, or a house or a dog. Something in me sets to wailing at the earth-moving profoundness of it all. That is what human kindness has become: an intensity of unlikeliness barely borne. Someone who found me worthy set her life aside and made a home for my bewildered self on the Pacific shore. Someone else who thought well of me put my wife and me up at her mineral springs motel in the desert, and we left her in a parking lot this morning. I'm moulting allies.

Now I'm at a Godless motel four hours down the road in central California, alongside railroad tracks and the town's four-lane main drag. The place has one area to linger outside, which doubles as the dog dump. No chairs, so I'm sitting on the grass, back against a half-height masonry wall, midafternoon, the locals roaring by to and from their lives. I'll have to go inside for a while. The southern California sun's too much for this white man, even in April.

All of which serves to remind me of touring *Nights of Grief & Mystery*. We'd be pending sound check, having begged our way into an early motel check-in. Or we'd be in the early hours of the sound check. I'd be a bit nervous, but not so much, pacing, making a few notes, watching Gregory and our sound tech, Charlie, practicing their craft, counting down the hours, me walking the main drag, sometimes being recognized, into the green room, questionable food, illicit alcohol sometimes, asking what time it was a dozen times or more, getting dressed, forgetting the suspenders, more pacing, forgetting the in-ears rig I have to wear under my shirt, getting half undressed then dressed again, and then we're in the wings, hearing the buzz, waiting out the intro, parting the curtains, out into the light and whirl.

I miss those nights, that camaraderie. I miss them intensely. I was doing some holy work in my sixties, when the usual trajectory is calming down. I don't know that I'll see such nights again. And there's no remedy for that poverty, no replacement nights.

Remembered happiness is agony, wrote the poet Donald Hall upon his wife's death.

So is remembered agony.

I've been asked several times if I remember when the Beast first came to call. As these devastations go, there are too many first times to recall. And some of them looked then like what most of them look like now. But the other day I remembered this:

> It's maybe sixteen months ago, and we're touring in the US. It was
> a good house, on a good night. Everything was cooking. There

was a moment when Gregory was grooving, as he so often did. In the early days I would lay out to keep the spotlight where it belonged. But as we got tighter, that got less real. On this night I grooved, too, finger popping in the pocket of the groove. We had in-ear monitors. You could hear just about everything that happened on the stage, so I could hear those pops. Or, one of them. I realized after a moment that the right hand was popping fine. The left, even though the mechanics were there, was all but silent.

It's been all but silence ever since.

I remember that right now, how unsuspecting I was at the time. I realize now how much diminishment was already underway, how true it had already become, creeping down from the crags on the mist bands at night, with me parting the curtains, stepping out into the light, the whirl, at the top of my game, keeping my end of that otherworldly deal struck so long ago.

An email came in today. Rather than coming to the generic Orphan Wisdom address, it came directly to my name. Out of habit, I popped it open. There's so little chance to change your mind with a screen. The wonks know that, too, built that feature right into the machine.

Next thing: I read it. I was for the moment only scanning. That's reading without commitment – like not inhaling, maybe. But the tar and nicotine of the thing entered the circuitry. It began with a few accolades. This can mean at least two things: there'll be accolades all the way through and the writer is just getting warmed up. Or the writer *is* warmed up and is getting the accolades out of the way so as to get to the main event.

Turned out she *was* warmed up. She was grateful in the usual way, but had grown increasingly frustrated with the latest newsletters. To wit: not enough news.

She used me against me, too. To wit: I have usually been forthright, as night follows day. I have usually been clear, she wrote. By those two semiaccolades she means that, so far, she figures that in the newsletters I've told everybody everything that's going on. And now I'm not. Not even close.

How does she know I've spilled the beans every time out? Does she know everything so far? Everything I've written so far? Have I really written everything?

The truth is that I've kept most of the stuff to myself. That's why the people who write in more or less satisfied are satisfied. They didn't have acres of my personal details to labour through.

Friends: this isn't a deal we struck, that I'll keep telling you what's happening, and you'll keep reading. I think my minimalism is kind, or kindly, just as the minimalism of your occasional accolades are kind. Let's keep it up, swapping out all the gory details for kindnesses. The world needs less of the former, don't you think, and more of the latter.

## 8 April 2024

I don't know just how closely I should be tracking the microclimates of symptoms and feelings that come for me.

Awareness or consciousness can turn into scanning after data, easily. For example, the big question might always be: Am I still me? And the moral order that drives that investigation is: I should however possible be me, retain me, sustain me. Any ragged philosophical or spiritual pursuit would countenance that goal, you'd think. Being nearly me had already been tried, found wanting. Hence, the quest to be true to whatever I gathered together by way of repeatable habits from which I made a self.

But if metaphysics give way to neurologics, when the mind and the brain are involved, what is the standard for being your self? The premorbid self is the standard, isn't it. It is Greece, it is Rome, it is Greenwich. If you were only 75 per cent you, you'd just be hanging on. If you were 100 per cent (always an exaggeration), you'd be doing well, self-wise. If you were 50-50, the authorities would have all but given up on you and turned you over to your next of kin.

For me now to strive after retention of my recognizable habits sounds criminal. The Beast sets upon my authorized self, and I dig my heels into quicksand to stand against what already is becoming of me? How am I to occupy the days granted me when the nostalgia standard holds firm? It's a storm I'm in, not a race. There's no winning. It'll be done soon enough.

It would be as though I didn't look my age. How much dislocation belongs to this affliction? How much of me do I owe it in the name of being realistic?

Look into the eyes of a sane dog. Not too hard or long. It's menace to them. Creatures do that when they've no sense of smell, or when they mean harm. But risk a look, and take the measure there. What you'll see is a creature who knows creation, and his creaturehood. What you'll see is a being not trying to look behind his own eyes to see his reasons for being here. Nothing, no ground, seems to have opened up between him being here – the same 'here' as you and me – and him being a dog. Same thing. It's not a default skill, not a species specificity.

You don't have to be a dog to be here. You do have to be here, though. All the way in. That means no future, no percentages, no point shaving. It means even your imagination belongs to the present moment. It means that you see your way clear by not holding out for a large piece of 'otherwise'. I doubt that dog hopes it'll still be a dog later on, or hopes that it's a dog now. Each of his moves – barring an extreme in gene manipulation or conditioning – is a dog move.

I walked a poodle the other day, a poodle that had, or sure seemed to have, these traits. Every bit a poodle, yes, but every bit a citizen of the breathing planet. I looked at him deep in his face. After a few seconds, he didn't like it, but up until then he just kept saying 'yes', an amber-orbed 'yes', a language which in my affliction I'm trying to learn.


# 9 April 2024

Yesterday there was a total eclipse of the sun in bright daylight against a clear sky. It passed me by entirely. I was out on the town today, and stood on the street corner like an uncalled-for wooden sentry, knowing full well what a haunt I looked and not moved enough by that to assume anything like a relaxed man stance. I am as alive as I'll ever be, as I ever was, with no prospects for an upswing in my fortune, and it arrests me.

Solitaire with forty-six cards and a joker is what seems imminent.

Days with a fixed gaze is what I fear.

But the fear is fixing the gaze.

That much today is clear.

Soon it'll be overcast, they've said.

Soon the eclipse. Or the storm. Or the gale.

Or the tower akimbo. Or the ghost ship set sail.

Could be the cookbooks now, and the newspapers, and not the classics anymore for a man who's traded headwinds for vapours.

The best of me seems to have waited on a time when the petty, the paltry and the grudge would be offered up for grabs, for keeps, and be gone.

The best of me might be the one who won't prevail or win, whose lingering places him last in the parade of grace.

He doesn't do pretty. Fixed face on a corner, standing stock still. Inside, he leaps.

# 10 April 2024

The deal you strike with life: that's your body.

The claims that gravity makes upon you – and equilibrium, hydraulics too – all dare you to find a way with them. The testing, the rising up of legions of impossibles, the sanctified boundaries, all of them hand over to you a self for safekeeping. You are your hand, your other hand, all the fingers, both thumbs. You are your reach's range.

The philosophers in your midst would have you understand that as error or illusion, that taking and mistaking of your body for a self. That body is more than illusion, though, more than noble conveyance. It is the ministrations and advent of limits. It is the guidance, the good governance that intrudes upon infinity, that parents your affinity for greater, and for more, and for the future. The body, the miraculous uprightness and work of it, comes to you incrementally, by unbidden limits. Abide there, and you might learn your lessons.

Let's face it: every success breeds striving. Failure, though, is how the grit and grain and girth of life call you to themselves. Frailty is hard business, though. Unwelcome, uncalled for, the seat of homelessness and its alien feeling, frailty and limits and endings aren't arranged for your sake. They are life's understanding of itself, levied upon the body in space and in time. And we get to overhear life murmuring to itself, and our body is the tuning fork, the dowsing rod.

You burn yourself, you learn yourself.

That's the body.

Which brings me to the dubious bit of design optimism called the button fly. The button fly, I've discovered, is all but eclipsed by that escalating device we call a zipper. A zipper is clear and present danger. It has a carnivorous design, a curious unregulated single purposefulness that reminds you of a chainsaw. It is ruthless, artificial intelligence. Its will be done, in a phrase. So it's not the most obvious preference to exercise when the nether parts are called into play.

But factor in urgency, and decorum, and compromised dexterity, and neurodegeneracy, and inexperience with imprecision and it's no contest. Even with the risk assessment, the zipper prevails.

I've discovered that almost every pair of pants I have are button-fly pants. This is where the renovation of life habits and deeds induced by neurodegeneration makes its claim. Because the undoing of a button fly I can expedite single-handedly with a deft application of a sheer twist of the fingers. The buttons just pop free. But, crisis averted, the restoration of the buttons in their buttonholes is an onerous, clumsy, two-handed job, prompting sighs and sideways glances from those in the lineup who are wondering what it was I could possibly have been doing in there.

'Buttons', I'd have told them.

## 11 April 2024

Volume. That's the temptation, to evaluate the walking by steps, or kilometres, the breathing by exhales per minute, the writing by pages, or entries or days. But you can't with volumes of elaboration put a record down on paper of being clobbered by something that dusts your brain stem. Elaboration is being clobbered too, don't forget. The tracking of the days hasn't suffered, not yet, though I am apt to track the suffering during the record keeping.

There's no merit in counting the days that go on. That just becomes what you're doing with the days that are left. A day comes to its end – yesterday, say. You watch the sun go down beneath the horizon, again. I did that. But this time you count it as something gone from you, as I did.

Is it true, that this day's gone from me? Did I have it all day long, and then just lose it there at the end? Is each day a refugee, an escapee disappearing down the dark street with a bit of my life in its mitts? Is it a thing come to take a few moments from the pile allotted to me? And where is this pile, and how is it that the thief finds it and I don't?

Could it be instead that each setting sun on the western border is a day added to what I am entrusted with? Does it mean that there's one fewer of the unknown days than there were? Or one more day filled with articulation of what I hold dear, or held? A little more added to what I've seen and done?

Your life is filling up, not falling down. Soon it will be full, as free of potential as an orchard in autumn is free of would-be apples, as the wine cellar is free of would-be calvados, as the tasting cups are free of would-be toasts, as the minds are free of would-be hangovers.

Red apples, strong drink, rowdy declarations, swoons the next day, the odd chance to do it again. That's the end of potential, the visitation of actual.

Anyway, friend; how did you want this time to go? In the days when you were sure you had a choice, what did you choose? I can think of different elegances, ones whose grace would be hard to mistake. But what did those elegances make of my days of less affliction? Where were the graces? When were they eaten? From what bottle were they drunk? Did I stumble when I did the drinking? How did I know I was done?

Less shaking would have made more what? Clarity of mind mid-morning? What? A better sunset? Once more up the hill? Did it help the sun to rise? A good day might be a stranger well-met, the best of you warning the rest of you: 'It's late.'

Have I been intact long enough, and at my life long enough, that I might finally and formally rest in the afternoon, as my grandfather did after his lunch, now that I'm his age?

## 12 April 2024

There is a head-on collision looming. I'm in one car, with my best effort to rise in the morning, and move the sand out through the machinery and do well by the upright days left to me. In another car are the claims I made about competence addiction in *Die Wise*, in *Come of Age*, the ignoble low-rent miseries wrought by the intolerance for limits that a be-all-you-can-be culture levies on its citizens.

Limits of this kind are new to me. I grew capable of being limited in height and girth – not a terrible limit to bear. I wheezed with exertion, was limited to running slowly, but learned ways to play anyhow. As a child whose parents weren't together – in a time when that was uncommon – it was harder, for it marked me as stained. Not disabled in any way. Marked by something like shame, like disfigurement that's more symbolic than functional, a disfigurement that people could suss, that registered for them. I ceased missing a father, so it seemed, and carried on.

## 14 April 2024

I've been offered the pharmacopeia. Not the whole thing, but several acres' worth of the stuff.

Now, I've thought of myself favourably in pagan terms, as one hazardous to the regime, who's loomed or lingered over the hesitant, standardized repertoire of responses that circulate over the day-by-day terrain, who's taken his chances with the citadel and its guards, who's gone the other way.

And now it turns out I am, just as surely, allopathy's native son. That bout with meningitis and its recuperative aftermath as a four-year-old, the recurring doses of adrenaline in Emerg after the wheezing race downtown, after being pulled over, after subsequent police escort, the dozen hospitalizations for leather lung later, the coming close to losing an eye, the tree knocking me down on my summer construction job, etcetera, all of it has had the surprising effect of making me a treatment conservative. People are shocked that I don't go all in on the mushrooms, the hallucinogens, the do-it-yourself pharmacopeia, the guy somebody knows who's gone across the border to a Tijuana clinic.

Hell, I'm shocked, in a way. But when it's treatment time, I go mainstream, as often as not, and look down a long lens at the jungle juice, the psychic surgeries, the tropical transplants. Somehow my calculus goes like this: when in working order, I'll ride the rails with the other outcasts, but when I'm ailing, I play Go Fish in assisted-living game rooms.

So, why? My associations with near death and near life are Teflon. They'll talk, but they won't give way quietly. They're persuaded of their time to shine, and that time is crunch time. It's a kind of fearful moral code, and it keeps its dreadful promises. Allopathy is, I presume, for one who is making it through. It goes down in the concrete bunker with me, when the drones rain down.

It takes a true shaking of the branches, I've found, for this to go otherwise. So, I've begun to practice divorcing my willingness, my allopathic eagerness, from my hand-to-mouth herbal behaviour. I don't require of myself that I believe in the efficacy of the bitter herb. I've become an agnostic when it comes to my disbelief in these things. My current repertoire of convictions is addled by the Beast. That much is true. So I try door number two, plan B.

At least until this morning. This morning, a long-studying naturopath afforded me a consultation on the scrambled matters at hand. She had in tow a dozen or more agents of herbal restoration, none of which I recognized. I took 'em on the spot, after a cursory thumbing through of the allegations on their behalf on the labels. I felt foolhardy, easily won over. But I choked 'em down. Later I walked her out to her car. The goodbye became a bit unwieldy, both of us alert to the stakes. 'Well listen', I said. 'You came a long way, and I see you know your stuff. I'm not sure about any of this, but I'll try.' 'You know what you said', she replied. I didn't. I shook my dopamine-deficient head. 'There's no trying. Only doing,' she said.

I don't know if that is paganry talking, or allopathy, or what. Strong stuff, though.

# 15 April 2024

A year ago, I was in Tuscany. A year ago, people paid me to do things, to talk. In fact, I got paid for things I hadn't done yet.

A year ago, I learned firsthand about Parmigiano Reggiano – food that was so good you didn't need an appetite to marvel.

A year ago, I had a public life and stood for hours in front of roomsful of strangers, lateral thinking on demand. I could speak as though I had a calling. I took my chances. I spoke across thresholds. I spoke in the crosshairs. I called up a storm.

A year ago, I toured with artists decades younger than I am. I was the only one up at two o'clock in the morning. I could not find reason enough to sleep. Such was the thrill of a *Nights of Grief & Mystery* tour. There was only joy to recover from, joy and being paid to do what I was born to do, on the other side of the ocean, the world.

A year ago, I sharpened the old Japanese chisels and took another run at carving the beams in the teaching hall on the farm, and reclaimed my membership in the chip-makers guild, remembered the Old Worthies and their handcraft, and sent them a struggler's love.

A year ago, I saw an old barn come safely down in pieces on the other side of the river. I saw it safely borne over to my side of that river. I saw this barn raised one post at a time, and the beams heaved up to bind over and steady them, and the hardwood dowels driven into their same old bore holes. High, dry, a new old barn's hard to come by.

A year ago, I wasted time, I'd guess.

A year ago, I talked about endings.

A year ago, I worried on a dollar.

A year later that memory's a calamity.

I have the stranger's grudge. When the topic of the Beast comes up, the diagnosis, I listen intensely for what people say about it from where they are, on the healthy side of the haunt. I listen for fidelity, something authentic in their talk. I'm ready to pounce, as if I'll know what fidelity would sound like – me, who doesn't yet know how to make that authentic sound. And the hurtingest thing by far is when people seem to blithely acknowledge the bastard fixity of the Beast, the fact of the matter, the incontrovertibility of the thing, as they might the day's weather.

'It's all work now', one long-studying healer said to me yesterday. Not a glimmer of 'we'll see' in her. Just, 'we'll see what you do.'

It enters me like betrayal. I thought I was the one who occupied the place of no return, and they the palace of possibility. I thought at least a few would talk me down from that place – better informed, persuasive, moved by intelligent love. I thought some would be hopeful. I'm holding out for that, and it doesn't appear. And I'm run through by betrayal.

I don't have the hang of this thing, this affliction, at all. I don't even know if it has a hang. I don't know how to be afflicted this way, with the loom of mental wreckage close by. 'You're early in this', an acupuncturist said today. I'm at a loss as to know what kind of news that is. Am I keen on more time, more of this, more getting the hang?

In a bookstore I looked through a big picture book that came from Leonard Cohen's last tour. I caught a line of his I'd heard before: 'If the machine functions well, the third act can be fine.' But Leonard, I'm not even seventy, and I suddenly have a disease that will make me old and unable at the same time. 'We all know how the third act ends', he also said. I'd really counted on one more tour, as an old man, to ride out the afterwords, tired, sure, but upright, and retaining the lines.

## 16 April 2024

There's something ultimate about an ultimatum.

That's what I thought when I started working through the short list of contenders for media interviews I might consider giving. It's what I thought two days ago when I joined a study group that has been making its way through my work: what do all of these limits do to the moral calculus by which I might decide what I properly owe these people?

I was not someone who fancied a public life. I never trusted the spectacle, nor the autobiography. Nor, if I'm honest, the throng. I knew approval was transient, leveraged, a goofy metric, a miserable map. Still, the public life happened, and I cooperated with it. *Die Wise* found its audience, and I was in the hurly burly then. I was there, but in truth I didn't notice it much. I was zoomed in on the gig at hand, and never did the exponential math. Never did have a sense of momentum, or the big picture, or the career. Testimonials have come in, in small droves. They open me up to the clutch of consequences I've had a hand in stirring. What might I owe them for that arousal? I've transgressed upon the short term of their visions and their plans. Do I turn now into Hammurabi's column, a sombre list of dos and don'ts? If I'm coming to my ends, to the drop off of my articulation and the articles of my faith, is it an example I owe? A cautionary tale, a get well card, clarity about how on their own they are again? A clean getaway? An invisible turning of the key?

Where does this 'owing' come from? 'Debt' is a lousy integer for this. There is no transgression. There is no theft, no seduction. The ending was there all along. I will say that I am shocked that it's come so . . . what? Unannounced? But it was announced in scores of ways. Suddenly? By what measure of time is a near seventy-year-old 'suddenly' relieved of his duties? As I've said often enough, 'sudden' is dereliction of duty, not a condition of information inadequacy. It comes from inattention, or from clinging to preference despite any sign otherwise. 'Quickly', then? Quick, starting when? There were signs, I see now, for a while. There may even have been causes, though pursuit of them in the rear view seems criminal.

No, I think 'shock' is the first layer of 'bottomlessly sad'. It's the layer that tolerates your feelings, credits them, employs them.

All of the sadness comes calling again when I am about to travel, leaving a place where I sought shelter from a primordial Beast: that's in truth an old affliction. That leaving is hard days. I've laid myself down to rest in these places. I've lived by their ministrations and been nursed by good people here. Now I'm to tremour my way into my next near future, and I'm weak-legged about it.

## 17 April 2024

A younger man from across the Atlantic and far across Europe was on a video call just now. News of my frailty has reached him, found him in a rough place. His dreams for a better day are snared and snagged on the wire of daily life, and marriage and kids, and especially the refusal of his pals to live out the proper thwarting of the schemes for success they once shared.

Mostly, though, he wants what he thinks I have: the plan, the workaround, the spiritually intact, righteous and intense way of prevailing – and he wants it while I can still talk.

I talked to him about learning to fail, about abiding a bit in the wilderness. He thought I said, 'Secretly succeed'. 'Ten years in the desert', I said, 'isn't weekends and holidays and time off for being clever. It's foreclosure time. It's the end of what you once gambled on. That's where I am, again. Not 'secretly succeeding'. Not being the boss. I'm behind the plough again, with the promises all but broken, again. I'm staggering. And I'm telling you to do the same. Start staggering. This is the guy you're asking for advice and a way through the rough stuff talking.'

## 21 April 2024
*Writing room, Orphan Wisdom Farm, Ottawa Valley*

I am back at home – that's what well-meaning people call it: my home, although I've scarcely been here in years. If I must have a home, for legal, for citizenship and for sentimental reasons, this is it. I've spent years packing to leave, unpacking to stay.

Though I could leave it in a moment with no hesitations, a brief blister of regret. I could leave it this evening, and not think of what I'd miss, nor think of coming back soon, or at all.

Was this me readying myself for my passing, so as not to be surprised?

'Being ready' mostly makes things less so, less of themselves, less consequential as you're more apt to be unsurprised.

The house has been quiet for months. Apart from my shuffling occasionally, and the sound of this pen on this paper, it's quiet again, now. My wife has gone to Paris.

Her father came to fetch her to the airport. His heart attack some years ago has winnowed him out. He's like a man looking out from under a hat, or a tarp. When he speaks now, he chirps, like a wee thing. He is wee in his clothes now, as I'm likely to be. And yet, when I meet him at the door and ask how he's doing, he says, 'Just great'. He means it, which is nine-tenths of the way to it being true. When he asks me, I say 'Ah, not so well'. And I am not so reduced as him, or so I think. But I can't manage to be great, not hardly at all.

He sits down. I'm pretty sure he knows about me. He looks at me briefly, as if from a great distance, or from another land, and waits for something else. He's eight years my senior.

One of us is winnowed, the other afflicted.

I am, I think later, too cooperative with this thing. I'll have to try being 'just great' off and on tomorrow, in this silent house people say is my home, with my wife in Paris.

For example: the western sky is ablaze, flaring. I told the sky, 'Goodbye' just now. The vastness of it was such that, far from stealing my hurt, it asked instead if I meant to hold on to it so tightly still.

## 25 April 2024

The Beast is a hungry Beast this morning. Alone in the house, the Beast makes for uncertain, agitated company. It's gnawing on this pen, for example, gnawing on the synapses that make the fingers go, disassembling the hundred tiny movements that make a 'y' or a 'w'. Thinking about the legions of pushes and pulls that make up penmanship – any child who conjures legibility from a pencil is a marvel. That conjuring is going away from me now, plainly another kind of marvel. Where is it going?

Some people's arches fall. Others' gums recede – to where, nobody seems to say. Some people's hair recedes – same mystery. Where things get serious: some people's hearts attack. Some livers go sclerotic, the only time almost any of us use that word. Some breaths get short – a feat of back and forth without any rival I can think of. Some eyes go dim. Some healths fail: we leave it at that. No elaboration. Oracles, like all things ocular, degenerate.

It is not only flesh that goes the way of all flesh. The mind, I'm finding, certainly has its way of disassembly. Some small part of it – the self, maybe – watches the rest of it go out, like a flame, maybe, or an equinoctial sunset. Time doesn't go out, but it does go by – by each of us, maybe. It does the moving, we the standing still. Days pass, until they pass us by. The heart fire goes out, like the sun will one day, they say. Out of what, they don't say. It won't much matter, given the other bits of terrestrial and cosmic business that will attend its passing away.

We go out of our minds sometimes. Sometimes it's for keeps. Where do we go when we do? Out of our mind, into what? God willing, we'll be beyond caring by then. Having done so, do we ever go back, then? Are the ties that bind stretched like the elastic waist on old foundation garments? Will our minds take us back, once we've philandered? Does being in our mind ever lose its appeal? Is it like going out of business?

We don't say we go out of love. We fall out of it instead. Again. It makes you wonder how much falling the heart and all its ways can take, how much of the involuntary plummet and descent, before you're done.

I've taken many an unfamiliar road in this time of contending. There is an official shelf in the house for my alternative bitter herbs. There is something afoot called the Joy Programme, that unofficial programme of affixing 'amen' to bits of life going by, to give my remaining dopamine choices, or something to do. I've the discipline of this book, which I'm unfaithful to. There's chi gong, for which there is a bamboo stick called a 'bang', or 'bong'.

I went outside with it this morning, instructed to face the sun while going through the motions. I finally feel unself-conscious doing it, largely because there's no one here. Or, so I thought. I rolled through the devotions as best as I could recall them, as best as the dervish nerves tolerate. I turned to find three cats lined up, mesmerized. I'm guessing on how mesmeric it was for them, as there's not much affect from a cat. Their eyes were locked on my every devotion. I saw myself through their eyes.

I am now officially taking a Jesus amount of supplements. I almost wrote 'supplicants', which would not have been inaccurate.

Now, 'Jesus' is not often in my corner of the world a vehicle of emphasis. It is a vehicle of exclamation. There is a difference. I mean 'Jesus' here as a means of achieving exponential increase, beggaring the norm.

So yes, a Jesus amount of supplements, mostly ochre-ish-coloured powders and viscous capsules. It is the best part of a forty-five-minute affair of preparing to leave the house to work on the abjectly elaborate coop I think of as a chicken palace down the lane. It's a workout of measuring, tracking, apportioning into a blender. I can trace no efficacy to the regime, nor do I feel better in any recognizable way. But I'm all in, for now, on the alternatives to the pharmacy.

The point of this story is that the whole thing takes a lot of liquid to chase down. Which requires a strategy of management, should the requirements of the day bid me rise and drive to town, to the bank, say, because it's remittance day, say, for the taxes. It requires deliberation, attention at this level of detail, calibration and calculation according to my proximity to porcelain. On the farm it is a nonissue. There are sixty-three acres of opportunities for self-care in this regard. An embarrassment of riches in terms of casual relief. Not so in town, though.

In town, there are no facilities, no chances for anonymous self-care. So if this stands any chance of being a challenging trip, duration-wise, I've got to be diligent and well-timed. Leaving the house, I thought I was. This was my second time driving since being diagnosed. It was grinding away at my sense of well-being, which ironically threw me off the scent of self-care, somehow. Once behind the wheel I knew that I knew how to drive, but there was a kind of soft delay between awareness and the next new thing arising, like a turn, or checking the rear-view. I couldn't quite tell if driving was something I should be doing.

Now town is about a twelve-minute drive, not a lot of time for things to turn bad. But four-fifths of the way there I started to intuit that maybe the swamp of bitter herbs and their smoothie chaser were coming around again. No problem, I thought. Time enough for an efficient encounter at the bank, a quick visit to the health food store for magnesium, and I'd be homeward bound.

Once through the bank doors I went from, 'Great. I'm the first person here at this early hour', to 'Oh, it's empty because it's not open yet.' At this moment, two old guys from the men's hostel down the road shuffled into the bank vestibule behind me – my age, give or take – and started going through the process of withdrawing cash. Life has been neither easy nor kind to them. Shuffling, layers of heavily employed clothing, hard on the edges. Actually, I don't know that they're old. Aged, maybe.

We small talk: 'Hey, leave some for me'. 'How can they not be open? I got an appointment.' I have to go to plan B: the health food store for more bitter herbs and Jesus compounds. I'm sensing a 'first time in public' anxiety come on, and it looks like I've miscalculated how I'll do out here. I come back to the bank in ten minutes. The aged guys are in the bank manager's office – they did have an appointment. I don't. I'm not sure I can work the delay. I deliberate asking to use the employee bathroom, leverage my status. I decide against it.

Anxiety on the rise, driving a strange car, and I'm chilled – a bad combination that the Beast thrives upon. I wonder how I come across now, how I look, what gaps in personal grooming present me as now just another old guy upon whom the subtleties and signals are lost, another spent journeyman people look through. Not many people start life off broken. Not many of us have practice at it that doesn't count against us later. It's an unravelling ligature when we join the ranks of the shuffling and walking wounded, without warning, without instruction.

Grace looks so much like frailty now.

## 2 May 2024

Yesterday, all day, was May Day in so many places.

Solidarity in some places, communion in some, reason to rise in others, not entirely in eclipse.

Yesterday evening, after dark, I'm in a darkened house, a single light to contend with the stairs and my wife's frequent rearrangement of household goods and furniture. I hear a strange sound, which I decide must be a cat or two on the porch moving their equivalent of household goods around. But wait, I thought: cats don't labour. They don't work. They connive for their food, bind themselves to your leg when they want feeding. Cats working on the porch at night was an unthinkable thought. I got up, prompted by this anomaly, and was about to open the porch light when I heard it again.

'Cats dragging things across a hollow wooden floor' was all I could manage by way of an accounting: a strange place to use up my creativity. In fact, there were no cats involved. It was the first staccato rolling thunder of the year, making its way to me from the west.

It was as if the Old World was heaving itself up for all the sakes forsaken over this last hard winter and the dawning of the year. It was as if the Old World was on my porch, and chose this moment of aquiline darkness to enlarge the frame, embolden the terms. The Old World was unshackled by tremours, and drawing its name across the night sky.

## 4 May 2024

The relative merits of diseases: it's odd calculus. I'll not be trading places with any other afflicted one, so the figuring is probably for naught. My reckoning of a cancer, say, if generalizations are fitting, is that the mind watches the encroachment, the metastigmata rolling in as they do, takes the poison pills and the radiation, or not, and as often as not, slowly the waters rise. Cancer or not, you are you until the end times. Unless the cancer is in the head, I suppose.

A swooning neurodegenerative condition may resemble all other swoons in that there might be a kind of unfailingness until well into it.

But then the pillars shift and fall. There may be a through line by which you'd recognize yourself. There more likely won't be.

Today I had the first encounter with a kind of word/thought bottleneck through which nothing could shoulder its way. It was a simple social moment with the semi-hermit living down the road. Nothing but easy banter was called for. I waited, and nothing. I said something unachieved, designed to dismiss the strange silence, fill the lacuna with dredged, easy gestures. It was like looking into an abyss. Cut loose, in free fall, every reliance upon the word hoard and the agile alchemy I'd resorted to in my stand-and-deliver days gone for those moments, traceless.

Later, I described the moment to my wife. 'Welcome to how it is for most of us, most of the time', she said. If that's how it goes for many or most, I'd never have survived membership there. I am so much a son of devotion to the spoken word and to Those from whom it comes that it pained me in a haunting way over the past decade or so to be visited by the looming likelihood that the visitations from those Gods would end unspectacularly, in the form of a brain bubble.

Now that those bubbles are in the cerebral plumbing, I marvel at the ease with which a word ceases to be at hand. I marvel, too, at the grace that kept me from word silence until now, when the meningitis could have done that silencing work sixty-five years ago.

## 8 May 2024
### *On plane to Boston for an award*

If you combine neurodegeneration with the miracle of flight, you have hieroglyphics for written notes. That's what happens to your cyphering. Add weather, add a small engine plane, and you'll have no written communication to speak of.

I am reminded again of that talk I did, perhaps in Sweden, or somewhere at great distance, the late middle-aged woman sitting to my left, in active distress throughout. She looked wan, grim, set upon, drawn down from within, a host to misery. The well-ordered, well-practiced story of medical mayhem and malfeasance, her summary, that one-line rending of peace of mind:

'I'm afraid it's too late for a lot of things.'

This is as authentic a confession and a prayer as there is in this world. You don't say this because you're afraid it might be true. You say it because you've seen it. It's there before you. Or, it's gone from you. And it isn't coming back. It takes a rendering of the heart's mind to see this. It is the limit of courage, the bleak landscape cleared of fairness and civility, readied for mercy, or gambling for it.

And she was right about that. It's already too late for a lot of things. That's what I said in response. 'Nothing to do with your health, or your age', I said, 'or mine. Just the march, the turning of the page, mercy when it's prayed for, relentless when you're pleading for more.' It's too late for the both of us.

I'm in a hotel, second floor (not high enough), in an American city on the Atlantic coast. I'm in town to receive recognition from the Harvard Divinity School for something I may have begun forty-five years ago, or may have just begun – some achievement which is only now showing itself, the way mist shows best when sun shoots through it, or when it hangs on tall grass in a field like clothes on the line, always in the morning. Maybe this is a morning, my work the dew, recognition the sunlight, the disease the turning world.

Having rained all day after the fashion of maritime towns, the evening is full of hissing tires searing down the pavement. It's the magnified sound of snack bags being torn open forever. The second floor isn't high enough. I'm waiting for the cars to finish their tearing of the road, and they don't.

This puts me in mind of having given the left side of me over to the Beast, not for safekeeping but for taking, the way you give a finger to keep a hand, or most of it. I don't think of it as sacrifice. More like stronger and stronger lenses to see what you saw unaided a decade ago, watching all that watching go its way. You can make do, you can make as-if, but the trust isn't that benign. I'm not really bargaining to keep the right side of myself, for now. The right side is showing little signs, hints, that it doesn't quite belong to me. The hymns I hummed in the early days – ha! A few months ago! – I'm only whispering now, and only to myself.

There's something about the notice of others, the unsuspected regard of strangers when it is trained upon the work you took up in private years before. It steals your spent anonymity. You don't know your real look, the enduring way you might for a time occur to others, what you mean, until that notice comes to you.

Gregory Hoskins, who's seen me in action, the public and the private me, called before I left to come here and receive this award. 'You never knew if you had it when you walked out into the lights,' he told me. 'You said it every time. Every time you did, but that didn't change you. So I gave up saying otherwise, left you to your calamities. You still don't know, see. Nothing's changed. Try to remember that.'

This is me trying, Mr. Hoskins.

I wonder if that's not the secret strategy for laying the fight down.

I was always fending off, always feisty first in the storm. There was always an adversary, a menace of some kind. That just seemed to be part of having a public life. But that's not a life's work. That's a habit, a swamping of dexterity. Nobody worthy wants to fight an old man – worse still, win. No honour there. If there's grace here at the end, it's leaving younger strangers to their victories by being their secret ally.

Someone sent me a book that says there's something to be done about the Beast, something off-road and alternative. 'Your life must change, though. Regardless.' That was the punch line. Could me putting down the habit of fighting be a start? Let it be.

There are moments when I am unclenched, and I forget the affliction utterly. Some part of me rises to the chance of me and Nathalie being in Istanbul again, or somewhere in Portugal. And then I remember the diagnostic truth, and ratchet up again, and then almost nothing is possible. There's nothing at all to be done. Everything likely has already happened. Then I obey the tremours like a monkey on a chain, or like the tufted, leashed, mangy auburn bear in a nineteenth-century sepia postcard, begging for scraps in a Balkan city square by doing tricks while upright on two legs, muzzled and not a bear, not really.

## 10 May 2024

I am here to be feted for a life's work, to be fussed over. I am wondering how the etiquette of admiration works in contemporary English, thinking of the signals that our speech has left to us. After we force most of our world through the gate of our lips, focussed our prayerfulness and profanity across our larynx, what nonverbal repertoire is there beyond the shrug, the brush-off, the blank stare, the high-five? There are places that are less burdened by the book and standard speech. They have enviable hand jive. They have dozens of finger signs for fornication, friendliness from a distance, flirtation, the sheer riptide of emphasis.

The rest of us have a beggared repertoire. But still, there are moments when we discover the power of the slight bow of the head, the palms-up plea or protestation, the one hand behind the back, a willingness to be one down to the other person. There's full-torso bowing at the waist for maximum grace, the hand on the shoulder or the elbow, the eyes downward cast.

Your merit, or the acquisition of office, can spring loose the hoard of silent signs. Debility can do it, age can, too. Has. I'm someone flirting with palsy. This matters.

I am visibly older than many, or most. My tremouring stands in for the slide of fixity. I am grey in the beard. I've little or no sense of being old, until those gestures of deference from younger people come on. Then I know that my job is to be the reason they do. Like a blank canvas, and in a simple palette arrayed, I'm the activation of grace. I hold still now when it comes on, or nearly still. I don't try to compete for who holds the door, who outwaits who going through it. I'm first fed, first feted, first warmed and warned. It seems premature, hasty and uncalled for. The necessity isn't mine, it's theirs. But I all but love them for it, their falling over the right thing, over me.

## 12 May 2024

Stillness was always a potent thing to me, though I was no good at it really. This could be no elevating thing, just an aversion to yammer and the fray. I loved the stillness of raku tea ware. The cup would sit quietly, neither waiting nor satisfied, just a citizen among things, as we are if we only knew it, if we only knew our country. The kettle will come, or will not, and still the raku cup sits in its place, full of emptiness, already ministering to our busy world, two hands gathered around air, already calm, a teacup before there is tea, a watering place before there is a thirst.

Stillness is beyond me now, for now. I get close sometimes. I hold the cup. The tea graphs the seismic stammering of the hand. But the cup neither contracts nor expands. It is still.

It's a wonder, it is.

I took a gouge from the flesh on my index finger, the size of a pearl, bigger, deeper. That was seven days ago, while guiding the chisel along the bush rafter's beam, readying it for the chicken coop we're raising, crafted as might have been done before stick lumber, before easy money, out here in the bush. A chicken coop for God's sake, getting this treatment, but to me a rustic palace, dovetailed, precise, already bleached, etched by the hewing axes.

Seven days later the hole is flesh-filled, all but healed, pain gone, blood staunched, ready for work.

And I can't do that for my mind, the palace of my concertedness. Not at all. For my finger, yes. But that's where it ends.

## 13 May 2024

Let's say you have something wrong with you. Let's say your judgment is involved, or will be.

Let's say there was a time before this was true.
Which confuses everyone. You look more or less the same.
But you move a little slower. And your figuring does, too.
Still, there's enough continuity that you could pass for you, for the same guy.
That same guy's not in the house, though.

Here's where you have to make a big move.
Somewhere in the circuitry of concern there's someone caring for you.
Far away or close by, but they're rising to your trouble.
You take that constant part of you, and
with it you turn that person towards their life.
Tell them to take that restaurant gig in Tuscany
that will take them from you.

Or you go along for the ride, a diminishing guy in an
eternally cool place. You'll cook, too, somewhere beyond
not feeling like it, not up to it.
That somebody will treasure that memory
someday.
And you'll be sick, or sick enough, though not soon,
to tie the world in a knot, with the one caring for you
in its middle.

## 16 May 2024

Where I went once to school there's an art museum –
not a fine place to have art happen. The shuffle of the
foot and the mind induces fatigue and intolerance, and
there's not much in art that can prevail against overwhelm
and ennui.

But I was there unexpectedly last week, and I went to the neoclassical set
piece museum anyway, and I checked my umbrella, went into the first
salon, and there, alongside pieces by Picasso, was the self-portrait that
Van Gogh had given Gauguin, garish emerald background, Vincent

bearing down with his implacable alertness, an alertness that would kill him a couple of years later.

Did he know this about himself, how untenable, how sheer and lacking in gun shyness he was when the push turned to shove? How poor was his aim when he turned inwards? A worker in despair, trustee of joy, he was better at irises, black birds rising up over fields, the full radius of night sky. A patron saint of the hard focus, unawares.

## 17 May 2024
### *Home, again.*

It's evening, sliver moon through cloud, peepers
in the creek calling out for moonlit love.
Who doesn't understand something of that longing for life?

The farm dog is by the door, as he's been his 80+ dog years.
He remains handsome, singular wisdom in his face, barely walking.
I mean to learn from him while both of us are still here.

News comes from Israel allies: a fine, full-throated woman friend
has died in the last hour. There was nothing in
seeing her last year in the Negev, singing Cohen songs, that meant
I'd see her again. I won't, now.

With all of this going on, there's a two-hour call with
a medical advocate that prompts dreams of what I can do about what
I can't do anything about to prompt this body a bit
further.
That arousal is of the kind, as Eliot knew, that makes April cruel.

## 18 May 2024

Walking without purpose through the house when two claims rose up in me. The first was winched from the depths by the younger man I work with on the farm looking across the hewn beams meant for the ongoing chicken palace and asking me with neither warning nor prelude: 'Where do you get your stamina from?' It wasn't pure admiration. He's no longer young, and is questioning his old mandates now. And I thought, 'Yep. Maybe that stamina, the unwillingness to rest, is what got me here.'

And up wells something like a revolt: 'I don't want to work!' I say out loud, to no one, to hear it, for the first time, as I recall.

Prayer is like telling the truth. It doesn't begin with the praying, the truth telling. It begins in these times when you're doing neither, when you don't know you're doing neither.

## 23 May 2024

Your life, and mine, they're collections as much as they're anything. We've gone our way, cadging bargains, working angles, settling, doing the right thing when it presents itself. The wardrobe fills, top and bottom. A lot of it at least is 'just in case'. The odd thing goes, replaced by two odd things.

Something happens. The old staunch reasons don't hold. It sends us to the closet. With grandiosity we open the doors. Two thirds of the stuff – more – doesn't belong there, doesn't belong to us. By the armloads we sweep through and empty the hangers. Down to the psychic Goodwill we go. We just give it away.

The way by which we made our way: its merit is faded. To a great giveaway in the sky it goes. Watch it walk out the door. The old standards that made everything gleam with purpose: now, no shine, no necessity. What we rose to then we lose to now.

## 25 May 2024

It doesn't take much, not anymore. It gets cold out, it sets me to shivering. Reason evaporates from my plan, my plan falls. All the years of dexterity, grace, cursive moves, elegance, crossovers, arpeggios – not to overstate, but there were years of it. And all that elegance and the measured and meted holy sequence that underlay the order, the chemical array in the everyday: I counted on it, took it as a given. By that sequence, the fingers knew the hand, and the arc of movement through the random span got me where I meant to go.

It doesn't take much for the grand mosaic to lose its pattern. The parts are there, but now in partition. The scheme doesn't hold sway, and a distance of some sort grows between me and what and when I mean to be true – between azure and indigo and blue.

## 26 May 2024

Dogs, like people with Parkinson's disease, have to walk. When they're old, it isn't clear they know this necessity anymore. They have other mandates. Not walking much, for one. Not walking far is another. Not walking fast. Or uphill. Or through snow. Any perfect storm of all these conditions underfoot at once is a recipe for defeat, or for a day indoors.

Today I am alone on the farm, a very unusual condition. If anything were to happen… But this is high planting season, late spring. Something always happens. And there are animals here. This is a recipe for things happening. If I stayed put, looked out the window at spring occurring, probably not much would happen. But I have an old dog, Boss, whose entire life has been lived out here, and even old dogs need walking.

Boss has a powerful ability to magnify and broadcast his inner life with the merest movement in the muscles around his eyes and ears. As his age has come upon him, his repertoire includes sighing, groaning and fully implementing the 'hangdog' look when walking time comes.

I have all of this in my repertoire, too. I scuffle, involuntarily, as if walking in weighted boots. Boss hangs his head when walking's too much. Or he walks so slowly that you can't walk with him and still call it walking. It's stepping, and then waiting.

I sag in the direction I mean to go. People here at the farm just eventually go ahead without me or they'd never get to where they're going.

But today it's just him and me. Some of the corn we hand planted didn't take, so I have to go out to the teaching hall and pull seed corn off the cobs that have been drying there since last fall. When I built the place, it was a fine walk from the house. But now, afflicted as I am, it is – to use a term of particular emphasis that Boss's eyes sometimes convey – a Jesus-long distance this morning. Boss has to come, for therapeutic reasons, and because he's been on the chain all night and to leave him here wouldn't be kind.

I'm maybe fifty steps into the project of going to get seed corn and I can already see that, at Boss's pace, this could easily be an hour of shuffling through bush and field. Shuffling must have been an urban invention. It's a cruel business over uneven ground. Another hundred steps, just into the bush, and I realize I am making my way to folly: the neighbour is up for the weekend with his massive, barely contained mountain guard dog from Uzbekistan or somewhere close, and it will be a desperate and one-sided pissing match if we cross his path – and I have no leash. Back to the house, slowly.

This is probably what indecision looks like from a distance.

Boss is looking at me this way: 'Didn't we just do this? And now we're going back?'

'I know', I say to him, 'but you don't know your pissing match limitations, which you now have. It's on me.'

By the time I get the leash I'm rethinking the project. Maybe he's had his walk – he certainly thinks so. So I leave him there, go and get the seed without incident, and think that having an old dog and Parkinson's at the same time is a kind of two-for-one crimp in your lifestyle. There are so many chances to see yourself in three drastic, merciless dimensions.

## 1 June 2024

The truth is that we don't have much ability to faithfully picture our diminishment. We picture what we can afford to imagine, what we can already see, and then we go about things.

A neighbour dropped by the barn today, someone I don't know well. He is genuine and kind. We talked about the old people who are gone, who lived the principled life of obedience to the savage limitations of a place such as this, who knew how to do such things as put up barns. The neighbour and I are on the same side of a merit-bearing life. There was no affability strain. Yet, maybe three times I couldn't find or welcome an easy word or phrase. I struggled, groped for the word, in the same way my left hand can do.

That was far from spectacular, or unravelling, but in my understanding, it was diminishment nonetheless, clear and progressive and unrelenting. If you haven't struggled to speak – I never have, that I can recall – you can't picture the goneness, the silence of an unavailable, ordinary thought. I never struggled that struggle, so I never imagined – successfully imagined – the struggle. As of today, around late morning, I don't have to. I'm free, however, to imagine it getting worse, and worse again.

## 8 June 2024
### *Near Plymouth, England*

I've flown transatlantically for the first time since getting my news. Now I'm far from home in many ways. It's that condition of 'in many ways' that settles upon my extremities and me in the presence of others. I'm feeling exposed, glass housed, unsheltered and prone without explanation or recourse.

The people I'm with are kind. We spent some time together in the *Nights of Grief & Mystery* days and the Orphan Wisdom School days. These are not those days, it's clear. When word got out that I was in town, people came around to drop things off – alcohol mostly, and dairy. My host said, 'Many of the people who love Mr. J are doing so by leaving things for him and staying away', a strain of sorts on the usual understanding of how one is to be with those who come from away. So, many of the ministrations are at a distance.

My host emerged from another room with a very elaborate, articulate stick. It was made for me years ago by a scholar, a four-foot walking stick. A cane, with a knob end, striations cut through the cambium. A cane made for you years before is a beautiful option, when an option it is. A cane as an obligation is something else. I've come here to pick it up, it seems.

## 10 June 2024
### *County Clare, Ireland*

It staggers me at times, and at times I forget utterly this thing that's come down on the mist bands for me. It is, by itself, throwing to have to remind myself of this affliction. Which may be mercy, or it may be affliction. I don't know what I'd rather be: constantly in the hurt and fog of it, or drawn back into it by an act of voluntary memory.

The devices for remembering that I am afflicted are peculiar and utter and far from mighty. The deities of a devolving mind are far from here, like a capital city I've never seen.

The other day I was in a Devon church full of people who'd come to hear me speak. We together had the sense that maybe this was it. The applause at the end was fond, raw sorrow.

## 21 June 2024

Had I slept, I'd have slept through it, the solstice. For a working pagan, this is dismaying. I think now that I've been vagrant or unvigilant much of the time. Year upon year, the lost, altered, starving days which were my little life. Rooms of regret now, ready for moving in.

## 24 June 2024

There were a good handful of people staying at the Devon estate to accompany me and be in on what might be the last of my UK gigs. They continued on to Ireland with me, filmed some interviews.

Now the last of the people lingering here have left. The etiquette of 'last times' was a strained thing sometimes, and I had more compound farewells to manage than normal life doles out. By such inexperience we are scuppered, staggered, censored. In the long goodbyes the unsupple, unsubtle clinging to last moments went on, bless them.

With the quiet now in the big house, sitting down to write, I have the feeling that, unmedicated by allopathy, yes, I am watching my handwriting go. And something may be going with it. With the great fondness and sense of well-being with which I once came to the writing table, I could always hear the music of a sentence before the syntax settled upon me, and the pen – always a pen, always recognizable ink – was the baton. The music of the sentences came before the sentences themselves. Every time. I heard it first. Without the pen, without legibility, I'm not persuaded the music will come.

## 28 June 2024
*Toronto, 5 a.m.*

I went across the North Atlantic to see
if I was really there.
To find out whether the word hoard had
been broken into, the gold plundered and pulled out,
the illuminations dim and faded and curled in on themselves,
the zoomorphs broken through the fence, the
wild things gone.
I walked the fields of St. Dyffd, St. Patrick, the
cliff perches of those saints who were born and leant life in the tempest,
out in the open.
I stood in the stone circles, the tumbled famine cabins
downy in moss, and the booley hut ruins and the lazy beds still
scoring the shaley hillsides.
And the holy wells all but dry now.
I stood for the trial blessing of the roundhouse at Trefacwn,
the old laying on of hands, the trace of my ancestors looking long and
hard at me in the eyes of those who gathered to hear.

To my wife I said, 'I'm ruined', as I walked to the roundhouse.
'Walk through the ruins', she said to me.

## 30 June 2024
*Home, again.*

I am missing the old of the places I was just in, now that I'm here again at my house in Tramore.

I was there in Ireland with a hazel rod weaver, with a child Viking on her hip, and she knew me. I was with a coppersmith in his sooted shop. He was shy, but he knew me. I asked him for a brick of the turf that heated his wee house and he gave me one, the old growth stuff, the six-feet-down-in-the-trench-stuff, the bog black peat that sprang up in the wake of the glacier. 'Celtic incense', he called it.

I was with the people who could just by speaking coax their apothecary into you, work you over by their gnawing, Inuit style, so that some or enough of life's benedictions obliged your hide to suppleness. Such was the conquest there in their language.

I come from that. I was, when I was able, summoned by that. It was my work. A life without it dries my words, scatters them.

# 1 July 2024

Just now I saw a piece of film, grainy home movie stock of young men playing soccer in an open field on a stormy afternoon somewhere in Africa. The lighting was uneven, it came and went, such was the haphazard autofocus. There was a moment when the camera seemed to have hiccupped, or blinked, and then three or four players slowly laid themselves down on the field, as if they'd suddenly grown tired or dismayed, or unenamoured of the game. Other players looked down at them for a few confused seconds, and then began to run in no particular direction in a kind of freeze-frame slow motion. It was as if everyone on the field had ceased to be persuaded of the merits or the necessity of the game, at more or less the same moment, as if the substrate of something had given way. As if the spirit of their mutual life had left them in an instant.

It's what spells look like when they take hold.

The field it turned out had been hit by lightning. Several of the young men didn't survive the encounter. If you were there you could have missed it altogether. Some part of you went out for a beverage at that moment, and you saw nothing. Just some young men unexpectedly taken over by dropsy, lured into slow motion by a dispiritedness nobody noticed. As if life blinked. Or an eclipse had come on – a sudden, unforeseen one that occluded some and not others.

Or it was like this: I had some ceremonial responsibilities years ago, in support of some wedding preparations. People came to the farm from different walks of life, with different persuasions of belief and conviction, including convictions about marriage, and about masters of ceremonies, or masters of any kind, or about people who looked like them.

I knew that certain extremes of heat and thirst and sitting have been employed for eons by masters of ceremony to conjure and spell break and choreograph this world for the sake of another world.

And so I went at it this way: 'We will meet tomorrow, early, just before first light.' It's another extremity, the precise imprecision of first light. It's easy enough to miss, or sleep through, or misunderstand. We congregated in the gloom, shadows all, shuffling through the uncertainties.

Now somewhere between a lightning strike and a first light, this thing came upon me, this Beast, in ways any sorcerer would recognize.

# 4 July 2024

Candour is the refuge of the unerring. For the rest of us, any arousal in the extremities, a dalliance with the extremes, and we're in the land of ambivalence and shadow.

'There's no cure' isn't certainty. It's spirit annihilation. There's nowhere to go when 'There's no cure', no thoughts to think that stand any test of purpose.

I assume – conspiracies aside – that they're right when they say, 'There's no cure.' In the same breath, there's this: 'There's nothing to be done.' Which isn't mellifluous, but malignant, malfeasant. At its very core, if it has a core, 'there's nothing to be done' is moral trespass, egregious, a lair for wrongmaking.

'There's nothing to be done' doesn't mean there's no way to win, no way to get back the life you knew yourself to be performing. It means there's no life to speak of. It means eclipse, occlusion, shuttering the openings. If 'life' is sails, a rudder, ropes, a hull and the wind, 'there's nothing to be done' means 'there's no sea.'

# Scaffolding 3

Seven months into whatever degeneration means, and the degenerate wonders accidentally, clumsily, whether there are signs to read, whether he can know if the onset is truly on. For that is the mercury of the thing, the mitre and crown of it, the mystery: Can the afflicted know the affliction? Or is the knowing afflicted too? It isn't a question when it's the lungs that are compromised, or the liver. It's a question of the mind though, a question for the mind.

They call it 'grey matter' when it's well and working. They call it 'white matter' when it's drying up and dying away.

At this point, seven months in, I'm running my fingers over the fetters, trying to find a language, a code for disassembly. I'm turning to the mechanics of what I know how to do to track the compromise of what I know how to do.

I'm posture compromised now. Unawares, I'm curling in upon myself, contracted around a core of devastation. Time going on doesn't dull the concession to compromise. The writing is as dense now as my entrails are, as my psyche is. It is twisting in on itself.

There have been apprentices gathered around me from time to time, when I was in my strength. When one or two gather around this waning, who've come kindly to what remains of my mind, it stymies me. Such kindness turns me towards my work, to inquire after its worthiness, after whether it can bear the scrutiny of the kindhearted.

Without knowing what's called for, what to do, I've drawn back from the public life, the interviews, the teaching, after a quarter century of it. I've no angle on anything that might count. One day, I leaned on the closest of these apprentices, in a moment of clarifying, magnifying, awful sorrow. 'Stay close', I said, 'in case something useful comes from this.'

And this, seven months in, is me trying to take my own advice, and stay close. I think. In case.

## 13 July 2024

Rising up now behind the scaley Beast,
  the sloe-eyed One, the degenerator.
In the wake of the one who's come for me
is the plumed inquisitor of a Beast.
The adjudicator,
chemical fury that would course my neurons,
leap my synapses, hex any redemptions.
I will cease in some fundament,
and I will stagger and roam, chimera-like.
They say so, anyway.
Out at the edge of the professions and what they profess,
beyond the habits they make of the eye and the mind,
out beyond the barrens of allopathy: What?

## 14 July 2024

I'd no idea there were so many people who'd lent an ear to me over the years. I still don't know that it's true. I don't know what it makes of what I've done. Are they witnesses? Are they auditors, spectators? Rumours? Whoever and whatever, the postman is busy bringing their claims and accounts of me. Amidst the correspondences, I am in receipt of a great number of near-obituaries. It's a pre-mortem vigil that's underway.

My first response is of being very moved, in full lament over the occasion. These people were flowers rising up in the far field, volunteering their hue, their pollen, the very fact of their lives, to the air. They're testifying. 'You're there', I thought. For years I didn't know, and now I seem to. And now some things are different. They tell me that I've had work, that my having done it matters. I see now that I never did stand all the way up and look out across the waving grasses towards what I've done.

At first, I didn't think much more than that.

My second response: a mild agitation at the edge of my heart.

## 22 July 2024

Now I have grown a commitment to chi gong. That is of necessity, since I have no way of moving available to me that is efficient and good and smooth. That is partly because years ago I turned down the plea of an old flame to take dance lessons, and I've never been proud of the decision. And it is partly because this Beast is slowly taking the oil and fluid from my joints, and I imagine I'll have the gait of a paralytic who's at last entirely persuaded of his frozenness.

They say chi gong is good for the seizing up, that it sends the vitality up and down the circuit and gives you a good riling up. Which on more days than not I could use, and might welcome.

I took some instruction on the matter while in California. The instruction included the use of a piece of stick, in case, the instructor said, I'd like to go the weapons route. The stick is the length of your forearm, thick as your two fingers bound together. When I have facility with this stick, it rolls nicely between the hands, like it's a part of me. I double back on it, rotate around it like a dance partner I forsook.

So the other morning I was on the back deck facing the river and the rising sun, and I was doing the chi gong fairly and faithfully, by turns devout and desperate. In the mulberry tree behind me there was a fracas of birds. I knew what they were after. They were after the berries, the same berries that year-upon-year – except one – I'd never gathered and brought to the kitchen. The whole of the futility of this moment in life came for me, and found me and laid its claim upon me. I was riled, and I was unthinking, a loaded combination, and I took up my chi gong stick and drilled it in the direction of the birds, as best as I could determine where they perched in the foliage.

The stick was eaten up by the world. I heard it bang around in the branches, I heard it fall in the weeds, and then it was gone. Instantly, I felt the bitter tang of crude measures taken in mindlessness – measures taken against the innocent. I went to reclaim the recklessness, withdraw the evidence, and could not find it. Back and forth I went in the brambles, but no baton. Every made thing around me, all of creation in that moment looked down in insinuation, or so it seemed. The birds themselves hadn't gone far. They waited me out. Not a berry to show. Not a baton.

Now, each time I assume the chi gong position, I see myself flinging the baton birdward, and scramble after that biblical passage about the birds being so indisputably cared for by God, as they were on that day, and how could it be different for us.

As of yet, no baton.

## 25 July 2024

I haven't been still for weeks. Not a contiguous minute in all that time. I watch the people around me on the farm, as we separated the ewes from the lambs this morning, with the work done, an arm casually draped across a fence rail, or leaning on the truck's tailgate, unmoving, satisfied. I wonder, will I have a moment like that again?

Acres of discouragement, grains of longing for unremarkable days of standard affliction which, when I had them, were lost on me.

More than regret. Bitterness.

This is how you find out that you are a momentum junkie, have been for years. I'm mad for the next thing, desperate for it, for how it governs the drastic days, rules and overrules them. That's what's waiting for me, I fear, in the swath of psychedelia that is routinely offered by helpful people; the ravenous thing, the beige terror of the end of what bears me along, once the momentum is spent. Left as it is, this will surely be the terminal anxiety that will feast on whatever peace of mind survives the tremours.

My 'work': I wonder about its transferable merit. Even I, alongside the blessed eulogizers and the obituarians, seem to be counting on a bit of the old Death Trade moxie to come through. I haven't thought the thought until this moment, but I seem sure that the *Griefwalker*, the *Die Wise* guy, will know what to do.

But this is not like anything I've seen, anything I've been through. That, or I didn't credit the devastation I saw in others when I was paid to be there. I thought I did. But it doesn't look like that now. Nothing of substance looks like it did last decade, last year.

## 27 July 2024

That momentum business: it was about work, if I'm honest. The moral obligation to be employed. A window on the Protestant Anglo-Saxon mind:

The new snow was deep. I was young and I had a shovel. I went to several neighbours to move the snow for pay. I was at it a good many hours. When I got home my mother berated me for moving other peoples' snow before our own. Not a trace of immigrant pride in a kid's hustle there.

I've worked, and measured myself against my work, and so little of that has changed since the news came in. That seems criminal negligence. It's not my work. It's the keeping of that strange faith, that so long as that continues, then I continue. But my continuity is a tyrant and it takes on no education.

The ever-petty crime, says my lack of education, is doing nothing. With my wife gone overnight, so rare, I mean tonight to do nothing. But I am doing this instead, wrestling nothing, wrestling the doing of nothing, while the sun lets himself down towards the river, the practice of ending there for anyone with slow eyes to see.

I kept a farm from subdivision, but I can't say I farmed. And me with no tractor, sure, the farmer next to me wouldn't say I've farmed. What now? Shall I garden? Is this what the storm of stillborn activity is called? Weed pulling, moving things aside, devotion to an unchanging patch of sandy ground? Gardening ideas? Then shelter indoors, windswept, panting?

Grim thinking there. Not final. Not fair. For just now, I checked on the chickens, seeming to be riled up by settling light, and saw a white rugosa rose, the kind least sought, barely opened, and bent to it in a gardener's way, and drew in the scented persuasion of life, and it spun my misery off its axis. Smell the roses, they say. There's that.

## 28 July 2024

I was doing nothing, or practically nothing, down by the river just now. And then I remembered something from years before: the roar of a neighbouring hovercraft, a monster unfit for this run of water, my wife breaking in bits, postpartum, post-surgery and nothing to show, unable to bear this travesty too. I brought her splintered convalescence to the neighbour's attention. Mobilizing his whim of citizenship he told me that this was – his words – a free country.

I slept a bit on the dock after the memory faded, ignoring the cough and sputter of a small outboard going by, but unable to sleep once the wake took up the canoe tied there, lifted it and drove it against the dock, which registered in my teeth and in my troubled parasympathetic nerves, and had me wide awake, unrested, doing practically nothing, and not having an easy go of it.

Doing practically nothing, I looked at the weathered boards of the dock, and it was as if I'd never seen them. For in their pith they were weathered and scoured by ordinary time passing, by weather, doing nothing, and the weather prompted the edges of the growth rings to rise, becoming whorls and what carpenters call live edges. And give it a moment of your clear attention, and the live edges of weathered boards, like weathered people do, seem to lift as continents did when the ice went back where it came from. The prints of what happened get left behind.

And all of this made magical the nothing practical that I was doing, the practical wizarding of time passing in just this unlaboured-over way. The beggaring of my working habit – for a few moments – worked.

I understand those people – or I believe I understand them – that are holding out hope that the particulars of our endings are draped in ordinary cloth, and that the ordinariness eases things there in the last times. They wring some comfort from the plainness of the thing. The seeking after comfort is proper and called for, and we could use more of it in heavy mortal weather.

But comfort is had at the expense of life as much as for the sake of life. And endings are considerable, and discomforting. And the Big One is an enormity of such unimagined thought and much-feared scale that it refuses the sackcloth. We do our death work ordained by that enormity.

I wonder if this is death work now.

# 1 August 2024

There is a great vexation upon me, and a tremendous fracas and seismic strain within. I've been so careful as to whom I acceded myself as an object of prayer making, careful not to just have anyone do that praying over me, me prostrate and sleepless and striving. What good? What carnage averted? What havoc waylaid by this care? I hadn't really sought out Rilke's greater and greater adversary upon whom I might dull myself. Maybe general, unregulated common prayer is good for you.

I was hard pressed to climb Mount Autobiography. I never did trust the lonely authority wielded by decrying any kind of 'personal truth'. I had a notion for decades that pushing around in the bright cage of the self-made life raised dust, laboured the breathing, but left much unthought. So I fought my way towards clarity. Like any lightweight thing, I swung hard to amplify the consequence.

I still don't know if the increments and details of the Big Story have their echo or twin in the mad leapers and unimagined animalia of the inner life. But surely there is something to the idea. I set about making a go of a preacher's life having never known a preacher, never having been to church, and was thwarted by those very reasons for a full decade and a half in the desert of disemployment, and upon disbarment from the medical establishments and with utterly no prospects, set out to make a school of a thing. That can't be stuff and nonsense.

Why is it that the lysergic possibilities recommended by colleagues and allies have ferreted up in me such a great foreboding? I stay clear of psychedelia, strongly clear, but I don't know why. I'm leery of psychosis, in truth. I'm leery of this green-jacketed book I'm writing in, leery of how many times 'I' appears. Now I stay clear of the teaching hall, and the writing cabin, too.

I thought that there was no such a thing as a *future*, much less *the* future. I thought *hope* was the ghost of that allegation. I stood on a *Night of Grief & Mystery* stage night after night, country after country, and rewrote our mangled take on fate: it's not the way things just go. It's what we do, once the Gods have spoken. Fate's not a given. It's not in the future, sitting by the roadside, waiting. I thought promises were promissory, and paled in their solemnity and their faith alongside vows, hankering after a future in which to safely appear. I thought faith was another promise.

I want you to know, in case it's been kept from you, that you owe nothing to consistency, to constancy, no matter what you think they've done for you up until now. You can decide that the time has come to third- and fourth-guess your wisest, staunchest positions, your foreclosed-upon futures, non-faiths and religions, your unwillingness to promise, your fated fate.

You could just arbitrarily decide that this latest misfortune is as close to the Big One as you need to get to be unstirrupped. You can be thrown, or you can dismount, or you can let loose the reins, open your arms wide, drape them over the crossbar of your cross, ride the uneven ground between now and the mystery days cruciformed, until these are those days.

So I take the position there'll be no cure, that's sure. But there may be respite. The torque may leave off my hand and my foot, and put them both in the manner of stillness. And if it does, what shall I do with that stillness? What do I think the tremours are keeping me from now, the arms of which I see myself running into? Is there a clarity waiting, of the kind that is elsewhere now but will be bountiful then?

# 3 August 2024

After one week of epic, gothic heat and dank undergrowth funk, it has in the last hour began to tympany in the far sky, and rain is on the tin roof now, and every growing thing is in exaltation.

I waited on the deluge, glad of it, until it's just now become a tumult. And I wondered: there could be searing silver, cobalt incineration coming down in this pent-up heat. The utter storm of our chemical mistreatment of the made world could bring incineration upon this age. There could be furies. There could be a peeling back of the skin of survival, the cranium of the world bared, and us clinging to it, or we could be primed and torched by the purifying chaos of survivorhood, cleared or washed or sheared or scythed of it.

Further still: What keeps us alive? If, as it seems, life is driven into us, uproaring the entropy of the flesh of us, what keeps it here against the hard weather and the hurt of the instruments and of the heart? Once the pilot light is lit, and we are here, what strange agency or edict bears down, bores into us and speaks its living piece?

Might it be the storm that binds us to our quick, our pith and marrow? Not peace, but the storm of it all, the seething overwhelm of the thing of being here? Is it the teeming uproar of how life comes over you? Is that my actual diagnosis: a visitation of telluria?

And where is the threshold that binds everything else to us, and to this, and to now? Is it our fontanelle, our parasympathetic nervous system, what we can bear? Or bear no more?

Now there is a storm breaking upon me, making a riot of my hand. Is this what keeps me here, as I begin the consolation of my days, and let in the choir of endings?

# 5 August 2024

What is becoming of the tea and the rice of me? I did once have a sense of where the pedestrian in me began and ended, where the civilian's outer edges were, the citizen's portion. Prowling the boundaries of public service, my hands running along the page wire, I knew the hard line of ordinary obligation, me a citizen of a troubled time. Now my ordinary stuff isn't working.

At mealtimes we have the old timer's plate on the table, the ancestor's portion. It makes the rounds at mealtime. The best bit of the best and the first of each person's food goes in there, and it's one of the first compound phrases the young among us learn – 'old timer's plate' – and it's one of the first bits of elegance and structural mystery they learn. It's real food they part with. And it's a bit of insurance, that they not become their ancestors' food for want of observance, gnawed upon by those Old Ones set apart and starved.

I wonder now: Am I set upon? Not out of vengeance but out of want. Am I my Old One's sustenance? Does it work that way?

It is the desolation that may be doing the summoning now. That falling quiet of this parched corner of the world. It whispers, 'Come hither now'. You choose it, or you agree. It's the wilderness, and you can find yourself there until the need for it is undone. But if you're dug in for the sake of more time, because you're not done yet, not entirely satisfied you've done well by your allotment, well it's the desert then. And you're not walking, you're not drifting or seeking. You're driven there. The wilderness is one thing; the desert another.

From here the desert seems a place of great magnification, in the way the dark can magnify a vole parting the grass to get home late into a stealthy, lurking assassin. There is often predation out there beyond the line marking shine from shadow.

It seems I'll cross that line as a man does in a strange house in the dark, shuffling feet across the floor, hands out in front so that they might contact the thing ahead before the face does, or worse, half-seized in a parody of readiness or aptitude, in a vanity of deciding. I am becoming a secret to myself, or a foreign country, or a rumour.

# 6 August 2024

There is this funereal notion, meant and fashioned I suppose as part-blessing and part-reward: eternal rest. The whole thing fills me with dread. What am I to do with this version of nothing? If I take it close to myself, am I meant to be rendered peaceful, unstriving, my burden set down, absolved of inwardness and outwardness? I mean, what am I to do with these notions now, in the whorl of being alive? Am I to loosen or lessen my fondness for the work of living, and take succour in losing the job of being a living man?

Perhaps it's that eternal rest is a form of kindness to those whose notions are spent, worn thin as they are so as to be translucent, unable to rise, unable to wish to rise. Is it reward to be absolved of the work that you cannot do anyhow?

## 8 August 2024

When are you healthy? Next to never, that's when. Being healthy surely requires some sense that it's true, that your health lives and breathes. But health is spent for the most part. You spend your health, employing it unto its limits. Until there comes a time when health is a fugitive, a memory, not a present-tense condition.

## 9 August 2024

Seventieth birthday. Teaching event at the farm called *A Handful of Endings*. This might be the Orphan Wisdom School session that never happened. Or it might be me practicing being over. Or it might be my version of the long goodbye.

## 12 August 2024

The people are gone now. The fields are clear.

I've heard that animals don't come down with the Beast. There's no such diagnosis for them. Nothing similar to lay them low. They are in the prey/predator story. They know themselves that way. When predation comes, there is a body understanding – the most persuasive – of danger. It is fitting that there is danger – it is a belonging. Should it happen that they escape, there is a short period of rigour, them laying stiff in the grass. Then, obeying some clarity of purpose, the animal rises, shudders head to tail, yawns and stretches to release the prey heart posture, and trots off. The place goes life-quiet, for the near-to-death of it all.

I'm sitting in the empty teaching hall. And it is quiet like that.

In the death trade days, I would ask the afflicted where in the arc of their life they thought they were. I was teaching them sonar. I'd have them send soundings down into the firmament, trace the shimmer of whatever returned, like Noah's bird, read the mud in the claws for signs.

Seismic work it was, to locate yourself here and now by sounding the depths, to change your mind without the instinct to do so, all preference gone scaley and arid, to agree to give the mind over to another citizenship.

I said to the people, apropos of *A Handful of Endings*, that were I to continue to present in the way of an able-bodied man, I'd thwart the design. There'd be persistence, but no obedience – and obedience is where the abundance that is in endings comes from.

Some things are as certain and clear running as degeneration. Not many.

## 19 August 2024

The near-obituaries continue and the love letters come – the kind that are prompted by foreclosures and movings on. They arrive at the rate of several per day. Requests for filming come. I don't know where these people were before all this, or how the passing of a bit of time adds a shine to whatever I may say. It may be coincidence. But it prompts me in the direction of summary. It has me wondering whether the oncoming of knowable frailty outfits one for the big view – the long-range, sky-high, fish-eye take on the whole onslaught.

I do wonder during the day when it is that my mind will begin to resemble my subdominant hand. The hand was early afflicted, its bird song in this open pit of my seventieth year a muted, muffled, inability to snap and keep time in a *Night of Grief and Mystery*. Now it has its own derangement, running amok sometimes, tapping out an accelerant of Morse code, metronomically in chains. It obeys it knows not what.

Does the mind in a trance of this go likewise, drawn in upon itself like a dead crowfoot, full of the last nothing it managed? Does it know the last of its knowing? Does it grow unto its mania, unable because of a mishap in synapses to obey its fatigue, its thrum uncontested, eccentric, routinized, unpersuaded by despair?

What will become of the filmmakers who've begun to come around, asking for last thoughts? Will I be fit for the summaries they seek? Or will my unspunness unfit me? Or will it equip me for inadvertence? Will the mind be like the dictionary of etymologies on my desk, spine stiffened and splayed open to the page with the last word that prompted investigation, the legacy workers stymied to get any closer to the last summary wonderment?

All of this prompts me towards the tally. Not to spare anyone their work in the time to come, or to solve things, or to cheat someone of their discovery or to set anything straight or mend it. To mind it instead, to gain a handhold in the clamber up the sheer rock face of swooning.

In this unfrequented cabin set up for writing, I have carved out several books. I held onto the hardwood of my ideas, parsed them out, parsimonious through the bounteous months, the drying stacks ready anyway and promising a rich man's winter that seldom shook out.

I came in this morning, the first cool day of August after the days of rain, and bent to the stove to ready the place for my unstill sitting. I meant to lash the waters of my once rising mind, to see what might still rise, with the chill and damp persuaded out of the shack, to uncoil my extremities a bit. I opened the stove's hinge door and found last winter's ash and char, tuft in the grate, an amateur's care and feeding of what he'd use to soothe himself. It was a poor find, a poor business, not fitting for a farmer, or a writer.

I scraped it and gathered it to the side with a bit of kindling, as you'd do to the clamour and clutter of your mind, to make a clean and promising place for whatever might gather and spark.

## 22 August 2024

The sundown belongs to the sun, I reckon.

The sun is just now down. I turned away, rose up from the dock, admired the river's day's work, saluted the blaze before it met the western shore, and walked up to the house.

While on the dock, I may have noticed the first tremours in the right hand, which, if so, will be a monument of discouragement. The hand-writing this evening is in disarray. I don't know what to wish for.

If you are afflicted, and it is the dog days of summer, and you walk your dog across your fields, and you are in a mire of synapse disarray, it is best that your dog is as old as you. Given the allowance of 'dog years', he is my age. Boss, still with us and eyeing another winter, is an old man, and then some. He labours going uphill. He moans when he lets himself down, grunts when covering flat ground. Neither of us needs to get anywhere, besides a bush for relief of the mandate. We are a good pair. We match, as if joined on a metrics-heavy dating app. If I have any love for him, and I do, I give allowance for his gone years, for the thirteen winters on him. I practice on him, so that I can walk myself slowly across the fields, and not break apart with sorrow over the sun going down on my early seventies.

Earlier today, I was in the village bank. My wife arranged a meeting with the manager. He's a good man, tried by family misfortune lately. In the country you know things about people that they may not have told you, and you hold them in safekeeping. This makes the prospect of meeting easier. I'd come from the drugstore where I got my passport photo taken. I couldn't make myself look at it. I suspected a lot of unwinding of the skein of my mind showed in my 'don't smile' look for the camera. 'Just look in the bull's eye', the clerk kept saying. I had to guess where that was. I just looked into the storm of the future, fixed my gaze there, saw some hard things, held on, tried not to shake. Last passport. Last photo, I'd say.

All that is with me in the bank, the likely lostness of my look. I realize sitting there that I don't get out much, intentionally. I'm unspooling in the chat skills. Can't keep the easy banter going. I don't seem to believe in it anymore. Or I'm saving whatever lucidity I have for the few interviews scheduled later this month.

I wonder if I should say anything about any of this. I wonder if the manager notices. And that's when it all falls into place: the question of 'competence'. I'm wondering if he's wondering, sitting there making decisions about who are the primary cardholders on the various accounts, how much of me is still there, still with the programme. Then I realize that I'm interacting with this wonder, this question. A mirror to a mirror to a mirror . . .

Bless him, he finally asks me how I am. 'Not good', I say. He looks down at his desk, giving my tremours their privacy. Humans in a sudden etiquette squall, caught outside without a hat or scarf: that's us together. 'If there's anything you need, you've got it.' That's his generous way of saying the first of a few informal goodbyes. I don't know the etiquette of this any more than he does. But he's got the fiduciary responsibilities, and I think I can hear him wondering when he might have to ask me if I understand what's going on. 'Not for a good while now, fella.'

As a mirror in a mirror in a mirror . . .

I wouldn't say it's all bad, this kind of a moment. It's clarifying, similar to the unwelcome way an argument clarifies whether you are still in the presence of a friend. My root condition still seems to be lucidity, alertness. I just can't find the vernacular sometimes to make the 'we see each other, right?' connection. Would that it isn't an overture of the near future.

# 23 August 2024

I'm feeling storm-tossed. I haven't my legs. My wife makes me soup. Soup seems convalescent now. It confirms the infirmity. 'Infirmity' is ironic, actually, since the particular infirmity at play stiffens the extremities. But she makes soup nonetheless, not knowing these associations of mine. It's good soup, has things I like. But there's the matter of a particular dry legume. Not garbanzo. Fava, probably. They are shucking their skins, most of them, but they aren't cooked, not as I understand 'cooked'. Even in my present state I can tell they aren't cooked. They resist. They fight back. I give them a try, but it's not going to work.

Next day, midafternoon, depletion comes on. Same soup is at play. Less soup than yesterday – less broth – but the same number of fava beans, no more cooked today than yesterday. I ladle it out. The favas vie for the ladle. A good number make it. I eat the soup, setting aside the beans. Because it's a bowl, they circle back to the spoon. At the end, I have dregs and beans. Unable to make myself throw them in the compost for the pigs, they go back in the pot. I could just cook them, but in my awful passivity I don't even think of it.

Next day, less broth, more beans. Now it's fava soup: mostly warmed but uncooked, shape-retaining beans, some broth to keep them moist and uncooked. Everything's exaggerated. This'll go this way until something gives.

That's how it is to be neurologically compromised for now. Not enough compromise to effect a change in personality. You think the same set of things, the broth of your days thinning, same uncooked thoughts there in the bottom of the bowl of your days, pushed to the perimeter, cycling back. You'd think this might be reason enough for the thought habits to cook, grow supple, not mess with the mechanics, go down easy. Different soup. But if you don't cook those thoughts, they'll be there at the bottom of the bowl, not going anywhere, pretending to be the broth of your days.

## 31 August 2024

I've a line of people arrayed to help me. I don't know how to be helped in tandem. It's rehab polyamory, if rehab is what it is. Or it's multichannel ambivalence. They are, each of them, a blessing. Separately and together, they are a gang of blessing, a havoc and a fracas and a blister of blessing.

Without intention, they contend, though. Not counting the prescriptions, proscriptions, supplements, and otherwise, they do contend. Their certainties contend. The dopamine enhancers, the neuroplasticity vehicles, the psychedelics, they contend. They don't say theirs is the one true make-do God of restitution. But there is a question of compatibility, or fidelity, or both. And I – I am the clearing house of conviction. I know that my heart and its keepers must be allies of this business of restoration. This requires choosing, submission. Restoration is by that measure a crisis, a prolapse of maybes who've met at the crossroads of my health and would have me, harried by information and frailty, choose from among them. Or choose all of them.

My symptoms – an awful phrase, a baleful one, a pillar of salt – doubled down upon me this morning. Mindful that I may be overly cooperative with them, I shadowboxed for a while, to no benefit. I rattled and I shook and I spun through nests of misgivings, and tried to make a decent go of my daughter coming over to say goodbye after a few days' stay.

That's when I had to 'fess up if I was wise to the unflattering fact that I was scared beyond eloquence of deciding what to submit my brain to. Currently up for grabs: giving in to the green boil or disassembly which I take to be ibogaine – the lysergic colossus of psychedelia, I'm told. Ibogaine is mainly available in a legislative and regulatory wasteland of do-it-yourself professional journey providers – earnest, recovered traumatics, well-meaning, limit-straddling self-improvers. From what I've heard, it's a clutch of people negligibly accountable for the services they provide, unbound by governance or tradition or profession. These are first impressions. Their services are sought out by combat veterans and others afflicted with the wicked compromises of the parasympathetic nervous system that cannot be persuaded – whose bodies cannot be persuaded – that the world is a kind place, or was, or may yet be, that they may safely seek their peace. It's strange, but minus the combat and the random news of death all about, I may be in their number.

I don't seek rest. It may be a sign. I haven't thirst. I am seemingly, oncomingly caught up in a habit of translating being awake into being upright, being active and bringing scrutiny to bear upon stillness. And so, I am not still. Or stilling. I labour instead. I labour, I see now, as the desert saints prayed, they say: without ceasing.

Relentlessly, I'm driven to labour. I fear a time without it. So, this is one of the nails pinning me to the shakes: no rest.

I think the ibogaine might nudge me to psychosis, just based on its spectacular reputation. Psychosis might be code for 'not inhabiting my mind' or 'no longer the guy I've grown accustomed to being' – the same guy who doesn't rest. The same guy who has cultivated a field of dread and fear. So now, whoever favours ibogaine in this pharmaceutical pageant to me favours a Beast at least as awe-filled as the one who brings tremours and mud in the machinery, a shuffle for a gait and idiocy and muttering and silence without quiet – an effigy maker.

## 2 September 2024

My time in the death trade made my thinking. I thought things before then, but there'd been little or no rigour or discipline beyond the university training. I needed adversity training, although I didn't know it then. To qualify for the death bedside, real loss counted, and collapse of argument, and the articles of crisis needed reading – and ambivalence. All of that came around.

Certainty was tempered and annealed, as was the opposite of certainty. With many of the trappings taken down, I went to work. An orphan wisdom, a formal engagement with the adversary came on. A forensic audit of conviction got underway.

## 4 September 2024

Now I am somewhere else, somewhere where the old skills do not enjoy ready employment. Many times in the death trade I would wonder: What does it take? How bad does it have to get before there are compelling, non-negotiable reasons for ceasing the regularly scheduled programme of your thinking, for taking another way to heart, another way to the heart of what's left? The habits of the mind and heart and eye are adamant, particularly in times of trial, and they are a poor stand-in for you, and for God and for necessity. To disobey them is to risk self-censure, and self-loss.

Which is what you should be bargaining for when the Rough Gods come around: self-loss. The self you've managed so far isn't called for any longer. That's what Rough Gods are. Mostly, they're endings. There's nothing in the enormity of goings that requires you to retain the habits you've managed so far.

And yet: What does it take, now that I'm here? The dread of idiocy, the dread of psychosis, of despair, of the insane prolongation of the machinery run down, of the running down of purpose: there's nothing much that's new there beyond the intensity. The dread of the medicine isn't anything I've just come up with. It's why I have no drug habit, no programme of self-harm of the usual kind. My current dread is habit seconded to novelty.

What does it take for the ordinary miracle of a fine day to occur, another day in which to be unspooled or unseated? What does it take for the mystery to see to the unswept floor of the mind? Everything should change when a slow-motion catastrophe of this sort comes round. Everything worth being alive with should register the tectonics of now. Of themselves, they do not change. They dig in for the black/white duration. It's stunning to see, to realize, to be unseated by. It's disappointing. It's a vacancy of grace. It makes you wonder what you've been learning all this time, and what for.

## 6 September 2024

A storm: it was as if the whole of a chapter of the Old Bible was tipped over and poured down upon the pressed tin roof of the farm's banquet hall, and it chaosed its way like remorseless feelings down upon the time and place where we sought shelter. Finally: something more persuasive than my hurt.

## 9 September 2024

I've opted for hyperbaric oxygen, though there's nothing in orthodox protocols that credits it for this disease. I'm in the dysphoria of 'trying something'.

Herded towards perfection, towards personal besting: maybe that's life in the wellness world. Still, you might trade mightily for a place in that world when you find yourself barred at the gate by stout diagnosis, baffled by etiology. The driver taking me to my dawn appointment is baffled: 'You're going for extreme oxygen and you've never smoked a cigarette?' Cause doesn't resolve itself with effect. It picks up passengers en route. Pretty soon, there are a fistful of drivers at the wheel, and nobody knows how they got there, or why. Neither me nor my driver get lucid on the matter, and I can feel him tense up at the thought that it doesn't matter what you do, not really. Nor does it matter how much of a good guy you've been. There are genetics, and feeling habits, prophylaxes. And there's luck, the sovereign dominion of the inscrutable, the beggaring place of merit and the fair shake. In place of merit, there's a shit magnet.

It sounded like make-believe at first: Got brain trouble? Try hyperbaric oxygen. Inobtrusive? Not intrusive enough is more like it. When it was recommended, I pictured trying to get in the way of $O_2$ the way you try to catch raindrops on your tongue in a summer shower. The other practitioners I tell nod at the prospect, and most don't say a word by way of encouragement or catharsis. I think I can hear their chairs scraping backwards across the floor.

Twenty visits, thirty-five hours of chamber time, dear frigging chamber time, is what they mean by 'trying it'. This outfit is on the western periphery of the city, part of an alternative medicine / parallel universe of a wellness strip mall. By the time I got to the front desk, to the masked receptionist, after more than an hour of expressway stop / start with the usual regime of supplements and dietary whole health add-ons left behind on the kitchen counter due to the early hour and some swallow fatigue, I'm a tremulous upright version of a vibrating bed in a worn-out motel. Not a good look. Not the first impression you want to make, even in rehab. Not at these prices.

## 11 September 2024

As it happens in many clinics that set out to investigate your striving for better health, this clinic obliges you to the blue scrubs and paper slip-ons. To get this look, you have to abandon the usual style semaphore, down to the ear studs, which they tape over on the off chance – no kidding – that they touch and set off an ignition reaction in this oxygen-rich atmosphere. 'If my two earlobes meet when I'm in this chamber . . .', I say to the nurse equivalent who's prepping me. She looks at me, waiting for me to make the syntactic link, to finish the joke. There's no playing to be had. I submit one lobe at a time to the tape job. Somehow, they get some unruly hair in there, so there's some tearing to be done on the way out of this.

To get to the chamber, you will catch sight of yourself in the full-length mirror, minus the usual stuff on, the usual talismans stripped away.

Why a full-length version of the patient version of yourself is provided, I can only guess. I look like a wet bantam rooster, sinew and jutting bone. Where the meagre fat supply went, I don't know, but it's gone, not a vestige. I'm scarecrowish in the fluorescent co-ed changing room. I'm a listing old man, an unlived-in inner city tenement, in appearance and stance. The blue scrubs hide that look and reveal it at the same time. It's sharp relief – more scalpel than kitchen knife. An intense, existential start to the day.

A word about urination: it isn't anything you think about if you're in usual fettle. There's no cause to. Young, or even well into middle age, you are typically urinarily sovereign. And then there is the odd circumstance that brings your bladder to the middle burner of life, priority-wise. Still, it's exceptional. It isn't you.

And then you're in the changing room, the blue scrubs hanging on yourself. The bathroom's one way, the hyperbaria the other. There's no pee on hand, none available to you, but you're about to be locked into an acrylic cocoon for ninety merciless, irreversible minutes, plus the blood pressure check on either end of that, with no urinary recourse. You stand in the bathroom anyway, filled with dread at the looming public inelegance that's possible, so you go through the motions of voiding. It's unfruitful, but you stand with the scrubs at your ankles, and you are an inner vaudeville of voiding. A bit of visualization should help, but doesn't. You are momentarily as dry as a stick. You couldn't offer a specimen if your life itself depended on it. Your dog back on the farm, Old Boss, has a bladder attached directly to his instincts, and can shower any plant or place with a provocative scent until he owns the place. You've nothing similar to draw upon.

So you stride out onto a well-lit operating theatre, gowned, cuffed, haunted by the real possibility of a violation of a lesson in self-mastery learned in infancy and held to until now. You're here to breathe deeply and long, in the hopes of reversing certain self-sabotaging habits of the mind, and to do so in a clear acrylic tube with a closed-circuit camera at one end, trained on you to detect signs of strife or reversal of fortune – signs like shifting from one side to the other, holding of breath, panting, counting backwards from ten, squirming.

## 12 September 2024

Progress is mostly an allegation, or a fiction, or a wishbone prevailed upon until it breaks into uneven bits. Progress is a conceit, a slide show that leaves out every other frame.

Unless you're talking about a diagnosis that involves your mind. Not your mood, mind you. Your very mind, the font of your feelings, the main frame of your peace of mind. If that's what you're talking about, then 'progress' is very much a moving, shaking, disconsolate ghost in the architecture.

Each of the well-spoken, well meaning, well-tutored professionals have found a glancing way to tell me that this will get worse, no matter what they do, very certainly. I'm told that. But I must not know it yet, for each time I'm shattered again. I think their education obliges them to say otherwise, as if 'knowing' is sand and 'but' is basalt. Knowing of this kind doesn't interfere with the facts of your life, not at all. It goes on and relentlessly on, progressing.

A force feed of pure $O_2$, and nothing to show for it.

## 14 September 2024
### *Guelph, en route to a recording studio*

Gregory and I – Gregory, mostly – are planning a recording session à la *The Dead Starling Session*, where we are to set about making a new *Nights of Grief & Mystery* record. I'd shelved this idea completely as part of the general collapse of my initiative, part and parcel of the dopamine compromise I'm in the midst of. I am utterly unpersuaded that I have anything to declare. In that condition, while on the train I made a list of themes we might peruse, or allegations or excuses for me being unable to deliver the poetic goods:

Seven spires

come sit alongside me.

We'll soothe our souls as strangers do.

These are killer days, you know. Killer days, it's true.
And lover days, you knew.
You understand, I know you do.
We'll go find the difference, if we can.
The time of the crow and not the dove.
A call from below, a prayer from above.
The spirit complications, the savage ministrations, plantations, gradations, dedications, pollinations, permutations.

## 16 September 2024
### *My son's house, Toronto*

Two afternoons at the Dead Starling Studio.
   Two afternoons of what's left to me.
Listening to our songs, the ones born fifteen months ago in Malibu
and then set aside as life blew through,
was opening a vault, dust mites dancing in the shafts of light, no
waft of time and love gone by, the audio of old skills, devotions
of an agile monk not yet bent by the damp of the cell
chanted on down the ages in my voice.

I was thrilled by it, stilled by it. I was once that guy.
I was taken up out of the shadows by gratitude,
and so I began to wonder on gratitude. And the wonder said:

Gratitude isn't a cancelation of debt. Or a forgiving.
Gratitude isn't a penance.
It's not settling oversight, although it may come to that.
Gratitude disturbs the ledger, it blurs/dims the accounts. It loses
its origins.
Gratitude upheaves in its chemicals, scalds the crucible as it scalds
the chalice.
It defects merit, very suddenly. It is innumerate.

It is beautiful trouble.

It is dowsed and dosed in grief. That particular hurt that rises from understanding the blessing of limit, of 'not now', of 'too late', the letting of blood.

Gratitude is durable, and doable and palpable.

It does its work post-facto, after the flood.

## 17 September 2024

I walk to move the instrument – not the needle, not the yardstick, not the goalpost. I walked three miles today to move my feet in some remnant of syncopation. I feel as though I'm throwing pieces of two-by-four lumber out in the swamp from a heaving boat. I can hear each foot slap the city pavement as if it never expected to land, as if surprised by something solid. With my distance vision compromised, too, I'm unable to make out facial expression, gaze, gender, most of the usual information from the person approaching on the sidewalk. I don't know what's coming. I feel like I'm in a zombie movie, where I move like the zombie.

Thank God the three miles were downhill. Who knows how I'd have made it.

I send most of this to the compromised limb or movement, to plead with the brain at this advanced time to learn the basics again.

## 18 September 2024

Time was that I would calculate the goodness of a day by what pleased me, or the labours I got up to, or the unsummoned grace that worked its way into the seams and the hours binding them. Other good days were mounted on the realization of my good fortune, or that of someone close, or someone being close.

The early days of this sickness had goodness in them, although it was lost to me entirely. They were casualties of misinformation. I thought everything was gone. I thought I'd learned that from the allopathic seance, where I got all this useless news. The goodness was that I was still here, and that I could have known that that was goodness.

They tell me that I'm in the early days of this. That's not any assurance that abides. It means, barring the parallel miracle of me being interrupted by some other insult that knows its business well and turns my turf, that this will persist and it will proceed in the fashion of degeneration. If my time in the death trade or in the spirit mechanics of teaching and exhorting mean anything now, I am supposed to find the goodness in the swoon, not in spite of it. In it. On account of it.

There are strategies for doing that work, doing those sums, I'm sure. I doubt now that I know them. Doing the work precedes any sense that you've got it right, I imagine. It is there, floating independent of any recollection of fitness. In this tremour-clad time, I collide with a good day. In my spirit, I lose my breath. I veer, and I am stiffened by this encounter with the wild. I pull over, out of the traffic. Bruised by the austerity of the blessing, I rotate my hands now to see if they're capable of transition, of a smooth flight from me to somewhere.

It's the same audit I did a decade ago. We were peeling old tin off the barn roof. Twenty-five feet in the air, I misstepped, fell from the barn rafters and laid bleeding from the head in the straw. I tried moving my fingers, then my hands. 'Am I here?', I tried to ascertain. 'Do I still work? Can I move? Should I reckon by the same devices?'

## 19 September 2024

Two weeks into hyperbaria. People ask: 'So, anything?' I have no idea. Are these things so subtle, the mingling with the brain cells so still a thing, that I've no business trying to find $3,000 worth of upside in this regime? Maybe you can't scale up the workings of hyperbaric pressure.

Or maybe Changeland isn't a place of reversals and restorations. Maybe it's a place of covert regime change, one cellular vote at a time. A perforation in habit.

## 20 September 2024

There's a look that you have when you catch yourself in a mirrored surface – at the mall, or downtown, anywhere shiny. It's detached and severe at the same time. It trades on familiarity – you don't look at most strangers that way – but it's lethal and lethargic. It means you no harm because you're slight enough to not mean so much.

Catching my look in the mirrored hallway today was scary, because I looked, for no particular reason, scared. I thought I saw the look of old people wary of the oncoming world, the look of being easily unseated, the look of being about to be upended by forces that most don't guard against or fret over or even notice. It was a look of capsize.

I am discovering, late in the game, that (although this was no doubt always so) my ex-wife is particularly good in hard weather. She's good in this hard weather, now, in particular. I just saw her briefly at a restaurant nearby on the occasion of her seventieth birthday. She was the model of workable concern for me. We didn't say much, but there was no shortage of history and life, with the kids there and the onset of all this. I had to leave in advance of most of the guests arriving. I'd not have fared well with the din and the strangers and the ex-family and me in the rise and fall of good days and bad days. But there was burnished tenderness there. I credit her for most of that. In a time like this, one combs the past for things that might properly endure. Our affability with hard weather coming on is one of those things.

## 21 September 2024

What is the difference between a bad day and feeling bad about the day? A bad day couldn't be otherwise. You could.

'Ooh', said the medical advocate when I told him about the ibogaine, 'that's the big one'.

Do you want to hear that from a doctor? If you're after structural change for the better in your neuroplasticity, do you expect to come by that from the kitchen tap?

Could you say to the 'dispenser': 'Maybe a half dose would be a good start' with a straight face? Or think very well of your prospects?

Ibogaine. It's part decision, part frayed nerves at the prospect of 'doing nothing'. In a week or so, I'm going the way of the broken warrior, as they say. Is trauma a kind of dark matter curled around the trunk of a malignant vine? Is it itself hurt, and yet doing the hurting? Is it habits of feeling and seeing born in misfortune or carnage or Jesus gone from you after a promising start – the same Jesus who promised the thief at his right hand to see him in paradise that very day?

If it is, then there's reason to believe that you'd need unapologetic spirit drink to get the hurt to go to liquid. And move. You can titrate the thing. You can. Save some medicine or save some trouble for a rainy day, which sounds judicious. But to break down to its constituent parts your hurt, your ancestors' hurt, and get the river of life running through it, you need some seriousness of intent, and follow through. Nerves or not. Broken warrior medicine probably comes from the war, the same place the brokenness comes from, just as curses and blessings employ the same codes and colours to do their work. It could go either way with that octane.

While tracking this Beast, I am bearing down upon a manuscript – the last? – about matrimony I started maybe four years ago. The old writing disciplines are unfruitful now. Up at dawn, well dressed for the work, silent on the way to the writing desk, a spartan glass of water and nothing more, seated and scratching away until noon's come: Gone, so it seems. Unsteady now in each limb, I seek strategies for still moments where once it was solemnity.

Lately I've taken to kneeling at the bedside, computer open on the bed, making manuscript corrections, a half hour at a time. Then I heave up and walk off the torque that's gathered in me.

Maybe that's fair trade. I've taken a knee to – and dictation from – this reeling. I've given the voluntary discipline of the scribe back to where it came from.

## 22 September 2024

Somewhere along this road I'm on, I'm going to have to decide what this means. Not how I feel about it. No. Instead, what it means that I'm this guy. I get dismayed sometimes at how readily people around me have adjusted, have gone along with this, have agreed it seems that I am this guy. They didn't get that from me.

## 23 September 2024

Each morning it's a new car, new driver, new way of eluding traffic to end up in traffic, me clenched in the back seat as the driver tries to make up time on the highway. When I first started the $O_2$ sessions, I noticed that a circus had pulled into a shopping mall parking lot along the highway west of the city. A half dozen big tops, trucks on the perimeter, RVs by the score against the fence separating it from the highway. Each time I went by, I thought about that life, the great handshake you'd have to make with your future, the peace of mind you'd have to eke out here on the edge of a big city. Circuses must be small town stuff by now.

Last week the tents were suddenly down and gone. The trucks were still there, the mobile homes. By last week's end they were gone, too. This is Tuesday. As we blew down the highway after the session, I couldn't recall which parking lot of which mall the whole thing had happened in and emptied from.

Maybe that's the lesson: the meaning, the 'why is it me, if it is', is fugitive, the mirth temporary, the floppy shoes and the big red nose of the thing already down the road, and me unsure of where the circus was.

This much counts, at least this much. I've a feeling often that I've been violated and taken from, that the chief injury begins now, that all those about me enjoy their range of motion and their steadiness unawares, that this is injustice and injustice is newly minted in my seventieth year, that something is awry just now.

But, of course, most young and midlife people see the aged as spent or all but spent, a paltry rag on a stick. And the aged have always book-ended the last of life's chapters with infirmity and rupture. Failure of the instruments is not unique to the aged, but it is typical of them, of us. This poorly timed thing isn't unjust. Grievous, and exceeding in its dislocation from the parade, but not unjust. Grievous. Today. Tomorrow I will lose the thread, and hurt the best part of another day away. Unless I can recall this.

## 28 September 2024

Last day of $O_2$ sessions. Last day of getting up as if for the school bus when it's still dark, oatmeal and out the door. Last day of remote drivers, traffic snares, tremours in the back seat, calculations of liquid intake to avoid bladder challenges on the highway, last day of my day beginning simultaneously at 6 a.m. and noon.

I tried to leave the clinic quietly. I sat for an exit interview with an $O_2$ allopath whose look said:

'Well, we told you there's no evidence this works for Parkinson's.

No hard feelings?'

Which was reason enough to just bail. But I went back into the humming cocoon room and stood awkwardly trying to figure out how to catch the nurse's attention enough to say goodbye. Finally, I did, got three or four words out, started crying. She started crying, too, others came over, and we stood in understanding. They know that nothing much for me changed – not yet, anyway – what I was up against, the likelihoods. I know they know. For a moment, the place went quiet. We held our hands up to each other, hands on hearts, hurting for it being over, understanding how over it was, in the way those who've seen things know.

It took me that long to realize how many childhood hospitalizations – meningitis, asthma – I was living all over again, how heartbreaking it is to lay your well-being in someone's hands, again, for a time. Nurses will always bring the mercy of that heartbreak to me – and maybe me to them, something I hadn't thought of.

# 1 October 2024
### *Plane to San Diego / Ibogaine sessions*

A pocket full of goodbyes yesterday – son, ex-wife, daughter – three weeks of 'maybe this'll help', $4,550 of what I earned to do something else with. Cried with the nurses, cried cleaning up my room at my son's house, cried with my wife in bed over what it's all about, cried at the inflight movie where Anthony Hopkins is so old and so good. Didn't do much of that when I was well. That's some of what it's about.

Now on another plane with my wife heading south, bargaining for some redemption of what the root of it's all about. Scared stupid over this way of getting to that root, scared stiff but not still by the prospect of psychosis. I think that's what it is. This morning she called it a holiday, but it doesn't feel that way. It feels like roulette. That's as far as I can take it on my own, it seems.

I know there's more. When your fear says, 'Yep, you got me. That's it', there's more. That's the wound speaking, the broken wing, the damage that shows, the poor soul you can afford to be. The tight chest says there's more. The knot in the lower GI says so. The haunted vacancy of my attention does.

There's a bottleneck of realizations here. There's me satisfied with the easy defeats, the usual ones, strenuous cooperation with the customary adversaries. Even that confession doesn't confess much. There's something in the habit of hurt and fear that safeguards it. Something about the familiar ground, the familiar groove and the rudiments of suffering that promote the suffering. Not the rudimentary one, the other one, the one I'm persuaded I can't afford to see, can't survive seeing. If 'seeing' even begins to describe the encounter.

Fifty years ago, off the coast of Malta, we were thirty hours in a force-eleven gale in a hundred-year-old Danish ketch, nearly shipwrecked. That 'nearly' counts for a lot. I didn't see the great fateful face of Poseidon. I have to make up his attributes, his mesmerizing repertoire, just to tell the story. There's what I can afford to remember and manage to recount, and there's the rest. It's just too awesome, the overwhelm of near death and near life. It's a beggar's dance, speaking about unconscionable things when you are bound by conscience.

Do I qualify for the psychic extremes of ibogaine? I don't have the chemicals to give up, nor the drugs to put away, nothing to pour in the toilet. I don't have ravaging trauma. I have – I think I have – a faceless, odourless, tasteless set of heart/mind habits I am deeply persuaded by. All of them stand to reason. All of them have earned their keep.

I am nosing in the floating wreckage of affect, wondering what I've done to prompt neurodegeneration in a mind that seemed serviceable enough, guessing at the patterns in the prompts, surmising the roiling firmament from the mess and inaction of what might be a half examined life.

## *Later, landed in Tijuana*

I am in a residential multiplex in a Mexican suburb. I am here for five days, to be prepped and counselled and administered ibogaine, and to be closely monitored by medical people for the duration of the encounter. I've had my luggage examined, my supplements catalogued and stored away while I'm here. I can tell from the questions at intake that the staff is used to dealing with addicts, self-harmers, extreme characters. I'm the only patient, or client, or time traveler or psychedelic cowboy here. I don't know what I expected, but the sheer ordinariness of the place, the furnishings and paintings, clashes savagely with the storied, primordial, miasmal spirit I've daydreamt. It is as if I'm going for chemo in one of these recliners in an outpatient clinic. That, or I am going to meet a God by the thermal springs in the backyard, and the furniture is a cover. Or something else beyond me and my imagining – the more likely thing.

# 2 October 2024

I t may be three decades ago or more, that I was in a shop that sold ceramics, the proprietrix a Caribe who was speaking to the woman I entered with, a Jamaican, in code, signaling some safety and fellow feeling between them that I could feel. Nodding in my direction, the potter said to the woman: 'Oh, he's good. He knows how to wait.' Which could not have been all that true, but was true enough that day to be seen and found unlikely in a white man.

It's gone from me now, that waiting skill. I am too unstill in my extremities. I am uncool. I can feel its rareness, its fugitive state in me. I cannot manage lingering anymore. Drifting is as close as I get to waiting now, frozenly staring sometimes, stiffened by calamity, by the stock standstill of no volition.

I know now that I did treasure that cool, that beautiful centrifuge of going but not having to go, that beautiful breaking even. I dressed for it, stood for it, counted it as an unerring blessing. Now that it's all but behind me, it's more than that, more than being able to hang.

Should there be vigils sat for the coming days? The want of vigils troubles those around me, especially my wife. Am I in need of prayer here? Is that good? Am I in Gethsemane here, or am I in Mexico? Should I be prayed over now, as I once prayed over dying people in the last pages of *How It All Could Be*? If yes, it is not for me to do. That's akin to being uncomfortable and comfortable in your discomfort at the same time.

I've no witnesses from places I've known here. I was dropped off, my wife and companions gone to wait these days out in a beach condo. I am an unknown. This is a clinic. I'm bereft of the rhythm of ritual. Ceremony is reduced to industry here. Tempting trickery, that is. I am on a pilgrimage now that has me sitting in my room, and then driven through a mangled, urban countryside to a temezcal, and then to my room again. I am going over the rough acreage of the psychic habits of the life that got me here. Maybe appearances are only that, and I'm in the home of an old spirit, the kind the black-robed missionaries were kept employed by. Who is there, I don't know. It's an African/Aztecan ensemble. There's an uncommon mix of good intent, big business, smooth marketing, with a volatile mystery medicine in there somewhere. I rely now on some old courtesy that's come to me these last twenty years as I mucked about in the precincts and the profanities of ceremonials. I am utterly adrift, in another country older than my own, in the hands of strangers in scrubs, waiting.

# 3 October 2024

Waiting on an IV port to enable fluid intake quickly. Almost surely, I will feel like a sick person, my associations with IVs being what they are.

I am the only person undergoing these ministrations. There are two nurses, both one-third my age. This is a considerable operation with many moving parts. The management has let me know that I am among the oldest that have ever come here. This seems to make them slightly nervous. They have me sign a sheaf of documents absolving them of everything untoward that could befall me. Which makes me nervous. They have also told me clearly that there's precious little evidence that ibogaine is a merited treatment protocol for neurodegenerative disease. But they are all but certain that it is. From this and other things I gather that they think ibogaine is a merited treatment protocol for just about anything that troubles a body or a mind or a spirit. Which makes me nervous.

I'm wrestling with all of this, every waking moment, since well before I got here. The prosaic miseries that come find you in times of gross uncertainty must certainly be an obstacle in themselves to whatever succour might be available in the medicine. The habits of the soul are amplified by drawing close to this jungle magic, this green God. I see this now. The troubles that bring you here are what gets in the way of being here, of gleaning merit, of being saved. The medicine is a Revelator God, part pacifier, part placebo, part plenipotentiary, part psychic pandemic.

There are plenty of opportunities for vanity here, but precious little employment of them for anything that matters. Do I want my personal style unmolested, untested by these adventures, everything as it was plus understanding this time? These are times for renovation, rehabilitation. Not everything is pending or up for grabs at every turn. Some things about me will abide. But I am not here to persist in all the ways I know. The ibogaine frequent fliers that I've been teamed up with (I think that's everybody, since having been a time or two waylaid by the medicine seems a company prerequisite for working here) keep asking me what I want the medicine to do, what I want to be done with and throw away. It sounds exorcistic to me, and I can't find my reasons for coming here in it. I am not here to mine and strip benefit from the made world, including this medicine. Taking dictation from the great beyond is work now, and this is the Great Beyond's world I'm about to enter. It doesn't seem to be a time for covert treatment goal certainty. Nothing goes away just because you can no longer see it, or don't want it any longer. This is where refuse comes from.

My stance, I see now, comes close to 'not my will but thine', or the nonaligned variety of that. If you petition the Gods, I think you have to leave room for the answer – if there's one forthcoming – and make room for broken translations. You don't leave the room in doing so.

Is not wanting to shake in the extremities the same as 'getting rid of what you don't want anymore?' How do you find the web of your habits but by detonating them, by crossing their wires so that they don't work anymore, don't make the same claims upon you? Am I playing placation with a disease, or a demon, or a bad habit?

In these last few days, I've been regaled with exceedingly positive test results. ECG: bloody marvelous. Blood pressure: superb. Heart of a younger man. They seem a little concerned about what this might do to my heart. So now I am, too. But all those excess-free years are paying dividends now. It didn't seem fun-less at the time, though I know I've wondered.

Now I've so few things to get rid of, so few poisons to swear off of. Makes me wonder how far down I keep the junk. Is there just always junk?

I've grown very fond of that meningitis kid I once was. Sitting here, waiting to take this medicine, I find myself thinking about him, about how he managed to be alright, eventually. He was four. That was sixty-seven years ago. Since then I've carried the idea that I was all but congenitally weakened by that illness and the near death of those days, that nothing of my constitution can hold up under pressure or scrutiny. I was warned about it by the only psychiatrist I've seen. When I mentioned the frailty spell I carried, he said: 'Interesting mythology', meaning: 'That's bullshit.' Bless his oblique self.

Man, it was persuasive, though. Every bit of bad luck, bad news, bad blood fit the description of a body and soul beset by early onset hairline fractures in the firmament. And I did cooperate with that. I was persuaded by it, found all the proof I needed for it.

Mostly my luck's been good, though. Rescues, near misses, the odd blessing abounds in the biography. It galls, how compelling an idea personal frailty can be, how much good luck you can just not notice at all because of it.

Now that young boy seems not as flooded with frailty as I'd thought. He resoundingly didn't die. Minus heroism, there's luck. And there's constitution. He's hovering here with me now. Perhaps there was goodness that came for him then, some kind of mercy or meant-to-be, and perhaps I'm heir to it now.

They say, 'If I'd known I was going to last this long I'd have taken better care of myself.' I say, 'If I'd known I was going to last this long I'd have taken better care of what that meningitis kid passed down to me.'

# 4 October 2024

The habits are the hauntings, I suppose.
   Or not the habits themselves.
The having of them, more like,
the deciding beforehand, that leaden certainty,
unfailing prejudice that meant to get there first, to win.
That bow wave of my intent,
solid, like the jitters, the jags,
strong frailties, washing up on the distant shore
well ahead of my arrival. Debris first.
The challenge of sobriety, the making sure
in a heaving place, the brutal balancing
is this habit work.

The time is short now. I've been fasting all day, vigilant, at an unusual kind of attention.

Unable to sit any longer, I go for a pretend walk through this house. Running out of places to go, I step back into the room. I've disturbed the charwoman who was sweeping in the bathroom. She scurried away – 'I come back in a moment', she said. Now I'm watching the doorway for her return, for signs of life, as I must have done so often in the hospital, waiting for company, dreading the needle poke or the test, back and forth on the hinges of patienthood, the forced inaction of the body driving all the starving for sunlight, for air on skin, for the rumour of life alive and not a rumour.

Things are officially underway. I've been fitted with paste-on electrodes or something, to hook me up to a heart monitor for the duration, 'in case', they say. Then I was brought out to the back patio, where a small fire was sparked, and I was obliged to put that 'wish paper' with those things I want rid of in the flames. There were some murmured, perfunctory prayers from the night shift staff that will oversee me. Then a glass of water, several gelcaps. Then a feeling of being irretrievable. Then back to the room to wait for the main event to begin. They tell me it could be a few hours until there's a sign.

The medicine – the old man – is with me now, and I await the beginning of his mercy and his ministrations.

I am softened to life these days. The neighbourhood dogs are barking up a fuss in the road outside the treatment room. This should be good. If it seems in keeping, I'll try to come to this book as things unfold, but 'all in' might make that unwise. It's a powerful business, this dose. That's what I'm told. Twelve hours of an utter encounter, at the minimum, they say. 'Don't even try to move', they say. 'You'll retch for what seems like forever.' 'It's a wild ride. You'll be okay', they say. How can something this powerful be inevitably 'okay'? And the electrodes on my chest? I see the fret is powerful in its way, too: it was quiet for the last hour, but then active again now, claiming its portion. Such are the habits.

I'm advised to pray.

*My boat is so small. Your sea, so immense. Help me in the hours and days to come. Help my family, and those gathered for my work and our common trials. Help me help them.*

*Bless these young people and their training, who gather around me now.*

They come to my room to check on me. Nothing yet. I'm asked if I want an 'adult diaper' to contend easily with the mobility challenge which is a standard part of the encounter. That is a first. I tell them I'll wait until a more pressing need of that presents itself. 'Not there', I don't think. The offer invites a bit of consideration, though.

# 5 October 2024
### *Ibogaine aftermath, back in my room*

I am a flayed thing left on a beach. The skin has been lifted off me. There's stunned silence and a dusty lakebed where there once was me.

Charred, ruined. The carnage of that encounter can't be approached voluntarily. You wouldn't crawl into that hive of riotous green antiphony because you thought you could use some adjusting, or that everything'd be fine. Everything's never fine, and that being so is the end of the line for my self-determination. The drench of it, the firehose onslaught of clusters of montage vying for the portal of my mind.

I move at my peril. A finger's twitch puts into motion cascades of gag-prompting vertigo. I am pinioned to the salt pan of a blasted place. 'It's like a roller coaster', they told me, 'It'll go up and down, and you'll go along with it. Just don't get off.' Which was brilliant advice. Just hold onto that useless strap of plastic that is meant to be your handle through all this.

Reams of this existential carnage came on with a roar, as if I had joined a programme in mid-transmission. They had me seated on a mat facing a mirror, shaking a rattle in time to a recorded, zithery African bee–sounding soundtrack. Then there was face heat, the first sign, then some kind of intuition – the last one – that I ought to stop shaking that rattle and lay down.

In the few seconds it took to lay down, I went from mildly altered to being entirely in the sway of the medicine. It was like falling backwards into a boil of liquid mercury. Every chamber, every crevice of me was filled at once with the stuff, every other possibility I'd have for myself gone. The passage of time ceased. A churn, a roar of unrecognizable being pressed in on me.

The only clear direction that I received from this riotous vegetal presence during the entire episode was: 'Smile'. Of all things. They didn't say why.

At that moment, I realized that I'd had a terrible grimace on, a rictus, and must have had it on for a long time, since all the muscles around my mouth were stiff and sore. I'm sure I looked like those pictures of people on roller coasters in mid-descent racing down the precipice, mouth driven open by the wind and the flex of zero gravity.

I wonder if this was a plant spirit, the enormity of the green life. The smell coming off me during this encounter could have been fear. There were headfulls of the smell wafting up. It's there still. But it could have been something like primordial life. I wonder if it was a spirit of place roused to coiling and uncoiling by being so far from its Bwiti home, or by me being so far from home. A Black man emerged as the first clear visual agent of turbulence, an old unimaginable man, as old as life. Near him was my mentor and the true storytelling father of my soul, Brother Blue, looking at me, saying nothing. They seemed aware of each other, though they didn't interact. On each of their faces, something like curiosity, and a kind of companionship that neither favoured nor menaced me. They looked at me as one might regard an unexpected newborn.

Even with no grimace, I must have been a sight.

One this-worldly moment: I had expected to be utterly disembodied through this, but that's not what happened. I was as present as I could afford to be, you could say. At some point I realized quite clearly that I had to urinate. At tremendous effort I raised my left hand to signal to somebody seated behind me. It was then that I realized that the sound I was hearing wasn't Godly. It was an alarm going off. The machine monitoring my heart was screeching its red alert. And everyone else in the room was sound asleep. I was alone with the crisis. I remember thinking: 'Huh. This is how I'm going to perish?'

## 7 October 2024

More tremours now than when I got here.
'Trust the process' – that's what they say here.
Being picked up by my wife in a half hour, to work my way back to the ordinary world.
Which will be a decision, not a given.
This is all but done.

I wonder what mercy is now.
I wonder what it means, what it was, to go down this road a bit
and not know what found me.
I cannot believe that the ones who've held me these many years, who've burdened and entrusted me with the makings of a life and its work, don't hold me now. But I don't know where they are. I don't know if they were in the parade of phantasma, or what they thought of it, or who I am to them now.
I am not retaining much of the substance of what I saw.
My limbs, not much used here, are performing as if they've never met. I feel like an invertebrate.
Maybe this is all discharge, the being let go of.
Am I strong of constitution?

*Now in a condominium, ten floors up,*
*at the edge of the Pacific Ocean, facing Japan*

The Atlantic is European, the Pacific Asian. But this medicine was something else. It was as old as the waves around the Cape of Good

Hope, old at least as the phytoplankton whales are made of, old as chlorophyll, as photosynthesis, old as that first scaled life that crawled from the surf and took breath.

There was no moral code relied on or hinted at, no transgression or penance presumed in what I saw. No 'thou shalt' or 'thou shalt not'. I was worthy and peripheral at once. There was me, seventy, and there was as old a presence as has ever been. There was me, and there was what the Gods mean by 'old'.

At one moment: a notion that there was no such thing. At the next moment, there was nothing else.

It was an utter thing. This must be birth of the injunction to fear God.

With me in that state of revery and awe, my wife took us to a local restaurant. It was a Mexican din, hard surfaces on every plane, remarkable garish lighting, raucous music. It was a staunch re-entry. She said, 'Is it all at a distance from you now? Are the memories already going?' I said, 'This is going.' Meaning: the calamitous world.

I sat there, found no kinship with the distracted, distracting fracas.

## 8 October 2024

I'd be naked of credibility if I said I am patiently awaiting the corrective outcome of the last week. As the handwriting slowly goes to shit, perceptibly to shit, as the left limbs go their separate ways, I am quietly beginning to mouth the possibility that in the smoldering aftermath of an encounter with moulten life, I am shaken but habit-ridden even still, unspectacularly afflicted, reaching for the guardrail, hand rail – interrupted by the thought that the brain needs its time, that the old spirits haven't moved on, unproductively interrupted.

The sussing out of magnitude is a crazy business. Where's the scale? This is an affliction compared to what?

Should that help?

# 9 October 2024

On the second morning, on the other side of the embrace, the onslaught of the mad green life, I sit on the floor, back to the chesterfield, the ocean at my left, the thunder maker of last night, the high and dry penthouse at my right, tea, books, the churn of the unassured. Once gravity was the guarantor: things would remain where you put them. If you didn't move, you'd still be where you last were. That was the deal you struck with life early on, that through line of constancy that comes with being upright, mobile, willful. You'd drink when thirsty, sleep when tired, lift up and put down the things of the world.

No more.

The ocean fed upon the shore last night, marauded the verge, swamped the shanties, and as it did so, I laid in bed, and my stillness was drawn, a few grains at a time, into the dark and the deep.

You'll find out, when momentum underpersuades the limbs, that the mechanics are marvelous, have always been, including the marvelous coincidence of getting where you mean to go.

Sanity employs gratitude as the gait employs an ash stick, chest high, carbuncled and, for all of that, straightening if not straight. Or it should.

I am at a swoon-making height, ten stories over the Pacific. The safety railing is barely at waist height. And so it was a few nights ago, after the fire ring council, the incineration of shucked-off reliances and stuff I didn't want, the go-around of intent, the witness of nurses, the swallow of alkaloid powder, the return to the room and pacing, seizing upon each sensation as a sign to be brought breathless, being fetched again from my room to be induced, shaking and rattling before a mirror, a tumult of African bee sounds within and without the ear, and the first flush of the hierarchy of earth: after that, a railing barely waist high is a suggestion and no more, and no impediment to flight or fight – within my rights to stay, or to storm away.

## 10 October 2024

It was decades ago when I began gathering the hair that fell from me at brushing and shearing time, and also the nail parings. I don't know what the cue was: magical thinking, the stirrings of my animism. Or menace in the cloisters, or in the firmament, magic at large that could be crosshaired on me. Or something witchy. This might be the other side of being saved from death as a child, the suspicion I nurse that nothing is quite done with me yet, that there's more where that came from.

I'd gather it all, burn it mostly, bury the ash, persuaded I was shielding myself from arbitrary harm, from bad juju, from the darkness in some. Maybe it worked.

But now that harm has come through despite the crossed fingers and the diligence, maybe it's a sign I was untutored in spells and their undoing. And maybe now I am more custodian than sentry, neatening up the stray signs of my having passed through.

## 11 October 2024

Wave upon wave for close to forever heaped up on the edge of this most recent continent. 'Pacific', we say. Not so much, in how it comes on. It is neither pacified nor pacifying. The fringe of the land runs through the fingers of time with sand as the only witness.

The night's percussion played upon the shore, one staggering wave at a time, free of beginning and end. It was one load of the land shelf we're perched upon clawed out to sea, destination everywhere else, all but never to return. And then one load of land waterborne, thrown up on shore, a ton at a time, one grain deep once the wave's work was done.

A night's work done as you sleep, and you awaken to the edge just where it was, all down its length, torn down and put up along its entirety, prelapsarian life breaking even, give or take the ruckus of storms. Not restless. Not forlorn. *Arriving and departing.* That is the unpacified life of all of us who are made things.

Thoughts might be like waves: bearing down upon their edges, bearing away by asymmetry the usual thing. Or they are like the grains, the granular proof that life is persuasive most when it's coercive least, at once incrementally true and faithless.

## 13 October 2024

I'm working on a series of talks about grief, dirt, home, belonging – the usual thing. This morning, I made a list of 'first inklings' of the body as a separate and separating thing, which I reckon to be the precursor of 'home'. Most of them include disturbance, like weaning, or a breakdown in pattern recognition, injury, sickness. Not all, though: eating at a friend's house for the first time, sleeping over, making a 'fort' with cushions. This is how you find out your family ways aren't the universal constant you figured they were, that there can be homes inside homes.

The body is a searching thing, looking for its coefficient, the asymmetrical turn that affords it a place in the flux and the filth of life. When the body's fortunes turn, the mind has some deciding to do: 'Now where and to what and to whom do I belong?' it wonders. 'Does the old learning about home and health still hold sway? Is it done, too?'

## 17 October 2024
### *On the farm, Ottawa Valley, Canada*

Try.

That's the bottom rung epithet for the afflicted in a time of choices. 'Try' is the moral order of the 99 per cent who will not be the ones who make it, nor the ones for whom the dice fall with favour. That's why the 99 per cent don't tell stories about each other or about themselves. 'Try' doesn't mean 'test' or 'adjudicate', not when you're stricken. 'Try' means 'get to the bottom of what's possible', 'elude what's likely'. You try when you're up against it. You try in order to exhaust, so that you leave no money on the table, so the underside of every stone shows. Nobody's likely to say it, but you try for the sake of those drawn in around you, the ones who'd trade you places but can't. There's no surrogacy in trying.

In trying, you see. Trying is mostly merciless, most of the time. Trying is a krieg light trained on your nerve. It shows you what you've actually been thinking all this time, the habits of how you ponder.

I tried hyperbaric oxygen, forty or so hours' worth. I went two countries away and tried the earth octane ibogaine. I tried to break the habit of 'likely', of my damage control figuring. Was my habit stronger than the medicine? I've wondered. I tried the benign winter of California. I tried horseback riding on the Pacific shore. I tried joy. *I tried trying*.

There's an oddness to this all. The years have assailed me. Good fortune has been a companion. I've been murmured to by the saints and surely by the spirits of place. Their company isn't something I choreographed. I've not been sure of my end of things, whether I can eke out or insinuate any merit on my part. But I've been bolstered by that companionship, and often their affirmation seemed to waft through the proceedings.

But I recognise my makers and their hands or prints not at all in this affliction. They may have been here in the trying, and I've overlooked them. But that would be odd in my days, to have no sense of them at all even as I set about trying to survive the last ten months.

All that seems sure is that I am shaking, that whatever governs the involuntaries of my left-handed self is being denied the necessities of life in the executive branch of my functioning, contracting as if under an awful pressure. The company of spirit and saint, to whom I credit so much of my work and life, is hard – bordering on the improbable – to trace now.

## 21 October 2024

Two years ago, a Viking-like child was born to us here on the farm. He's Viking-capable, even at two. He lifts things that outweigh him, goes out in foul weather all but undressed, seems undismayed by any reversal in fortune that comes his way. They had a fete for him in the last while. I was reluctant. I'd no gab in me, I was shrinking at loud voices, coming off the San Diego / Tijuana venture and the Green God. For some reason, I went anyway, the whole walk to my neighbour's a wrestle with my wish to be anywhere else, knowing my wife wished for me to come as much as she wished for anything from me.

It was the strangest initiation. I sat on the side of the room seeming to be set apart for the afflicted and their caregivers. I felt old. Oldened by it. I was spoken to with a kind of deference offered to those who aren't likely to fend for themselves. Respect was there, surely, and compassion, and surely, too, some cultivated . . . I don't know. I've never been there before. I've never been offered that seat at the table. It's the difference between 'honoured' and 'honourary'. 'Honoured' means venerated. 'Honourary' usually means 'not quite' or 'not really' or 'no longer'. This is where age and affliction meet, and meld.

## 23 October 2024

The wind has shorn the trees in an afternoon. From today, we'll make the sound of dry and fallen leaves every time we walk. We, and this place, are naked now until April – six non-negotiable months of the drearies.

I remember that during my time in the death trade, I came upon a kind of conceit: oblige the dying to declare what the likelihood might be of them seeing another winter, another spring, or birthday or the like. The purpose was to have them locate themselves seasonally, rhythmically, not diagnostically.

Now I am trying to calculate the value of any given idea, or enterprise, according to how many seasonal carbon credits it might burn off. This has come to include movies and books, screentime, time spent in anger, in customary pursuit of revenge paradigms, in poor posture chiropractic and spiritual, in looking down at the dirt road as I walk the farm. I lingered upstairs in the barn today, wondering if I am old enough for this beautiful farmer's chapel, finally, the rays of sunlight coming in sideways through the one-eighth inch between the boards, and now because it's mid-fall lower down in the sky, as am I. There I found thirty bales of alfalfa, two dozen bags of kindling wood, a new yurt kit from Mongolia, drying racks for herbs, a bale elevator. I wished it all well, climbed back down to ground level, rejoined the living, saying grace on the dirt road, side-stepping the updraught of exhaustion.

## 24 October 2024

I suppose now that wisdom is lightning: erratic, volatile, uncontained, ramshackling, incoming. Poetry is the translation of wisdom speaking creation's tongue: cursive, measured, strophic, spiralling, subversive, subliminal. Wisdom is for keeps. It comes to humans. Poetry comes through elders. It's for later. It's for the depths. Poetry is to wisdom as electricity is to an electrical storm. Wisdom, yes, but poetry too is called for now.

## 26 October 2024

A year ago, I was astride the *Nights of Grief & Mystery* tour, night upon night. There were pieces meant to slow the heart rate of the people, the birthrate of their ideas. 'Still' was one of those. It fell to me after writing a kind of pause in prose for a film. It opened up before me, within me, alongside me. I contemplated the contemplative life, which I've only ever viewed at a considerable distance. I sat beside the sitting, complicated the monastery cell's simple air. It was during these transgressions that I wondered upon 'the prostrations and the stations of the evening, and the toiling and the tolling of the bells'. No one from among us living in the throes here can manage having left the world behind. It's too severe. The skeleton of the schemes for the day, the armature of the evening are for governance, and for fair compensation for a gone world. They employ the soul, give it its recognizable work to do.

My work is now in the throes of being collated, catalogued, translated and given the scriptorium treatment. But the summation itself is an allegation. There was never a scheme, though scheming may be drawn from it, or forced upon it some. The work has been my armature, my exoskeleton, my master's voice. The work was the bones of the day I lived in, the cover of evening that I rested in. I was no monk. I didn't even think of living without it.

I'm thinking about it now, though.

# 28 October 2024

No new thoughts for some time to drape these deranged letters across. Inspiration may be drawn to the agile of heart, mostly, leaving the rest of us unqualified. These tremours seize up the limbs, seize up the heart. Kind people send in their convictions, their remedies. I'm leaving behind that guy chasing the naturopathy, chasing the laying on of hands. I write that as if I had other things to do. There aren't many choices neurodegeneration hasn't already chosen for itself.

Then there is the seasonless notion that, given everything, I am otherwise healthy.

I may persist in a state of dissolution for years, they say, barring further extremes of fortune. There is great drastic overthrow of the heart at this prospect, an astringent laid upon the mind. Nothing goes kindly when considering that grey prospect. Even heartbreak goes cold.

I heard something yesterday that was a beam of some other possibility that hadn't found me yet. Gregory was speaking with Nathalie about the mixed blessing of the advent of his grandparenthood and the goneness of his mother in the same half year. He said to her, 'I make my sadness work. I take it to the studio, do work. I take it to the workout place, workout sadly.' It sounded as though he was employing the sadness, given that it doesn't of itself relent. It's stuff like this that persuades me again and again to work with him, should I be spared.

I've a mind to try that, to work the sadness, to nurse it to health, as one would an antithesis, an anti-Christ, an antidote, a wayward want, an antediluvian, an antebellum, the Antarctic. Here's a dream worth dreaming: a working sadness. No routine. No momentum. A laying on of the working hands of sorrow.

My son's grown sure that I over-agree with defeat, so as to manage, maybe. So as to elevate the pessimism that looks so much like learning, maybe, so as to not be caught unawares. The hollowest of wisdoms. He waits for me to ask him about it before he tells me. Then he unblinkingly tells me. That's his love at work.

# Scaffolding 4

The onset of disease brings out the barrister in some, the sorcerer in others. 'If you can, you should': that's the moral code of the med-tech regime, the haunting, looming *Materia Medica* of the tech-besotted. That's what the illusion of life mastery sounds like: a mound of spent possibilities. I was not immune, it turns out. At a loss and nonaligned, I *tried*. That's the last ten months: trying.

Years ago, I was surprised to find that a room full of educated people at the Orphan Wisdom School divided neatly along generational lines as follows: the older people were either dismissive of, or spooked by, the advent of artificial intelligence. The younger people took it as a given, and were weirdly impressed more by the 'near real' of the artifice and its phantasms, and grew passive the nearer they drew to 'reality'.

'Real', though, happens because there are limits, not because everything's possible. The borders and edges are where you work your fate. The slow-motion dissolve of disassembly – neurodegeneration – is where you work the handshake deal you made when life seemed mostly possible. It's the walk you take through the ruins of Maybeland. When the novelty of crisis wears off, it's worn off. The debris, the sand, is in the hourglass. By now I'd 'tried.' I was crossing palliations off an imaginary list. Ten months ago I felt preyed upon, sought out and hunted down. Ten months later, I was trying to figure out how – or whether – to occupy an ordinary life that at times seemed to be a rattled cage, at other times a fallow field.

I took pride during my sojourn in the death trade in making a language to speak with dying people where the realities of dying survived the utterances, platitudes, bromides, hopes, laws, prejudices, untutored sufferings so often brought to bear upon them. Now I seem to be having one more go at that kind of word work. But I can't untremour, uncontract, ununcertain the measure I take of things here. Or I won't. Looking back, you want to straighten the lines you drew. But that's not what neurodegeneration is. It isn't straight lines. That's the deal I struck with writing things down. That's the 'neuro' part of the thing. It's not a limp, or a trembling. It's what's left of what I've got, as grey matter goes white.

Now, this is where I'm working out what kind of intelligence – moral, ethical, aesthetic, semantic – I'll be left with.

## 29 October 2024

Am I hopeful?, I wonder.

About what?, I answer.

Am I hopeful that the diagnosis is wrong?, I wonder. 'No', I say.

Hopeful that the prognosis is unnecessarily occluding and bleak?

That's akin to asking whether I hope that what's happening isn't happening, that all down the line it's an information problem, an occasion of that famous assault of misinformation we've got in high places and low. It's unlikely that the diagnostic systems are in tatters enough to have placed me at the wrong stage of my life.

Am I hoping for anything? I don't think so. Any skill or capacity I might hope for I think I'm working on now. Or I should be.

I'm thinking again about what being hopeful does for people who are in for it anyway. I think you occupy yourself in the work of not being who and where you are when you hope. An alternative: you occupy yourself in a citizen's work, the work of seeing things for what they are when you'd want otherwise. I wouldn't know how to show up for duty and occupy this life as it is and – at the same time – hope that this is not required of me, that this isn't my little life, too.

In my best moments – there aren't so many – I am a man afflicted in his health, not so clearly healthy in his affliction. Hope strikes me as it has for much of my life: a laying on of hands upon the allegation of a future to secure a foothold that looks like a present, one I don't have.

## 31 October 2024

Speaking of disguises: does there come a time when I go from 'this is what they told me' to 'this is what I am trying' to 'this is who I am'? Is it best to get to the third thing quickly? Is there a skin to shed? A skin to wear?

Where is the line that marks me as having happened this way now? Is it different from going through a windshield? Is the shakes my catastrophic mutilation? My wheelchair-assisted living? My handi-capped parking privilege? My differently abled?

I fretted that the ibogaine could prompt psychosis. That was a con-siderable fear. I prize my mind, as it is – which prompts all kinds of fixity in a time that recommends moving like time moves, like a breeze in a field at dusk moves.

No psychosis to report, no unravelling. The meagerest of insights, and no noticeable restoring of the myelin on the nerve endings – which, given the psychic enormity of the ibogaine encounter, is hard to credit. It was so enormous I opted out of a last morning dose of toad. I felt like I was playing with fire. I wonder about that now.

There'll be no prevailing here, my son
There'll be no foresight to banish the unruly
No intoxicant, no tidy chant to lift the heavy, dark wing.

This is what I am, now
Trial and fire and error
This is what has come.

## 2 November 2024

The ram is among the ewes today. He has his work. Spring will be theirs. The farm's future is taken up in their instincts, the proverbial, ordinary miracle of their obedience – the ruly mandate. The force majeure in the blood, the blood we'll spill once the weather promises no flies, no waste in the slaughter. In five months, we'll be up all night, the amniotic vigil.

The calendrical uprising and downturning, the quickening and the melancholy, they're with me now. I watch the place from a greater distance, now that my strength is not what is called for. The others move around my stiffness as the river around a dead, fallen log moves, unhurried and distancing and complete. I am less responsive, more obedient. In the city I'd be an old man doused in uncertainty in a doorway, nothing needing him. What graceful alchemy that I had money, didn't keep it, and bought a farm, that a few people stayed.

Pigs and sheep, dogs and ducks are in general agreement with my presence here. A new barn agrees, the last act of my dexterous solvency. Another year and I wouldn't have done it, gathering my ducats in close, as if that was wise or prudent. But prudence is a pall on the proceedings now, and the best wine's to be tasted till the bottle's upturned on the trestle table in the teaching hall.

I catch sight of myself every so often. I am as a man pending, perched on an edge no one can see, hunched around a prized possession no one treasures or wants. I move carefully, but it wears. I walk as if something strange and vital is at stake, but I can scarcely do otherwise. The resemblance to age is so faithful, and so sudden. I am in a storm that has no stillness at its centre, driving me to its edges.

Today, in the coming of the sharpness in the fall air, I break wood with a maul, a medieval man-severer and destroyer of a thing, and then stack it by the house. That's my provider gene at work, provisioning my wife for the cold days ahead, in case my arms or legs fail. You'd think, with all the wagging of my extremities, I'd be all over the place with the blade and short a kneecap already. But there's no wavering, not for now, and the edge lands where I mean it to, hardwood and soft, morning and eve, and I keep faith with that brassy claim I made in *Come of Age* to be after the hardwood now, while there's still a writing shack, and writing to be done in it, and a hearth and need for warmth.

# 11 November 2024

The soot-grey light of earliest dawn has come stealing. The duo-chrome of the days' gathering is so silently here. With the leaves down, the tree silhouettes are distinct. Splayed as hands are when pleading skyward in rapture's indecision, they are the truth test of what endured, what agreed to stay in another kind of dark. A duck on the river now sheds the night's timidity, the risk taken by those mated for life in this, the hunting season, when camouflaged death dealing is in the rushes and the weeds. The closest trees are pushed forward by the two-tone contrast, black out of the grey. Another day's overture wicks away this eleventh-month twilight, and the orchestration of remembrance has come, the scrim for fortune's tally, the eleventh of the eleventh. And in the time it's taken to describe all this, it's gone, an orange streak in the east.

On day one of the official diagnosis, almost a year ago, the neurologist talked briefly about 'dopamine deficiency'. He said that I had a com-promise of – and here he made air quotes – 'the joy chemical'. Jesus, I've walked around with a sense of personal failure when it comes to joy every day since. But I don't think it's joy that's compromised. It's some-thing closer to initiative, anticipatory engagement with the possibilities, the feel of being drawn by the current of life, the quickening of it, the keenness. Maybe joy's an offspring of the keenness. You've no idea how rudimentary those things are to your little life until something turns the tap off, the volume down. Joy scarcely stands a chance when these mechanics of joy are brought low.

For a full seven days, I've gone without recourse to this book. For the first time in almost a year, I let this book go. I was nagged by the habits of conscience a few times: 'Get to it'. I see now that this was those joy mechanics in abeyance. It was like how I am sometimes with the supplement array. When your life becomes ground zero for remedial strategizing, some part of you takes a step back. I must have been objecting to this book, objecting even to the discipline I'd agreed to, the regime of reflection I'd signed up for, the work of seeing and bearing faithful witness.

But I didn't even see that. I just stopped writing for a while, without having decided to stop. Yesterday my wife went down to the writing shack to fetch a lectern that would allow me to stand for the podcast *Never Land / Sever Land* I am due to give with Kimberly Johnson. After a few minutes she came back with this very green book in hand. I looked at it, had no idea in that moment how she came by it, what was happening. She gave the book to me and said, 'This was outside, on the porch of the cabin. I don't know if it's still good.'

*Seven days in heavy weather.* The ink didn't run.

*Seven days in the wild.* The bindings held. The paper didn't curl, didn't delaminate.

It is a portent. It is something merciful. The timing of her going down to the writing shack, the lack of rain in what is commonly a rainy time: merciful. Timing: it is God's middle name this time, not God's middle finger.

Let's see if I'm still good, if I can hack the suburbs of my habits, while my wife finds what I didn't know I'd lost.

## 15 November 2024

I now have a forty-year-old child in the world. Our way of life – this liberty fantasy of North America that we count on – has marauded across her well-being, as it has so many of her generation. I've hectored and extolled so often for their sakes. The stakes are always high, but it isn't so clear I've done well by them. I was out on the barricades for decades, and meanwhile my own kids were ailing with the malady. Forty's not young. She may set about 'working on herself', but like me she won't be able to start anew. So much of our hurt in these troubled times seems more personal than it actually is. Much of our hurt is cultural. 'I haven't liked myself sometimes this year', she said – an affliction or a self-assessment I've rarely, if ever, consciously made. It isn't as though you can be wrong about not liking yourself, so much as you might err as to your reasons why.

You don't really 'grow infirm'. There's no growth in it, no increase. There's no measuring negative space, I wouldn't think. Still, something is amassing because of the disappearances, the gonenesses, the graceless-ness of what's left of the commons, and whatever that is, I do wonder if my children are old enough to see that happen without the world grow-ing increasingly hard for them to be in. Whatever's happening with me, the increments of sorrow are gathering in their lives. No matter what work I've done, that gracelessness in the culture is deepening.

How then was it supposed to be?

Most of the sorrow comes from the unexamined grudge, the secret one, that it wasn't supposed to be this way. 'Supposed to' abandons you to the thinnest gruel of choice: take it or leave it. But 'supposed to' is something you do, something you pull on one leg at a time, that you hitch up and zip up and belt up, until it suits you.

That's what I'd have for my kids: that this unspooling of mine would suit them, suit their ages and their lives, that they'd find a size of it that would smooth into a fine gait over time, inseparable from how they'd walk, and that there'd be peace for them.

Hanging in the rafters of the banquet hall tonight are the gutted sheep that are to hold us over in the hardening of winter's grey, ill-lit days – remains of what was once the farm's nobility and near future. Some sixteen in number, they are lambs born seven months ago, grass gone into them, and the oldest of their mothers.

Because of this life I've lived, I've missed most springs and almost as many autumns on this farm, making me a benefactor and a well-wisher and accomplice to these proceedings, and a chronicler and advocate and visitor. You scarcely want to be a guest to your designs, but those days and nights are gone now, traded for wise dying, and coming of age, and grief and mystery, and a bit of adulation.

## 16 November 2024

The carcasses hang there, slaughterhouse chic to an outsider, to someone looking for a fabled bucolic life. Without the machines that are common to most farms, we are Iron Age in the harvesting and the culling we perform. We need the cold weather to save us from the salves and additives of preservation. So, we half freeze while doing this work.

This morning the sheep will be stiffened, waxy tubes of bone and flesh, and I'll stand at the stainless-steel table, stropping the knives, scoring lines down muscle sheaths to turn out the meat that the pasture grass and imperative mystery of life made of them. I'll be stiffened as I do this, a sagging version of a farmhand, titular now, honourary, lapped by the helpers, deference of another order – disorder – coming my way.

The farm is a drastic revelator of limitation. Town is made in the human image, and comfort and convenience are the way of the place. Suburbs, more so. But the farm only looks to be serving humans to some other outsider humans. Here, every decision passes through the eye of consequence for animal or crop, as best as we can figure them – or pasture, wetland, woods, verge. There's little or no business done here, no agribusiness, no bottom line to reach. We are beholden to the beasts almost entirely, and to the heavy calculus and the light hand they require, or their requirements require, which until the calamity of cities has always been the measure of human capacity.

So I am no farmer now. I am, instead, a consultant with a decent memory, a subsidizer doing a lot of leaning, sitting. I am watching the blessings of seasonally summoned work pass me by, resorting to people thirty years my junior for it to be done.

## 18 November 2024

Yesterday was the fifth and final episode of a podcast series Kim Johnson and I recorded called *Never Land / Sever Land*. About halfway through, Kim went off on a riff I didn't see or hear coming. As it went on, I waited for the signs that have virtually always come my way, signs of what I might do by way of response. I waited some more, and nothing was happening. The old alchemy that fired my conceiving and responding neurons was for that moment cold and silent and still. When she threw the discussion over to me, I was still in that state. For the first time I can recall, I had to cover for myself. Eventually I said something that amounted to this:

> 'Well, no one's obliged to weigh in on everything. The world doesn't need to hear from me about any and every fractious item on Ideology Main Street.'

The truth was that I couldn't find the thread. It wasn't so extreme as to call it nightmarish. Daymarish, probably. I had nothing to bring to the moment. I didn't panic, but I wasn't OK. Later she called it 'an elder moment', by which she meant that it was a moment in which she was encountering the parallel etiquette universe of elderhood. Maybe it was that. It wasn't a teaching moment, though. It was a survival moment. Or maybe these days there's a fierce resemblance between the two.

Later still, back at the house, I was explaining or describing the moment to my wife, who in response said something relentlessly, maturely kind and deeply informed. She said:

> 'You don't have to work anymore. There's enough money. It can be over. Unless you really love it still, it can be done now.'

I wasn't relieved. I was seen, though. I was loved. I sagged in a relief I didn't know I sought.

## 19 November 2024

That unrelenting, pulseless, remorseless bitch that is so often the spirit of winter in the north of the hemisphere has so far stayed her hand. I've just been outside exercising the privilege of land stewardship: urinating without recourse to any concern about neighbours. It is, by November's standards, warm – ominously, loomingly, wrongly warm. This is the stuff of melting ice caps.

The cold now sets me to tremouring something fierce, penetrating and enervating as it has become, so I know these warm days are a kind of exemption for me. Even so, yesterday's mildness proved to be a test of sorts. At one point in the early afternoon, I couldn't track the sequence of deboning the carcasses to end up with the cuts people preferred. I couldn't intuit the pattern, as many times as I'd done it. I stood there, twisted around an invisible pin driven into my understanding. Picking the knife up, putting it down again, by late afternoon I was defeated.

Grace is the work, surely. Grace is the laying down of what I no longer carry. Without grace my misery would be a moral order, probably for the duration, as it was in the early days of this diagnostic séance I've been in.

## 21 November 2024

Rain. Strange weather. Betrayal weather. Message weather. Angel weather. Winter is shy this year, keeping our blood thin, the heavy boots put away, the working gloves astray and unmatched. We scarcely belong here because of it. Our old, locative devotions to the cold have no home in weather like this, as much as we might bitch about it. And our abattoir scripture is unsure, unread, unintoned this year, like a bead string on a shelf, the beads uncounted.

We will come to the work out of step with things anyway, shirt-sleeved instead of shivering, discomfited with the comfort, mad to be concerned, a few words spoken of the 'It's not good, good as it is' kind. While Rome burns. We won't see our breath. It'll be unclear that we're breathing, or here. We'll set about the work anyway.

The women will ride the ewes into the old roofless shell of a barn where the milking was done in the summer months. It will be as in the days of guild and rank and papers of indenture, how the murmurs of aptitude were passed between those bent to the task, to the exact hone of the blade's inflection. Even here, with none of us having grown up in this, everyone knows the work to be done, their place in it. They will bear down upon the harrowing work, bear the ewes and the lambs to the ministrations of the shooting man. They won't look away. They'll wedge the sheep to a railing with their bodies. A rifle crack will rip through the old log barn shell, then there'll be the dumb slump of a just-dead animal on the ground. They'll step over the body, lift it to a pallet with effort.

They'll lift the stunned, blind sheep to me, and I'll do what these extremes of fortune have left for me to do. I will sink a knife into the carotid artery beneath the jaw hinge, pull up on the chin, let loose the iron oxide flood made of pasture grass and sheep ancestry into a plastic pan, wait for the rearing and galloping to ebb, till the sheep find their feet on the ground of another world, a world of sheep mysteries.

After, I'll wipe the blade on a handful of brown grass, cover the blood spill with dead leaves, watch as the strong ones heave the former future of the farm up onto the tailgate, tuck a twist of grass between the slack jaws, stretch the grim work from their muscles, ready themselves to do it again, and again, all day long and into the next day. I'll watch, no longer the mayordomo, the mantle passed from me without me seeing it. Along the way now I'll obey the quiet code of the pasture grass bent over and laid down by strong wind. I'll give way, let the young know that I know it is so, and for the best, that it's already prosecuted and done.

I think now on how old a moment this one is, how many grazing peoples saw the weakness in the limb of the greying shepherd the way they saw the weakness in the flock, and acted with a single mind to cull the frailty from the coming days. No one will speak it, and everyone will know the moment of succession is upon us.

Later, an old teapot will sit on the old wood stove. I'll notice the cant of the handle, how its skew keeps it just out of the heat's path, and like a phantom limb bears its bit of weight silently, remotely, for the pouring out for the thirst of the workers. And I'll notice how in a year I've become that handle, that limb. I'll notice how everybody knows, without a word of it being spoken.

Such is the natural genius of the old ways, unblinking and quiet, unspooling now in the unnatural heat of this November.

Yesterday I was on the screen call again after some months' hiatus. A young man was awkwardly seeking counsel to serve him the rest of his life. He wanted to get into the death trade, as I had done. He had no questions worth answering. I felt the swarm of his untutored admiration. 'How did you get like that?' he would have asked if his tongue worked for him. As if I'd know how I got like this. As if I was there at the time of my making. He was a good man, and good enough for the death trade troubles that awaited him. So off we went, me answering what he didn't ask.

We were on video. I was gesturing, two handedly. At least I meant to be ambidextrous. I caught sight of myself in mid-gesture. The right hand conducted the orchestra of the notions that were for the moment coming to me. The left hand hovered in the air, waiting for instruction, all but still, like that awkward man at the dance who can sense the thud of the music in his feet, but not on the anvil in his ear.

I told the left hand to lower down, out of sight and slight, out of indictment and camera range. Down it went. Still some obedience, even if recalcitrant.

## 22 November 2024

If God is a crisis . . .

## 24 November 2024

Two things.

My reed basket is taking on water from the river of life. Years ago, I was at a men's conference in rural Minnesota. There was an afternoon off. I'd brought with me a birchbark canoe I'd made or helped make. It was a sight. I paddled the lake, gave some of the men rides, answered the how-to questions. Hefting it out of the water, I saw something in the weeds. I put down the canoe, parted the shore grass, and found there the remains of a birch bark canoe, a carved thwart, several ribs. I knew by then how much work and love went into the making of a canoe. I was unnerved at the prospect that someone could have abandoned such a beauty to the weather and the vagaries, dumbfounded by it. Something inside me figured that, given the skill and devotion needed, the canoe should last a good long forever.

Years later, I go to the back of my house, to check on the well. There I find a couple of trestles under the eaves. Spanning the trestles are the disassembling remains of the finest birch bark canoe I have ever made, or seen. The eaves were never deep enough to safeguard the canoe that I stored there for protection from the elements. The canoe suffered most from want of water. I worked all over the world. I wasn't here enough to get it in the river, and like anything made to float, it dried and contracted and withered.

To my own disrepute I know now how and by whom such beauty can be forsaken. Anaesthetic: to be desensitized or disabled where beauty is concerned.

My craftsman's conscience is taking on water.

Knowing in a general way isn't knowing. It's growing habituated. It's ceasing to inquire.

So, start again. The failings I made in caring for the beauty in my hands transgress upon a moral order so remote now as to have become a suspicion. That is largely true because the harsh, merciless injustice at work among us now dares the conscience to attend to beauty.

If this is true of aesthetic things, then it might be true of my slow disassembly, my taking on water. What moral order, I wonder now, does this affliction resemble, or stagger out of, or tumble down from, or transgress? To what does a personal, temporarily treatable, ultimately undeniable unravelling belong? What universe of purpose does it hint at? Is there a deity involved? Is it a question of belonging that doesn't itself belong? This is an unhandy way of asking 'why me?', or 'why this?'

I was thrown in the early going by the suggestion floating around that there's a Parkinson's personality profile: intellectually adroit, emotionally aloof or illiterate. Not dopamine deprived, but joy deficient. Diagnosis: unable to party. So I've examined myself in these terms. It's a joyless exercise. Is joy celebration? Is it thanksgiving? Is it the bright side of every street? Is it saying 'yes' more often? Is it play? Good luck?

At any moment my inquiry could be beggared, my shattered sorrows untented. At any moment my old certainties could powder, old momentums go to the doldrums. I've asked of mayhem, What does it take? How badly off the rails must it go before the stall and still stalling and stilling in me roused by big unalterable questions finally reigns? Resigns?

## 26 November 2024

First snow.

It is that indecisive kind, rain and hail and slush and clumps of grey sky bellying to earth, the kind that keeps your head down, chin tucked, hands buried in pockets.

I have the blessing of seasonal work here. The discipline that comes with harsh changes absolves the mind of deciding. Obedience finds favour here. I roll through. I flirt with despair. I dress for work, my footprints scuffing the snow. I'm still walking, out to the fields this time and taking the measure of the regenerating bush. We'll push the frontier back some years, cull the saplings, ready them for the hearth, for the smokehouse, pine needles set aside and dried for tea.

## 27 November 2024

Nothing of the snow's firstborn lasts. We're soaked in the field, gathering up the prunings, leaving shade trees for the sheep come the heat of August, planning ahead, regretting behind, figuring by the unsteady hand of the sun's work. It is a strange flexing of the mind: planning for a time in which I can plan no longer.

My fears and chagrin are nonsensical here, in my fields and in my house. There is, instead of ordinary fret, a farmer's love for what can't be wished away or altered much. That comes my way at the end of the day, when the weary investments I make of my waning energies ought not be asked more of, when sighing down to a supper's table is prayer enough for the givings and takings of the day.

There's a second snow today. But there's nothing that's cold enough to hold it. We're all but a month late now in butchering. That means that there's a month's more feeding and expense and tending to, a month more for the heart to hover over its work. This may be how it is when 'more time' seems benign, or merciful, or just, or a general amnesty, reconciliation and reparation. You thought you'd be full enough with more time, that that would do. But I saw what I saw in the death trade, and when it comes to 'more time', just be very careful what you wish for.

I'm trying to be careful. Being here must do. Maybe more of being here doesn't work like skill works. Maybe it works like a fever works, teeth chattering, hot and cold at the same time, catarrh on the walls where there should be the sepia of belonging. Belonging is sweet some-how, like the ambered insides of the smokehouse, the tang of another autumn there and the fine shanks and bellies and promise hanging in the maple smoke and the grace.

When you're in the autumn of a life now mostly lived, you have memories hooked and hanging in the smokehouse, old certainties smoldering, giving off smoke, griefs finally going sweet, taken down in time to make the promise of a plate, and cause for thanksgiving and rising up again.

More time is more of what prompted you to want more time.

## 28 November 2024

I signed maybe twenty of my books yesterday evening. They're on their way today to their buyers, despite a strike at the post office. There's strong evidence that my work is sought by a few. Evidence of the work itself is there on the shelf, drawn down in the days of optimal health, though I never thought of it then. But these brief updates I write to the buyers, in the form of inscription and signature, are executed in contraction, as if by a frozen hand, or a hand unaccustomed to the fine points any longer, or a hand grown unaccountably timid, now fonder of speech.

But there's ink in the pen, and it leaves its mark, and the particulars of a stranger's request for the work are there, about to go out into the wide world. 'For Christine', says the inscription. 'For Jake', says another. 'Bless', it says, and then my glyph, and the month and year, signature and sign that for now we're both here. I used to write paragraphs when inscribing books. The mind is willing still, but the flesh is weak.

Nose to the smarting ground, the harsh of frost upon it, I'm walking unprompted by a destination or purpose. I am for reading signs of what awaits me in the stranger days ahead, the captivity of cold, the stiffening until fingers curl like planed curls of wood. I'm there already, I think to myself, minus the hard cold.

Later, there's no dinner made. Thinking I've been left to fend for myself, I'm blind entirely to the possibility that there's purpose afoot in the foregoing of the nightly meal. Another signpost on the usual road heeled over in the weeds, I think. Until I find out that my wife's fasting, old order penitent that she is, for me and for my sake. Her quiet at the time of repast is a prayer. Perhaps I'll be borne up by that intercession of hers: perhaps that's what awaits me.

## 29 November 2024
*Day three of snow*

Fat pieces of the sky, untroubled by descent, come straight down from on high. There's no thudding, but that's surprising, given their force, their free fall. Being that it's still warmish for November, these won't last either. Even now they are not lasting, like sighs. Like promises.

This winter is like a guest unsure of its welcome, stalling at the door, tongue testing the air, the tone of the place. It doesn't bode well at all, this long lapse of the season. Utterly comfort driven at times, I don't mind. Pushing through snow on the way to the pigs, slippage underfoot, would – will – be a drastic more of the same for my already taxed gait, like extra weight unevenly fit on my frame, like extra clothes someone's rented for a wedding.

Then, later in the day, as if a decision was made somewhere, cold came down the valley. And it ordered the snow, and separated and firmed the flakes. Like the force of its twin, the vegetal God, the snow multiplied. The marl of leaf and mould is covered now, en route to spring and dirt, like the face of God with the eyes suddenly closed, drawing even light to itself.

I might have slept through it all, the face of God and the eyes closing and every living thing drawn to that God's face as if it were wisdom itself. I might have panicked my way beyond all that, or beneath it. I might have carried the sorrow burden all through the storm and the night and, bent over with the weight, missed it all.

But I didn't. I headed out into it, grief intact.

That's the work sometimes: not blinking, not turning away long enough that the world firms again as the light draws in. You just go outside and lift your eyes to the world continuing, as it will do without you.

That is mercy: leaving a book in the rain, and the ink not running and the binding still bound, to take note.

## 30 November 2024

The pasture grass at the edge of my field here remembers the unremembered Irish dead, laid low in the first winter of their pilgrimage from the old country for increase's sake to this spot, they and their young and their religion, the first wave of Europe on Algonquin land, two hundred or more years ago. There's no bone yard, no mound or marker. But I know that the harshness of these months delivered some of them into this ground. I've walked through it in the fall. I went that way again now. Wonder of wonders, that path is there when the new grass comes the next year: the grass's memory.

I may fear the eclipse of my memory, though I don't recall fearing it. I don't remember the grass's memory, either. But when I wander this place, tallying the mysteries transacted mostly at night, I see traces of who's come round. The path made in habit is furrow enough that you can follow it in the dark. The bent stalks hold the murmur of who's gone through, as the phosphorus holds the sea's wake, its disturbance.

I go for a night walk in my field, a good place to bring a sadness this big, to move out beyond the brailing hands and the blind man's shuffle, until my eyes finally make peace with the dark. I remember putting a match to a small pile of refuse in the spring of the year, and then an errant spark, and in ten minutes that same field's stubble was up in fire, how it nearly took the old cedar barn but didn't, the flames pouring upwards, inextinguishable, that distinct roar of uncontained, implacable fury, cindering our face and brow as we made to stomp it out, hollering down the river for help. 'And what happened?' asked the volunteer fire chief when all was smoke and cinder and saved. 'Lightning', I said straight-faced, as we stood there under a blue sky in the midday spring sun.

I might have made a go of things, had I been taken in by one clergy or another, had I prevailed and gained the credential of the cross or the cloth. Something ecclesiastical might have nursed certainty in me of one creed or another, and I might have fought the fight of the warrior monk, a thing that's in me to do. If any of that had happened, I might have walked these nights thinking of sin and debt and trespass, of God at the drastic wheel, meting out temperate pay for transgressive work. And I might have had a malignant story I could tell myself about where this degeneration is coming from, or why. Or I might have joined the psychology brigades, or the archetypalists, or put my faith in the regression machine, and brought the dark fruit forward, and had the trauma frame for my holy writ. And I might have been nursed to a dark understanding, persuaded by a nascent and personal hurt.

But I am a bad joiner, then and now, and I have no programme I know about, not much of a scheme that explains all of this. I've already tired of the mechanics of sorrow. Be it now, at seventy, or earlier, or deeper into the fray, what kind of ending features more justice, more measured mercy, than this?

# 4 December 2024

Four days of hard cold, bare ground, trussed sheep, one of the pigs in a desperate, violent swooning, tearing up a bit of half-frozen swamp because of a gun's misfire on the bloody butchering ground, because the wound was cranial and not lethal. With that awful mayhem upending the good preparations, there were prayers and steady hands even still. The orchestra of succession has played its refrain. Each person on the farm can work longer than I. I manage the periphery, the nonessentials. I am fitfully leaning into my limits.

About seven years ago, I would come down to the banquet hall after six hours of writing, and join the farm folk for lunch. The first few days I'd paraphrase the morning's work on the elderhood book, *Come of Age*. Thereafter, I'd bring the writing book down, and as a digestif I would read a couple of new paragraphs. It was a wonderful hour. Before the ink was dry, I would get to hear how a barely born notion sounded in the world.

I'm writing this book now, one halting half-page at a time. There's no victory in it. No audience. I'm not inclined to turn it on the farm folk, oblige them to respond, compare then and now.

I don't.

So I don't know the sound of this one.

# 5 December 2024

Still, there's the work of age, once the witnesses arrive. That's a claim I made years ago: elders are made in the willingness of the young to seek them out. Elderhood is built by the witnesses, not the practitioners. That's what's left of my calling.

I know well how it goes when there's no old presence. Things get brittle for the young, as they are brittle now. Elders are the myelin of the culture's nervous system. As the working elders wane, the young grow edgy, feel threatened, abandoned to soulless systems of conviction and *techne*. If you're entrusted with a life in prolongation, you are obliged to draw the young close as the timbers buckle and the doors catch on the heaving floorboards. You are there to reward their fascination with the mortalities that seem for the moment to pass them by entirely, that seem to pertain only to you and not to them, confused by freedom and health as they are.

In these days, standing stock still at the butcher's block as the cold comes down the valley, going numb, forgetting the sequence of dissection from a waning competence, wayward of mind, I reckon they deserve a good, sound, concerted swoon-by-example. I write this irony-free. I don't know how else they'd come to their undoing as anything but truants.

So rather than write and recite from the vagaries, I mean to grow vague among them, and entrust them with moments of unsought, faithful witness to the sun going down. This way, they may risk twilight, and come to their eclipse as if it were something more than unprecedented emptiness. That's the bargain I would strike with the void.

I'm seized by the necessity to pass water, although I did so an hour ago, and I do so on the hour. I fumble for what seems like minutes with my button fly. No matter which way the wind prevails, I'll end up peeing on my boots towards the end of the stream. It's chronically a partial relief. Perhaps not the fault of the affliction at all. That's the kind of testimony to frailty I'm entrusting to them, the kind that's hard on the self-esteem. Self-esteem isn't as useful in times of frailty as I once thought it was.

## 6 December 2024

The cramp of winter is upon us and upon everything. Waiting for the cold is like waiting for a seizure. Or like waiting to fall down. You go about your work, but there's a stutter in your step. The monstrous anticipation contracts you. You are an uncertain animal, foreign and forlorn.

It is a morning of particular disintegration. I stood up, and the uncertainties began as if an alarm had gone off. Making a fire in the kitchen, starting the smokehouse smoldering now that the butchering's done, breaking kindling, quartering the wood so my wife can carry the pieces in, in case of . . .

Well, there it is. It's not 'in case of . . .' Not at all. It's 'when' . . . It is disarming, how provisional you can be when the information is at hand, how conjectural, how posture-prone. Grey matter to white matter, and still, I make oaths with 'if' at the heart of them. I've asked of the air and of the Gods, 'What does it take . . .?', and still I supply 'if' for an answer.

Coming around to the days you already inhabit: nothing certain about that. Thunder down the valley, ozone in the air, auguries and portents everywhere, and still, it's 'if' for an answer.

If only the work of it all was foregone.

The morning's din has worn off and left me to think this thought: I stand in the summer kitchen, behind the banquet hall where all the cooking for the Orphan Wisdom School happened. Today it's a frozen outpost where the last of the medicinals are being drawn from the bones and caul fat of the *matanza*. In my mind I am wandering, looking for some needed thing for me to do. In vain. It was like fishing: line out, snag/ silence, line in. Repeat until dark.

The others go about it all well informed and driven. I stand there as if I'd never heard of work – unclaimed, adrift, unfound.

Or:

I stand there in the cold, utterly unburdened by the laborious ethic by which I came to this visitation. I can still feel the current of the feeling habit, but I cannot locate this strident Protestant moral order that routinely bids me rise and flail, and turn the daylight into workings and tailings.

Maybe this is what voluntary retirement does to you. If it doesn't kill you with an anxious heart, or fill your brain with bubbles, then perhaps it exonerates you, absolves you of the bonds of middle age's performance. I was cold and I was still, and with this absolution at hand I was flirting with a freedom I thought I could live without.

I may have no need any longer of a weekday, nor a weekday of me. It may go the way of the appointment book.

## 8 December 2024

We drove all day to get halfway across the province. To the west a sky that is so low as to bring a storm, the kind trouble's born in. It's staying west of us, though, and we seem fine. Five hours from home, my wife and I have come to buy a lamb sight unseen, to bring strong genes to the flock, a milker's genes. We'll visit my daughter and her new guy for a bit, and then Nathalie heads home and I'm to go to Dead Starling Studios, Gregory's seen-better-days factory/recording studio, to lend my voice to a new record about love, somehow. He, bless him, thinks it's still in me.

A lamb in the backseat, all day, newly separated from her flock, driving at the edge of a winter's storm, with maybe six more hours on the road still to get home. What could go wrong?

## 9 December 2024

All seemed clear enough until, an hour from our destination, the highway veered northwest away from the bay's shoreline and upland, and we steered into the teeth of a blizzard. My wife and I were already road weary and done driving, there's maybe a half hour of daylight left, but we weren't far from my daughter's place. The roads were mostly bare, with snakes of dry snow writhing across them. 'Take County Road 4', the instructions said. 'The last turn on your left.' My wife said, 'I can't see the road.' Taking that as a failure of nerve I, in my utter doneness with being restrained in a vehicle, and being neurologically unsound occasionally, countered with, 'Just go. We've got four-wheel low'. She listened to me, which in twenty minutes proved faulty. We were literally ploughing up drifts on an unmaintained backroad, drifts that rose up over the hood and washed the windshield like typhoon waves over the prow. I knew almost at once we were done for on this road. The truck is powerful beyond reason, but it's low-slung, and it doesn't take much fracas or upheaval of the ground beneath to lift it up off its wheels and leave it gunning and thrashing like a cow mired in a mud hole.

Soon enough we were snagged on a drift, immovable, two humans in a ton of impotent, pointless metal and plastic. In another twenty minutes the snow had drifted up the driver's side, and we couldn't open the doors.

The daylight was failing, and even though we knew we could walk back down to the highway if we had to, it was beginning to feel like a doom/survival movie. We weren't dressed for bad weather or the blasted heath, and I knew what cold, wet and exhausted feel like in tandem.

The truck began losing its heat and light. Even with the cell phone seeming to work, still I could feel the cold hands of the Gods of the Frozen Fields close themselves on the place where we had run aground. A Great Lakes tempest was now upon us. Even with the phone, there was scarcely a way anything or anyone could get to us. It was a measured encounter with force majeure, with the ways of the sudden world and the sheer winds coming off big water.

The calamity was transparent. We were in strong and deep inconvenience, in vague but not inconsequential danger. The nearness of trouble, the coming in of catastrophe, they had my blood running, which this affliction quickly turns into tremours. Anxiety and cold aren't friendly to the extremities now, and I was rattling.

It was when we were chest deep into it all that my wife took my hands in hers, and with a penitent's devotion said: 'I'm so sorry I'm putting you through this. It's taken a year off your life.'

You see, you don't get to not be a burden to people when in the wane of your powers. You get to be a presence, a consequential one. You've got to live that out, to its unruly depths. We did eventually and adventuresomely get rescued by a Mennonite chap and his small tractor (blessings on the fact that he wasn't Old Order). And my daughter, who had headlines running through her head for a while there, asked me four or five times that night what made us try going down that road.

Sometimes you get to set it straight. I'm the one who said, 'Drive, already' into the tempest, as I'm wont to do.

## 10 December 2024

I'd like to say that I'm a purist in matters of self-care. No drugs. No smoking, all the rest in moderation.

The truth is, I'm a Puritan. There's a difference. I'm non-compliant with many presumptions of both the allopaths and the apothecaries, medicine men, bone jugglers and the like. Upon diagnosis of this visitation I was offered a prescription. I got it filled with anguish and bewilderment, although my bewildered self knew I'd leave it alone. There it sits undisturbed on a bathroom shelf, a year later, and here I sit, a year later, tremourous, almost to the point of fine motor failure, trying to write about it. I haven't taken the stuff.

This moral standard I can scarcely articulate. What faith it serves, I can't say. I think it goes something like this: the levodopa is palliative. It masks symptoms by temporarily relieving them. I didn't want to lose track of how I was. The efficacy of the stuff has a shelf life. If there was only so much help in the vial, I wanted to resort to it closer to the eleventh hour. The neurologist says it doesn't work that way. Get the benefit from it now, he says. You won't get more later by holding off now.

I wanted to try to hear this quiet of God in the bansheeing of the Beast, if it's there. That, as much as anything, is why I haven't opened the vial. But soon I'm going to have to bite the pellet, as my unmedicated self shudders and leaps, and see if I can buy a few stable years to go along with my otherwise healthy prospects.

# 11 December 2024

Three days and counting in the Dead Starling Studios, scene of my pandemic-era, feature-length filmed gig with the *Nights of Grief & Mystery* ensemble. Now we're deep into a new record, Hoskins and myself. It is a feat of groundless commitment, and the finest camaraderie.

I'm guessing that at some point in all this the thought of the last record, the last book or letter will bear down heavily on my otherwise ordinary days and press the well-being out of me. For a time, that will be as bad an any killing frost in the orchard in the spring. For a time, it'll take my breath from me as that frost takes the blossoms that won't ever open. And, true to my habit, I will mourn the things that won't be.

But there is a chance that I will have done what I can before the shifting frost seizes and snaps my mind. If I work into my work's verges, I'll have done everything, and the hard frost will shock my mourning into petals fallen into the dry grass. There'll be no cruelty, or not as much as I thought. Only another spring.

I am working mostly without melancholy, making the sounds that my days, fallen on hard times, bid me make. My comrade Hoskins is my reward. He's soldering the genius granted him onto that granted me, just as an orchard worker would graft a scion spliced into an old branch for the sake of blossoms, some for the birds, some for the pestilence, some for the frost – and some for the pickers next year, bless them, and their cider. More giving than misgiving. It endures for now.

## 12 December 2024

Recording my vocals for the new record. Studio twilight, and the boarded windows and the wine, and the hours fall away. 'Not sexy' is how Gregory describes the granular detail of audio capture.

Deep into the afternoon we get to *Wife of a Famous Man*, my elegy to Ruth's devotion to Brother Blue's calling, to her 'steel'. In its heart it is a love letter to people partnered to notoriety, people married to the ascendant in another person.

We do the four-minute piece in one take. My voice is raspy, as if having done uncommon heavy lifting. Gregory lets the orchestral part of the epilogue go on until it's only echo, and the sound of my breathing.

Usually, he'll let me know his feeling on the take, its merits and gaffs. But he's silent. Because of the mic stands and the baffles and the gear, I can't see him, so I'm waiting for him to say something. There's a kind of full-pocket quiet on his side of the room. It's then I realize that he's weeping. Not sniffling. Broken open weeping.

I gave a good reading, but he wasn't moved by any skill of mine. It was the echo, I reckon. I'd brought a death memory, a memorial, into the room. My old mentor, my elder, was there with us in the death story I told. Gregory saw in my fatigue and tremours my death coming, and the end of our beautiful run. He saw it more clearly than I have. He was, I think, grieving me, and us, and those fine stories of the road, and how remarkable and precise the ending around us can be. He was grieving the goodness we'd been visited and joined by.

I've a line in another piece about the man known to history as doubting Thomas:

*Endings die from disbelief.*
*It happens every day.*
*Faith and faithlessness entwine,*
*The wayward and the way.*

There's so much tuition in our ending, so much instruction and so much expense. It's hard work, and its hard on the voice and on the heart. People need from their mortal predecessors a 'first light, then wisdom' encounter with the real thing. That encounter has to be mediated by those predecessors' suffering until there's more clarity than endurance. It's one of the last gifts we have to give. It's the spirit patrimony of an age's spirit that they can render for the sake of those who are coming on, who are watching from the wings.

The apothecary left the potions on her shelf,
and said to me instead,
*'What if this Beast is God,*
*and it is God you dread?'*

Not summoned to the afterlife, not yet,
summoned still and all to this life
and to its quieting of me.

## 13 December 2024

I bought a blue tweed vest in County Cork in the summer.
It loves body heat, so much so that it gives heat
back, even summons up more.
There's a nice mechanism in back for synching up the waist to
your girth.
But there's a mystery at work with the County Cork vest.
Four pockets there are, for fob and pen and spare change, I
suppose. Not a one works. Sewn shut each of them is,

neat and sealed as can be. No slippery way in.
Real pockets that don't work. That's the way they send it to
you: warming, cinched up, sealed against add-ons with the neatest stitch.

What's that like? It's like life a little. Comes in working order, but without instructions. Ways in, gathering places. Seamed and tucked, sutured
against hasty addition or the gathering of oversized stuff. As much skill
given to the ways in as to the ways out. Alterations extra. And there's fine
design and handiwork in what slows or stymies you at all the openings.

## Last day of recording

Two things: I can't sing, and I don't sing.

I could say I left all that to Gregory, but the truth is that I had nothing
to leave. That was always his ground. Song composition, too.

So what am I doing here, in a cool recording studio, referring to this
as a 'project', with words I've written, laying down the vocals, all but
swallowing a microphone the size of a shoe box? I tried this months ago.
The affliction is in my larynx.

Who's kidding who?

Well, here's the third thing: the standards aren't quite what they were.
Vanity was a concern once. Credibility was a concern. Authenticity.
Most of the usual reticent person's repertoire.

But things are going from me, noticeably, steadily. I have to decide
on whether to obey the old character wrinkles that I decided were
authentic, whether to go out like I came in. Character change requires a
crisis, you might think. I'd say that it *is* a crisis, a wilderness crossroads,
an advent in search of a reason. In days like these, you could crawl into
your crawling for the sake of maintaining a self, protecting it against
other possibilities, trying to stay recognizable to yourself.

I'm standing at a microphone all day not to see if I can sound like me.
I already sound like me, have for a long time. I'm standing there to see if
I can sound like now, like this. In case someday I or someone else wants
to know what these times sounded like.

What about art? What about beauty, poetry, conjuring, alchemy?

Art is sounding like what's come to be, a refraction of the plate glass plane of inevitability, consistency, recognizability. Art renders out what prevails, by delivering up its constituent parts for perusal. Art is the periodic table of culture.

If God were in the house, would you want to sound like all your feelings about the house, or about God? Or would you want to sound like what life sounds like when God is present? The choice is a real one: autobiography or seismology. The differences are real.

Very hesitantly, inexpertly, unnaturally, I went after sounding like God was in the house; as if I were an echo, not an aftermath – a consequence, not a casualty. That's what I'd want to be for people listening: one filament, an eighth note of what being sounded by God is, dowsed and tuned and tempered.

The strain while recording was considerable. The microphone amplifies, exaggerates, expounds until you hardly recognize your voice. And I'm atremble. I still have to make an intelligible, this-wordly sound, keeping the same distance from the microphone, no matter the crisis. It is a fine crisis, a fitting crossroads. A proper catastrophe.

I hope it shows.

## 14 December 2024

Home after a week on the road, which in years past would have been an easy go, but now is a real stretch. Beside me the green three-ring binder I toured with that once held the libretto for the *Nights of Grief & Mystery* shows, but now is frayed at each corner, torn up the spine, sporting a fading stick-on danger signal of a capering skeletal being cloaked in red roses, *NOGM*, the show's acronym, in black ink above.

So far, I cannot soothe the sense that I have failed the new record subtly but utterly. Gregory played high and low with his producer's repertoire, his bag of singer tricks. I pulled up lame well before the end was in sight. I cooperated exceedingly well with my newly hatched limitations. Not the energy wane. The psychic disfigurement. It is as though a part of me has flown through the windshield, skidded face first on the pavement, left my likeness there. My voice is that disfigurement. I sounded like someone who didn't really know how to make sounds with his mouth. I was a mime. I was broadcasting on the frequency called 'Used to Be'. I thought I knew what the intoning was supposed to sound like: what I'd heard before. I balked. That's how it seems tonight, with no redeeming studio session in my schedule or scheme to make it good.

I was – am – glad to come back to the farm. The truth is that I ran back here, away from the concerned people asking how the record's going. I blinked. I persuaded Gregory that I was at my limit, that there was no more magic in the bag. The great dismay I have is that he believed it, or acquiesced. That's great yammer about God being in the house, but I didn't sound like God was in the house. I sounded like someone granted asylum on compassionate grounds. I made the sounds I am known to make. There were few sounds, or none, of a man made over, leavened, or marked.

## 15 December 2024

That is, if my recrimination is sound, legit, to be trusted. It could be that my standards for a working self are hardening and losing their suppleness along with my leg muscles. My fondness for old standards might be a strange defense against the radical reassembly – with a few pieces gone – that seems called for. But I'm not the best judge anymore. I don't have a lot of time in with disability. I might be nursing a prolapse nostalgia. You just don't know who should be the boss when the mind is drawn into the fray.

## 16 December 2024

When you have a love for the textile arts – the working arts, not the wall hanging decorative kind – chances are that you end up with a few pieces, or a few pieces more than a few. If you have done so, the chances are very good that you are troubled by moths. Moths eat beauty. They're drawn to it in the same fashion and to the same degree that you are. They inhale, scour and unravel woven beauty in the same way your appreciation might.

But moths do their work by night, in silence. When they're done, the light comes through.

That is a fair rendering of the ways of the progressive degeneration I'm getting to know. You collect your competences over the years, drawn by the fluid motion, the efficacy, the generosity of their distribution across the web and skein of the calculus of your needs, and of what the world and its gravity ask of you. You have the scent of beauty, and beauty has your scent. There's a place for your competence. If you're lucky, the world employs it. I've been lucky that way. From time to time, my little corner of the world has warped its loom with my ability, and I have trained my breath to waft across those threads.

Each time I took the weaving out and showed it, a bit of fibre went away, just in the revelation. Some people came to it with avarice, with sorrows of their own. Some came with wounds that would never heal. Their longing played across the weaving – working and weakening the threads. I pleaded, bargained to be useful, and I was used. Prayers answered are hard on the world as it is, hard on the beauty you are entrusted with. I meant to preserve it, but employment isn't preservation. It's slow-motion consumption.

I have sung the beauty I managed. I have wrung and strung the beauty that was entrusted to me. Fibre scattered, bits of beauty everywhere.

Now, the moths are at it. Like lawyers duly appointed, the white matter makers are at work in the night in the millworks of my mind.

## 17 December 2024

Friends of the Orphan Wisdom work are after making an archive of my troubledness. They're uprooting the interviews; that's one thing. But they're after transcribing the school sessions. Transcribing something of an afternoon – long harangue, off the cuff and off the clock, is akin to translating poetry: meant well but often treasonous none the less. The nuance of the placement of the comma, the difference between that and a semicolon: that's breath, intonation, eyebrow, vernacular, the sum of an arduous education. The standardization of language in a style manual deserves and requires raiding. Many a well-placed notion falls through the cracks when the raid gets standardized.

When people gather around the fire of a life's work with this project of tracking legacy in mind, it's usually embers that draw them. It is the beginning of a wake, orchestrated around the ebbing of the voice, the likelihood that most of what you were blessed with has been dispensed – that, or fortune has turned elsewhere. But the results are the same. When you're all but done, their labours are unlikely to be disturbed by a late-hour contribution from you that troubles the waters significantly, or in some unprecedented way changes things.

There will be what I intended in what I said or wrote, and that intent will be moot more and more as the legacy project wears on. And there will be what I've come to mean, which is in the hands of the scribes as they take up their work. They'll turn to me in their confusion, less so in their certainty, so long as they're able and I'm able. I'll practice the beginnings of standing down, and make room for them. My leaving them to their work will be my blessing. My blessing of their labours, their squinting and their certainties will be the way I practice my work's mortality.

No matter their motivation in doing so, anyone working credibly to summon a legacy from what I did and was not able to refrain from doing does me and my origins honour. I gathered errancies to myself, and I didn't start until well into the second act of my allotment. They are laying a laurel wreath upon my persistence, not my judgment. Just on my willingness to go on, unsure of the merits but more and more sure of doing so.

## 18 December 2024

I do not, near one year in, know very keenly the excruciata of my mind's departure. I've come onto the details of the unbidden dance of the extremities. The severity has obliged me to consider the allopathic palliation of symptoms, to see if I can recover mealtimes and handwriting. These are two places where I'm tempted to say 'I'm sick'. I'm having to do the symptom / side effect psychic algebra I watched so many cancer patients do, trying to suss the merits and demerits of securing comfort. The new year will be a year of drug sentry duty, vigilance on the cognitive parapet. Perhaps the grains of alertness will be prized off by such increment that I may miss the main event. I mean, I may be so taken up by this symptom vigilance that I lose the benefit I sought in doing so.

If I'm honest, I'm picturing some hell such as locked-in syndrome, or that endless turbulence of the man with brain cancer in *Die Wise* who could not imagine or adjust his way towards equilibrium, and rolled endlessly on the floor in search of it. The hell you conjure for yourself is decorated with achievements you think you can't live without, coordinated by an incorrigible, frantic architect who is pinned to the wall by futility. That's why every imagined hell is a personal one.

Maybe I'll find that cognitive decline, a phrase that still catches me off balance, has the soft-handed compassion of numbness, extracting from all involved a sequence of goodbyes, one station of competence at a time, fluttering farewells. Maybe it will be benign, or have the mercy of a pneumonia sedated but untreated.

Are you able to love your mind and not lose all credible humility? Are you able to make distance from the grievous and ill-considered of its doings and work, and still love your mind? If so, I love my mind. Deeply, dearly. It is a beloved of mine. For decades it was there, with me, and there again, like the come-againness of the morning. I used it so that it boiled and marled, gave off scent, capered until all hours in foreign countries, believed itself amoral and immortal at once. It was the blessing of my days, and blessed me with a way of working what I was born to do.

And now it is inconstant. It asks which one of the two of us was unfaithful.

I almost drowned once, almost took my arm off with a chainsaw another time, was moderate mostly, left the street pharmacopeia to others, was towed to shore in a sinking ketch at barely twenty, and arrested by Interpol, and schooled by an angel in Notre Dame, fell twenty feet and walked away and very nearly lost an eye all with no loss of faculty that I ever traced. I came to working the land in my fifties, perhaps late in the day for my mind. I did no or little toxic work, worked no corrosive or mean-smelling stuff. No chemtrail to blur me.

I more than survived. I persisted, as if I'd been spared the worst of what came my way. But I may have called out in the heart's night too often believing in the heart's might. I may have found my twin in woe.

I was fifteen, in the midst of my own season of psychedelic inquiry. I came home early and under the influence. I stood at the foot of my five-year-old sister's bed. She was of a separate kind, the kind children are keen to peck in the yard until there's blood, with no fear that the odd, separate one would rise up. I was awash in her disadvantage, in the caprice of it all, the morose randomness of how capacity is dealt. It all arrived at once, and I wept at the crisis of it all. My mother must have heard the travail. She appeared at the door. 'What is it?' 'She doesn't have a chance', I wept. 'What? Are you on drugs?' she asked.

Maybe heartbreak by proxy doesn't bring catharsis.

Does the mind have the equivalent of heartbreak? What would mind-break do to you? Is this what I have?

There are merits to endurance in this world. There are demerits. When the work of being here is on, the difference pales. Later it rises and darkens. In that darkening the moths are set out to dart, and to fray the warp threads that make a mandate of your mind.

## 19 December 2024

Three-and-a-half hours of a frozen afternoon, and the sun is flirting with the treeline, the crusted river already in shadow. The farm is curled in upon itself. The first of the hard cold is upon us now, and the work of winter is healing the ground from the exertions of other seasons.

Animals not getting Parkinson's disease: that's a very striking detail. I suppose if this is true it's because they've little capacity to disobey the redeeming mandate of seasonal change, what we call instinct. When the silent summons of the blood comes, they heed the thing. The light is their God, or the heat of the day, or the sound under foot going from silence to rustle. Their totem, that sustaining presence in the wild mind, might be the coming and going of the green life, the mandates of the calendar. They are at worship when they obey fatigue and lay themselves down.

I've had little obedience of that kind in me. I chased after anything that chased darkness out of doors, and I was insulted by fatigue.

## 20 December 2024

Forty-some weeks ago, my wife asked me to dance. I've let my dancing slide over the years. The opportunity rarely showed itself, so I didn't really know how gone my dancing chops actually were. We were in the desert, a week post-diagnosis, my defect complete and utter, shuffling and uncompelled by syncopated movement of any kind. I took her hand anyhow, the moon rising over the Sierras, and stood up, tried to find the rhythm in the music, anything I could lean on to move.

It was then I discovered how deeply the visitation of this thing had gone. It had made a stranger out of my left leg. There was nothing in the limb that obeyed, or heard the music, or remembered groove or how to syncopate. I shuffled in the gravel, held on miserably and for dear life to she who could truly move. I pictured my future, the vow made with this embodied self now broken and left behind.

Since then, I moved into the tenement of the future I saw so austerely and so clearly that night. I walked its trembling halls, its self-conscious stairwells, swept its commons, went down on hands and knees to scour its private places. I was at first keen to buy the place, sell all I had for whatever life might be left in that blighted certainty. I followed my own scent down. When I thought to think at all, it was a sequence of one-note / one-word supplications that I mistook for prayers: 'please', or 'no', or 'really?', or 'not now', or 'not this'.

The apothecary wonders why I'm so easily, readily on the side of defeat. I say I failed to make new sounds for the new record. She says that *wondering about that failure is a new sound*. I am silenced almost unto stillness by the insight.

I'm on the record as wishing I'd been an apothecary. Having an apothecary mindful of and ministering to me isn't second best. It's me benefiting from the Gods having chosen another for that job, releasing me, binding me now, to this one.

## 21 December 2024

I'm sitting in one of my fields, in the teaching hall wherein I held so many Orphan Wisdom School sessions. At this time of year, in this corner of the world, sunlight is brief but emphatic. The great cleaving of the year: there are few calendricals more generous, more fecund enough even in icy repose. It lends the human moment on Earth a human-scaled cue for restoration, for catching our breath and giving it over to the decision to live again. Just, given everything, to continue. Just to live again.

The darkness of this time of year has another kind of goodness, the one that marks you as one with time-in with the Adversary. I do recommend those markings, for the case they make for the overlooked part of life, the holy ground that is out there beyond benefit. They open that ground, that homeland of adversity. They situate you, citizen you. They're where you find out that no, they don't have the wrong guy.

On the way here I saw much evidence in the snow of the coyotes coming ever closer to the barn, the houses and sheep and crops, the farm's assurances against vagabondage. They have a knack for sussing out frailty in the farm and firmament. They carve up a farm's leavings, its loose ends.

On this place they've learned Boss's waning, the gauntness there in his hips, the deafness in his ears, the simple thing his frailty has made of his life. He has his teeth, but hasn't the strength to bear down. His chest makes a questionable sound where for a decade there was a stout, throaty declaration. On one of his dire patrols in these frozen months he may be tested, since all this catalogue of waning is the libretto of the coyote's call. Country people credit coyotes with convoluting intelligence, and those who don't lay out glass-laced bait or poison. We make the kind of deals with coyotes normally made in prayer.

Boss seems no more fond of me than usual, but I love him more in his unwinding than I did in his formidable strength. He comes to that love as he does his food: less frequently but no less doggedly.

He's no longer a farm dog, as I am no longer a farmer. We have seen the saunter pass from our field walks. We seem by the stoop in our frames more attentive to the ground below than to the sky above. We have our testament in the things we can touch, no longer in the things we can do. He groans when he rises – I understand – but seems untroubled by it. He starts out alongside us as we walk, but soon falls behind, out of sight, head a-bob and not unwilling. He seems to have figured a different purpose for his patrolling the field, less a creature now than a moving limb or wrinkle of creation, mindful but unhaunted by what he no longer summons.

I'm his companion now, impeded in my instincts, brought along by his.

These last lines come as the light is faltering. The old, pale sunlight of the winter is splayed by the bare saplings along the river, quieted and weakened in the frozen bush. The ending of a year is too vast an ending to see at once. It's like a life. Still, Boss waits for me at the door, alone with his twilight.

## 23 December 2024

I am today in the south of the province, orchards for acre after acre. The snow is wind-drifted across the roads, the mercury dropping enough to numb the saplings in the bush lots to dormancy. Family is gathered uncertainly around my trembling, which drums on the table. The challenges over the many moving parts of a normal meal seem to throw me. Because we don't all live together, nobody's quite used to the tremours. We're playing out a reprise of the 'weird' time together of a year ago, when our lives were doused in arbitrary overwhelm, bound together now by a kind of grieflove.

Earlier we visited a small town that is suffering the disfigurement of pandemic refugees from the big city now having bought up the place. Boutique upon boutique with stuff no one needs choke the main street. I'm in it, disconcertedly. I follow my family into a kind of gift store. A middle-aged woman eyes me up and down in unambiguous appraisal, and then cannot help herself. Feeling it necessary to report, and imagining that doing so can only compliment me, she says, 'I like your (a pause while she seeks words that might redeem this moment) your *look*' – which might be akin to describing me either as disguised or decorated.

Nothing rose up in me to say, for some reason. Not 'thank you', which would have served us both, nor anything more socially apt or convoluted. I just stood there, in my look, disguised or decorated, stilled, until the woman finally took offense, and went aggressive and dismissive, understandably, at my failure to roll with the festive holiday punches. 'Unnerved' I could say that I was. This might be the future: me not getting the signals in time.

Neurodegeneration, at almost any stage, will have you second-guessing anything associated with 'nerves'. There are messy, sometimes drastic sessions. Awkward social moments, which I seem to be accumulating, are easy to come by, but far from easy to perform. 'Unnerved' doesn't describe at all the goneness of the intuitive information which in the past helped me in these moments.

## 26 December 2024

The dark days condense memory, make it a solid, monumental cenotaph of a thing that we circumambulate and find ways to believe in. Family memory is magnetic north. A family's outliers are the Capricorn and Cancer of what the family is sure of. Its equator is that psychic weather that magically recurs when the family gathers again.

My family knew me as a flawed and capable man, in ways I didn't know. Christmas coalesces permissible memory, tolerable memory, memories steeped in health. I wonder in Christmases to come how these days and me in them will be lifted up. Already there are many who've gone to ground whom I don't take up into a festive memory, and they're not gone so many decades, never mind lifetimes. Human memory only has so much work room and storage room. It's porous, and there's mercy there. Imagine if you couldn't shake even a single memory, crowded by the insolubles and the inconsolables of the past? The good ones might be as tyrannous as the rough ones, standard-setters for satisfaction and solace as they'd be.

As it is, you have to reform how to care and credit, how to contend and give thanks and how to be sustained again. It is a wondrous labyrinth, a sojourn, an eagle's flight of the mind, to come again with purpose to the clamouring convictions of old family trespasses committed and endured, and to reconsider them. That's the thing about a mind in slow eclipse: you wonder what belongs in it, what to give it over to. Even those torments of genuine injury given and gotten that score and scour across the nerves, even their claim upon you seems properly up for grabs.

If forgiveness is too much to ask of the civilian and the middling in us, then maybe the flaws of memory could bless the proceedings. And a family's patrimony, stored in its memories, is saved and spent in what its members agree to remember and hold dear, and in what they agree to forget.

That's the trick to all this: agreeing to forget, agreeing until the tally is spent in the tale, that a lot of the hurt isn't what it was. This is a condition of our belonging to this world and to what and who came before us. We could, once infirmity comes, agree that we have forgotten much that could spare us and retrieve us and redeem us. It may be that our forgiveness is summoned by our frailty. I am finding that the ignition of gratitude for being alive doesn't come from things going well. Or even from being alive. It comes from the limits and the frailties and the endings we are heirs to. Seeing the end of what you hold dear is the beginning of holding those things dear.

## 30 December 2024

For some reason, the solace that's available to me now finds its distillation in, of all things, cleaning the copper pots in the kitchen.

I've waited too long to get at the bottoms, so I never get them in good showroom condition. But they do seem to look better than when in showroom condition. With some forgiveness in the eye, the use they've endured lends them credibility. They look as though they've stood testing. They've been in the fire of alchemy. They've held, and it shows. Generous conductors of kitchen heat they are, vessels, dense chalices, weighted things, beautifully bellied, every coaxing tap of the ball peen hammer showing, as the persuasions of the thumb show the potter's mark. The workman's beauty is as employable when they're empty as when they're full. Their wrought-iron handles work. They work elegance into the broth, the fricassee, the fry. Their weight invites you to bring two hands to the cooking, to the serving, benediction-like, blessing-like.

The secret to cleaning them is no secret at all: a benign acid that comes from cider vinegar, and coarse salt, and persistent rubbing through the early going when nothing seems to be happening. No steel wool, no abrasives. They'd scar the copper. Just leaning, coaxing until that light glows through the mire, like a well-wrought thought that rises again through the slogans and sloth of ill-considered words. It's like a daily dose of *being here*.

Caring for a copper pot is, I've come to see, much like caring for a mind. It will tarnish, it will dent and deform when in the heat of contention, until its maker's mark seems gone altogether. The temper will seem to go out of it. The smudge of use so resembles profanation or abuse or disuse that you have to pay attention to tell the difference. The mind needs its minding, its burnishing.

## 31 December 2024

The year's last day, the day's last hours.

I took myself down the lane – minus Boss, for whom almost any walk now is punishment – to the mishung gate, ajar. There I turned into the close acres of the far field. Even in this brailling winter so thrown by the December heat and rains, the far field in winter is medieval and peasant and Breughel in the north of the hemisphere. No matter how deeply running is civilization in you, the greys and blacks and the predator possibility of the bush will whisper and maraud across your nerve endings. As they've just done again.

I tried to walk upright, lengthen myself, but the tufts of grass left uneaten by the sheep in summer rose up under foot, and I was too stiff to do anything but stub my foot on them and stumble. A field is a place where my limits come on.

My ears are still ringing with the end of year well-wishers who came to call a few hours ago. 'I can't imagine what goes through your mind', someone said. I realized later, walking the field, that it's much of the same stuff that goes through their minds, plus some kind of foregoneness about a near future. Which is a bitter disappointment. I've counted on the drastic news of these last months to sweep at least some of the venal mental holdouts to the curb, but the force of habit doesn't blink, doesn't turn away. Unbelievable. With nowhere else to go, it slouches at the threshold of my having gotten used even to this.

But thank God for a far field. Once out there, so few of these disappointments counted. They persisted, but they didn't matter so much. I lurched inelegantly past the alder clumps and the cedar fence posts that would outlast me. I felt the old obligation to manage and care after these things. It felt like a bruise, like work pants frayed at the knees. It felt like a burr in the fur trim of my winter mitts. But the chemical claim of regret for all those things hadn't the range or the fixed state of other years. All the fencing decisions, the pasture calculations, the breeding calls and culls, they are already in the hands of others by now, have been for a few years.

Thank God, yes, for a far field, for the way it has eluded me, has won. One of the fingerprints of God, the maker's mark, the far field knows the way home. I walked it today, the year's last light going grey. The question I arrived with but didn't know to ask: 'What is life like?'

The far field said, 'Like this'.

# 1 January 2025

First light – a bare enough thing at this time of year – had us padding through new snow that had fallen in the hours before dawn, down to the new old barn and the yard, to feed the sheep and chickens. They are each time famished, devouring their high-priced stuff. This is their gratitude: still here. It has the makings of a eucharist, and we are the ones being lifted up. My being out here is part of the joy programme, that scheme for remembering the going by of days.

The anniversary of the edict is looming. I don't really know what to make of the day, aside from keeping my date with the end of this run of pulse takings, this book.

Phone rings. Gregory is calling. He says that he's been thinking about the fact that ten years ago, when I was his age, I was on a teaching circuit I dubbed the Mankiller Tour. He wanted me to know that he deeply esteemed my stamina and stand/deliver chops. I hear that and wonder whether I burned too hot for too long, whether there are only so many word horde victories per mind, whether I'm living out the intemperateness now. He's scoring a short film about me – another drastic sign I've made the last turn for home.

There are mummers due at the barn mid-morning, but I obey a nudge to check the phone messages before I go. A physician has offered his expertise and contacts. He mentions dementia, and I tumble into a barbed swoon, a two-fisted recurrence of the dread/doom complex of the past year, that savage anniversary almost upon me. I grow stiff and thick-muscled, and shuffle down the lane, seeming to be doomed to idiocy, decay.

Until I get to the barn, and the uncanny procession of a dozen people sounding and looking medieval and devout. They sing Old Europe blessings for flock and field, for the post and beam and the year to come. Wheat sheaf talismans, corn for the threshold. A young lad with a goat's mask is casting wheat and rye on the barn floor, sombre and resolute. He has a trickster's sense of things. It's all three-part harmony and angelus choir, and the saints and dusty worthies are in the rafters. It goes a bit off key, it's hesitant, it's beautiful. It's my kind of neighbourhood.

Where's my doom gone, now that life has come to call? I could petition my misery to reappear, but in the presence of these old singers, it is stymied for now. I'm shakily holding the sheaf, but the shaking belongs somehow, as the human hurts belong. The call and response is them translating the Old Terms of Engagement, hearth to hearth, and I've lived long enough to see the mummers let in.

Yes, the dread's still there. Yes, it's dismaying that a year later it can still be so close at hand. And yes, for a hierophantic hour it didn't hold sway, no longer so true. Have I learned anything worth knowing these last twelve months? Left anything behind no longer worth knowing? Is that the work, that winnowing? Am I to wear so thin that the Old Light finds its way out at last, and wisdom comes around at last, and the elder's bench is occupied, at last, just before it's vacated? The intact ones of this farm are looking on.

## 2 January 2025

I have learned some. Dread or no. Dead soon or no, I've learned temple talk. There's carnage to come, yes, and chaos in the winds, and catastrophe coming on. Still, I get to sound like God is in this house.

A year ago now, I was crawling, I was wreckage, I was dumb. Those things are all available to me now, and will be for the duration, it seems. Travail doesn't say, 'Just kidding', and then you feel better. I'll never feel better that way. There are clusters of little deaths before dying, it seems. Just as I figured. The stauncher habits seem harder to break, but their work is done. That's some of those little deaths coming on. Much of the old purpose is dying, going frail, taken up by the wind.

I see now that the verities of an ordinary life, no matter their persistence, don't really seem to win. Their beauty is this: they don't argue or contend. They leave the habits of personhood to your person. They're nothing personal. They give your heart its choices.

## 3 January 2025

How does it end? How does anything end? A day, a century, a millennium, a life, a parade, an idea, an era: we picture them building to a fever pitch, a crescendo, an anticrescendo, a spectacle of exaltation, and then to exhaustion, to exhalation, to extinction. Momentum alone, the entropy and the perpetuation of things, seem enough to guarantee fireworks, and a bow, and the lights going out.

But endings' ends are granular. The idea of *an* ending is rhetorical, pedantic, argumentative. The fact of an ending is putative, anticlimactic, clustering where we expect sequence. The crowd tires of the vigil, the uneventfulness of real endings, and like the signs of the ending it awaits, it begins to thin out and head for the exits. The dispersal is as much the ending as anything. But the witnesses are few.

A raindrop plummets for a mile. We see it go by our windows for the last few feet of its journey and say, 'It's starting to rain.'

The attention span needed to heed an ending is mighty business. The last note, the last breath, the last chance: their finality happens afterwards, in the rearview. 'Oh', you say to yourself, 'I guess that was it.' 'I guess': it's by default that we learn the art of ending. Never having done it before, we find it waiting there, after everything. It's that time before first light, beginning at sundown and stretching into that 4 a.m. infinity. No wonder we miss it: an eternity of practice looking, then a blink at a fateful moment, and that's it. You guess. We missed the beginning of the pandemic. We missed its ending, too. And I missed the onset of a disease that is emphatic, and unsecreted enough to show.

But like you perhaps, I've over and over again grown used to still being here, no matter what lessons impermanence offers up. I got used to this diagnosis, missed its onset entirely. I'll miss its end, too. I got used to this book being here, waiting, arms folded each morning, a chronicle of perpetuity whose end – entirely knowable – I will miss.

Seeing the end is a Godly thing.

Ending might be Godly, too.

# Epilogue

## 17 July 2025

I've had a lot of time in with finality, morbidity, mortality. Some of it's been my own. I learned well or well enough from those brushes with extinction, and I don't mind that they came around. If your private musings are draped over a public life, as many of mine have been, there is genuine credibility to be had from a full-throttle engagement with adversity. But the lion's share of my drastic education, the enduring and most persuasive part, has been in the precinct of other peoples' lives. There's a bit of breathing room that comes with seeing life's lessons coming on from a distance, through the mediation of others.

I saw a lot of other peoples' dying and death in my working life. I saw it from a way's off, though. It was the distance of health, of 'not me, not yet'. That distance has closed now. 'My turn' is my neighbour now. The abiding truth is that everyone's death before your own is your chance to get it right, to get a good long look at the way it is. The grace of that exposure is that I've begun to come to my days not as amateurishly as I might have, nor as authoritatively. There's skill involved in seeing your life unspool towards you, skill in living some kind of faithful amen to the fortunes and the slings and arrows.

I wrote this in part to trace a warm line, and a sane one, through the early days of genuine devastation. It's no easier now. It'll never be easy. Ease is not a good goal to entertain once the lights come up on the third act of your little allotment. I sent this out into the world in case I could be a 'someone else' to you.

Neurodegeneration, I have to say, is terrifying. The grinding, grueling prospects are occluding, eclipsing, enervating, eviscerating at times. When your brain's involved, and things aren't fatal in the short or even the medium term, the feeling of doom, of being preyed upon and hunted in the night, is strong. I lie down at night and wonder what will be left of me when I rise. My dreams were and sometimes still are spiked with assassins, predators, ambushes, and those menacings have had me down on the floor on all fours at 4 a.m., panting, dry mouthed, with no recollection of how I got there.

Losing your mind: that might not be the same as losing your personality, your self. It's possible that neurodegeneration is most calamitous because of the convictions we have about being true to ourselves. It's a loss of self, yes. And maybe it is rejoining that pool of sparks from which we arose. Losing the distraction of our allegiance to our particulars, might we come alive in a way that self-reliance forebade?

I don't know where the crushing, enervating misery of the last year has gone. It hasn't gone far. It's around. But it doesn't seem too interested in me for now. That word – 'degeneration' – doesn't detonate like it did. That's odd, because technically I'm deeper into the undoings that have been promised me than ever. I've more white matter. My legs are weaker, my gait gimpier.

It's more than terrifying, though. It's saddening, heartbreakingly so. I've never been sad like this. Sadness of this order is solid. It's bracing, truing even. It is clarifying, in a trustworthy way. Its hand isn't heavy, surprisingly. It's not magic. It's a revelator. It is as frank as frank can be. It's candid. It can make an honest person of you. The epic quality of this sadness: that might be me overhearing that old silence some know as God.

And – I don't know how this will sound to you – that sorrow can fit you out for joy. Maybe not ecstasy, at least not routinely. But this thing can give you an instinct for genuine, utter joy at being alive that success and ease and health don't know much about. It is a kind of sonorous punctuation, as if the scripture of your days is festooned like an illuminated manuscript.

So, I'm recommending joy, if you're asking. Not giddiness, although there's nothing wrong with that. Not breezy affability, although your kith and kin probably will be heartened to see that in you. No, I mean something that has a devotional tang, elegiac, rhapsodic and deeply fond of the wrinkles and the broad strokes and the heart-rending details, where the Gods live.

I didn't figure out the joy business on my own. I don't think I figured it out at all. I had a few people around me who did, and they just leaned on me to reconsider my devotion to misery and despair, the same way they leaned on me about my posture or my gait. Whatever sense of well-being I scraped up from the killing floor of this diagnosis I owe to those who gathered round to sit in sorrow with me.

Their companionship was in the early going exceedingly painful to be around. I'd all but lost my citizenship in the land of the living. But they found some other etiquette to practice on me, one that didn't need me to be okay, or think good thoughts. This is especially true of my wife, Nathalie Roy, and deeply true of Kimberly Johnson, and Gregory Hoskins, and the spirit of Brother Blue, and of my children, Jesse Jenkinson and Gabriel Jenkinson. This book, and this curious détente I seem to have with degeneration now, is unthinkable without them. Their way with me: I wouldn't be surprised if that is what the silence of God sounds like, this time around. I didn't welcome their distraction at first. I still bristle at times at the idea that joy belongs in a neurodegenerative day.

But it does, though. Utterly.

Very practically, I recommend boxing lessons, especially the footwork. It's called the sweet science for good reason. Your mind – and all it's attached to – will thank you for it. I recommend chi gong. It's an elegant workout, and your mind will thank you. I strongly recommend zippers over buttons. Your nether parts will thank you. And I recommend chuckling, wherever it seems called for, whatever your ambivalence about it. And getting dressed up, whether it's called for or not. And praise. Especially praise.

A little while ago, right around the time that the paralyzing devotion to misery I'd settled for moved off, I rethought my reedy, winded, drastic assessment of the sessions Gregory and I made for the new record. No, it wasn't great. It wasn't even all I had in me at the time. It was me being wrong about myself – an experience I recommend. It was frank, though. We had one more go, a few months ago, and we found another sound. We looked at each other frequently during that rerecording. 'Huh', one of us would say to the other. 'Who knew that was in there?' We wrestled with naming what became a love record for grown-ups. But once we outgrew the original ideas, the record named itself: *Caldera*. Of course. The mouth of a volcano, site of molten volatility and cooled for the moment and approachable. A sound the firmament makes once God is in the house.

I wrote a piece some years ago for *Nights of Grief & Mystery*. I was thinking about the young people coming to the show, that look in their faces, half-marvel / half-disbelief, a corrupted, overshadowed near-future almost upon them. I called the piece 'Fate, in Four'. It was a quartet of mea culpas on behalf of my generation and stout throwdowns in the direction of the young to reconsider fatalism.

Fate, it turns out, doesn't mean the fix is in, nor that there's nothing to be done. Fate does mean that *the Gods have spoken*. That's what 'the way it is' is. It's the givenness of things, the irreducible, three-dimensional facts and artifacts of life. That's half its meaning.

Here's the other half: So, *what shall you do*, and *what shall I do*, now that the Gods have spoken?

# Glossary of
# Called-For Words

There are extremes in a human life that hanker for their equal, their ally, in words. Sometimes profanity answers the call. Sometimes a glossary does.

There are times in the life of a book when the usual semantic limits of the language are legitimately reached, when the music of the language spills over the edge. When that happens, and as a public service, a graft of sorts, a burnished language, seems called for.

The editor of this book came across words that weren't in any dictionary. She very gently called them 'improvised words'. I think she was crediting them with perhaps having some secret, unauthorized merit. They were laid bare by the heat and fracture of hard times, children of the harrow. I'd call them 'called-for words'.

**ARCHETYPALIST:** a devotee of the notion that, come what may, everyone in every culture has a mutually recognizable psychic architecture.

**AWAKENEDNESS:** an emphatic form of 'awake' that registers the impact of being on the receiving end of a summons or call.

**BIRDWARD:** an Old English formulation meaning 'moving in the direction of a bird'.

**BONE HOUSE:** a transliteration of the Old English word usually translated as 'body', which magnifies the architectural facts of the thing.

**CALENDRICALS (ADJ. CALENDRICAL):** those seasonal, earthbound prompts that propel action; often the purview of pagans.

**CHANGELAND:** a mythical place easily found in contemporary North America and beyond, where fairly easy alteration for the sake of alteration is valued.

**CHAOSED:** to be on the receiving end of a ramshackling, disordering, unanticipated fact of life.

**CITYFUL:** both urban and urbane, burdened with a sense of obligation to become or remain current, influential, ahead of the curve, style-lucid or -addicted.

**COME-AGAINNESS:** the quality of givenness, of something being naturally occurring or required or called for, that lends a sense of being able to predict and plan accordingly.

**CROSSHAIRED (N. CROSSHAIR):** to be placed or pinioned at the point where two or more possibilities intersect, often mercilessly, without recourse or easy resolution.

**CRUCIFORMED (N. CRUCIFORM):** to be crosshaired at right angles.

**DAYMARISH:** after the fashion of a feverish, disorienting state of phantasm visitation, without benefit of any sleep that precedes or follows from it; garishly illumined psychic event.

**DISCHOREOGRAPHY:** the tendency of certain of life's events to cause the needle to skip, or the old syncopation to fail; a secular, disorganized religion.

**DISEMPLOYMENT:** the quality of being chronically denied employment or engagement with the necessities of life.

**DISPOSABILITIES:** all of the material world made to be disowned or wasted or done away with.

**DREARIES:** the plural form of those dispiriting weather systems, be they outer meteorology or inner feelings.

**EXCRUCIATA:** those sufferings particular to being taken down from any of the crosses of life, over and seemingly over again.

**GAIJINNESS:** a word taking the Japanese term for 'foreigner' and giving it a kind of involuntary, and possibly endearing (or just as possibly not), style.

**GONENESS:** a kind of utter encounter with arbitrary removal or disappearance; the presence of the absence of a person or thing.

**GRIEFLOVE:** an understanding of the confounding alchemy of frailties and endings that endorse the work of ordinary love; the lost and found of the human heart, where you're thrown together 'cause you're blown apart.

**GROUNDWARDS:** obeying gravity, willingly or not: heading for a non-negotiable end to flight.

**HALF-THERENESS:** the quality of bare attendance, or resounding frailty.

**HELLGATE:** Old English-sounding portal for entry into a place where good is unlikely.

**HURTINGEST:** the superlative of sorrow-making.

**HYPERBARIA:** the paraphernalia, accoutrement and existential dislocation of exposure to hyperbaric oxygen therapy.

**INNUMERIC:** the condition of being so vast in number or breadth as to beggar abacus or computer or telescope, or computation.

**INSCRUTABLES:** plural for that kind of addling encounter that compromises the fundament; the end of sense-making.

**INVOLUNTARIES:** plural for the irreducible, counterintuitive facts of life.

**LOSTNESS:** the acute encounter with displacedness. Often coincidental with 'goneness'.

**MAYBELAND:** mythical place of unconquerable though vague affirmation, where everything is possible as a consequence of saying that anything is possible.

**METASTIGMATA:** the tendency of the markers of suffering and sorrow to exponentially increase.

**MISHUNG:** askew, poorly executed.

**MYCELLIALY:** adjective invoking a subtle, sudden, anarchic, exponential and hard-to-explain growth spasm, after the fashion of mushrooms.

**NEUROLOGICS:** the granular details of the mind engaged in its usual calculus, otherwise that scheme of order or constancy inferred from and imposed upon the mind.

**NON-FAITHS:** a particular kind of faith devoted to the denial or defeat of faith; akin to disorganized religion.

**NON-FUTURES:** a particular kind of faith devoted to the fundamental compromise of oncoming possibilities.

**OBITUARIAN:** aficionado and practitioner of crafting death notices and other declarations of ending and termination.

**ONCOMINGLY:** the way of a looming, approaching, not altogether welcome thing.

**ONCOMINGNESS:** the quality of headlongness. See 'oncomingly'.

**PARTICULATE:** tendency to disassemble; secondarily, the elemental, irreducible constituent parts of something.

**PENDULUMED:** being on the receiving end of an oscillating, back-and-forth effect.

**PROMISELESS:** beyond the sway of 'anything is possible'.

**PROPRIETRIX:** female proprietor.

**RULY:** tendency of a person, place or thing to consistently present; a recognizable throughline in life.

**SCARECROWISH:** the quality of being two-dimensional, thrown together or threadbare, with the purpose of warning or driving off.

**SEMIACCOLADES:** lukewarm regard from without, typically informed more by approval than by genuine assessment.

**SHAMANESQUE:** the quality of shape-shifting or subverting the usual appearance of things, with a freakish or dubious tone. Something like 'burlesque'.

**SHAKENNESS:** the noun version of 'all but undone' or 'swayed against your better judgement'; derived from being shaken, not shaky.

**SHUFFLY:** to be unendearingly slowed in the gait, as if too much gravity is bearing down.

**TRAUMATICS:** plural of those unnerving, ensnaring, habit-loaded encounters with involuntary givens.

**TELLURIA:** plural of elemental, earth-bound; the disorganized religion of pagans and animists.

**TYMPANY (V.):** to concuss through force of one's declaration, or to declare in a bellicose way.

**UNDERPERSUADE:** the practice of lukewarmness in the hortatory arts, in the manner of a half sung song.

**UNDOINGS:** plural of that category of encounter which compromises integrity.

**UNFAILINGNESS:** the condition of chronic, repeating performance.

**UNFIRMING:** causing a flaccidness or destabilization.

**UNMOOREDNESS:** the condition of being set adrift, unanchored.

**UNSPUNNESS:** the condition of being disassembled, untwilled, unwoven.

**UNSTIRRUPPED:** to be thrown, or to be deprived of the mechanics of self-determination or governance.

**UNTENTED:** to be unhoused, or unshielded, or made vulnerable and exposed to elemental forces within and without.

**UNTHROWN:** to be challenged and ultimately to survive, without the grandiosity of the spiritual warrior in victory.

**UNUNCERTAIN:** the condition of achieving a degree of working familiarity with something after a period of intense doubt or credibility challenge regarding that something.

**WOUNDEDNESS:** here meaning the chronic, persuasive and often pervasive sense of primordial slight or disfigurement.

**WRONGMAKING:** the act of making things poorly, or of making things poor by doing so, or both.

**ZENNISH:** the quality of practice, speech or dress induced by a less-than-prolonged or -disciplined encounter with Zen.

# About the Author

Stephen Jenkinson, MTS, MSW, is a culture worker, author, international teacher and farmer. He is the creator and principal instructor of the Orphan Wisdom School, founded in 2010. He has master's degrees from Harvard University (theology) and the University of Toronto (social work). He is the author of *Come of Age*, the award-winning *Die Wise*, *Money and the Soul's Desires*, *A Generation's Worth*, *Reckoning* (with Kimberly Johnson), *Matrimony*, and other books. Since 2017, with musical partner Gregory Hoskins, he has produced four records and toured *Nights of Grief & Mystery* internationally.

For more information, visit www.orphanwisdom.com.